D0907849

FUNDAMENTALS OF PSYCHOANALYSIS

FRANZ ALEXANDER, M.D.

FUNDAMENTALS
OF
PSYCHOANALYSIS

SALVE REGINA COLLEGE LIBRARY
OCHRE POINT AVENUE
NEWPORT, RHODE ISLAND 02840

W · W · NORTON & COMPANY · INC · *New York*

COPYRIGHT, © 1963, 1948, BY

W. W. NORTON & COMPANY, INC.

131.34
Al2

**SALVE REGINA
COLLEGE LIBRARY**

W. W. Norton & Company, Inc. is also the publisher of
the works of Erik H. Erikson, Otto Fenichel, Karen Horney and
Harry Stack Sullivan, and the principal works of Sigmund Freud.

PRINTED IN THE UNITED STATES OF AMERICA

39900

Introduction to This Edition

Fundamentals of Psychoanalysis, originally published fifteen years ago, attempted to present the essential and best-established concepts of psychoanalytic theory and treatment in a concise and understandable language, and touched only tangentially on the still unexplored and controversial aspects of psychoanalysis. The hard core of psychoanalysis consists in the well-established principles of psychodynamics, which is gradually becoming one of the basic sciences of psychiatry, taking a prominent place side by side with neuroanatomy and neurophysiology. Psychodynamics rests on solid observations and generalizations; it is continuously enriched by details but its essentials have stood the test of clinical experience remarkably well.

But even in the recently slow-moving field of psychoanalysis, important developments can take place in fifteen years, and as might be expected, the area of most conspicuous development lies in the applications of psychodynamic knowledge to treatment. A better understanding of the therapeutic process has become more and more a focal point of interest. Many of us have felt that this problem requires a systematic observation of the psychoanalytic and psychotherapeutic treatment processes by non-participant observers. Most of our psychoanalytic knowledge has come from unrecorded observations made by the psychoanalyst while treating patients and later reconstructed from memory. Being himself involved in the therapeutic process, the analyst is not able to evaluate objectively his own reactions. Psychoanalytic treatment consists in a highly complex interactional process between two persons. Its full understanding requires a close observation of this interaction by others who are not involved in it.

The Ford Foundation has subsidized a number of comprehensive studies of the therapeutic process in several research centers. These studies have resulted in a vast accumulation of data, the processing of which will require systematic collaborative work over years to come. From our own research of the therapeutic process, undertaken at the Mount Sinai Hospital in Los Angeles and continuing over the last six years, certain conclusions are emerging which indicate that current views about the major therapeutic factors will require some revision. It is becoming evident that in the therapeutic process, non-verbal communication between therapist and patient reflects the emotional interchange between them more than does the verbal exchange of ideas (interpretations). The emotional experiences of the patient during treatment —as already emphasized in this book—seem to have a central role in bringing about changes in the patient's personality. Moreover, the significance of the therapist's concrete personality, of his idiosyncratic qualities, is becoming evident. This is precisely the factor which the therapist himself is least able to evaluate.

Fundamentals of Psychoanalysis ends with a paragraph stating: "Finally, it should be emphasized that psychoanalytic theory and practice are in process of development. To further this development a continuous revision of theoretical assumptions and generalizations, as well as experiments with therapeutic procedure, is imperative." This is precisely what has occurred in the years since this book was published.

Perhaps the most significant development in psychiatry consists in the emergence of what is commonly called "psychoanalytically oriented psychotherapy." This development in the psychological aspects of psychiatry appears to me even more important and promising than the more spectacular—because more tangible—progress made in the utilization of psychologically effective drugs. Psychoanalytically oriented psychotherapy consists in the flexible application of those fundamental principles of psychodynamics which are treated in this book. It applies these principles in various technical procedures which are precisely adjusted to the individual nature of each case. The routine application of the same standardized procedure (the standard psychoanalysis) gradually is becoming enriched by more individualized and more economical treatment. Through these developments the significance of psychoanalysis for the whole of psychiatry is substantially enhanced. Psychoanalytic theory has in the past revolutionized our *understanding* of mental disturbances. Now it is in the process of reforming the psychological *treatment* of the vast group of emotionally disturbed persons.

Franz Alexander, M.D.
February, 1963

Preface

CONFRONTED with the task of revising *The Medical Value of Psychoanalysis* for a third edition, I have decided to write a new book in two volumes. The first will be devoted to the fundamentals of psychoanalysis, the second to the discussion of the psychosomatic approach to medicine.

In the eleven years which have elapsed since the second edition of *The Medical Value of Psychoanalysis,* some of the fundamental concepts of psychoanalysis have been further clarified and can be formulated more concretely and comprehensively. It is no longer necessary or desirable to trace the historical evolution of Freudian theory in detail. Only those who have witnessed this evolution and have grown up with it can follow with ease all the intricacies of a historical presentation of psychoanalysis. They alone can fully understand why Freud repeatedly changed his ideas and steadily adapted them to the rapid accumulation of new facts. For others the conventional historical presentation of psychoanalytic theory is often confusing. The student can with greater advantage follow the pioneer efforts of Freud to understand the human personality after he has taken a comprehensive view of the present state of psychoanalytic knowledge. In this book, therefore, only a brief historical review is given, and it is related as closely as possible to statements of fact and the generalizations based upon them. No attempt has been made to give a comprehensive history of all psychoanalytic concepts, and historical discussions are added only when they appear to facilitate the understanding of principles. References to the literature are accordingly limited to fundamental contributions.

In presenting the theory of drives I have tried to formulate basic principles and to limit theoretical discussion of it to a minimum. Physicists still do not agree on the ultimate nature of light, although the laws of optics are well defined and generally accepted. Similarly, psychodynamics rests on well-established observations and generalizations although the ultimate nature of instincts is still a highly controversial subject.

Our views about fundamental processes such as repression, identification, projection, reaction formation, substitution, displacement and sublimation, which were derived directly from observation, have undergone little change since their formulation by Freud. They form the solid basis of psychoanalysis and have proved their validity in the study of both normal and abnormal behavior and in the treatment of neuroses. The main object of this book is a comprehensive presentation of fundamental theory and its application to treatment.

Acknowledgments

THIS BOOK has been prepared from the notes of my Introductory Lectures to Psychoanalysis, which I have given over the past fifteen years in the Chicago Institute for Psychoanalysis. In trying to explain to my students as clearly as possible the fundamentals of psychoanalytic theory, my own ideas have been greatly clarified. The reactions, questions, and comments of my students have been of the greatest value in discovering obscurities in my own presentation and in current theories. I owe a great debt to my students in the Institute. Equally important has been the exchange of ideas with members of my staff, some of whom have collaborated with me in research and teaching since the foundation of the Institute. Drs. Therese Benedek, Thomas French, Roy Grinker, William C. Menninger, Franklin and Helen McLean, Gerhart Piers, and the Rev. Robert T. Casey have read part or all of the manuscript and have made valuable suggestions. I am indebted to the editor of the *International Journal of Psycho-Analysis* for permission to reprint a few passages from my article, "Remarks about the Relation of Inferiority Feelings to Guilt Feelings" (1938).

Contents

Chapter I

The Position of
Psychoanalysis in Medicine

IN THE LAST two decades psychoanalysis has become progressively an integral part of medical theory and practice. Thirty years ago it led an isolated existence on the borderline of medicine, a fact not due entirely to the unreceptive attitude of medicine toward psychoanalysis, for psychoanalysts themselves questioned whether psychoanalysis was not a distinct discipline, related to medicine but essentially independent of it, just as archaeology, though related to history, is an independent science, or as paleontology is related to geology but is different in its methods and purpose. For even those psychoanalysts who, like myself, were convinced that psychoanalysis as a form of therapy belonged to medicine, could not ignore the fact that its subject matter, methods, and terminology were so different from those of medicine that its assimilation to it was difficult. For years a clear decision on the citizenship of this young empirical discipline was not forthcoming. Medicine aims within certain limits to understand the body as a physicochemical machine; psychoanalysis deals with psychological facts and tries to influence psychological processes by psychological means. This gap appeared difficult to bridge.

Psychological processes, however, are functions of biological systems and influence such physiological phenomena as weeping, blushing, respiration and the secretion of gastric juice. Furthermore, a number of diseases manifest themselves in mental disturbances such as psychoses and psychoneuroses. Even after the physiology of the brain has been highly developed, it is improbable that physiological or pharmacological methods will replace psychological means to influence people's minds. In influencing pathological mental processes, psychological methods are used which are similar to persuasion and explanation. Probably the best method of reducing psychological disturbances will always be through psychological means.

In order to preserve the homogeneity of medicine there has been an inclination to exclude psychological methods even when their scientific and therapeutic value were acknowledged, and to regard psychology, psychopathology, and psychotherapy as disciplines related to medicine, but outside its range. Gradually, however, the artificiality of the separation of mental from physical diseases and of mental processes from physical processes became apparent through an appreciation of their interaction. In therapy it is not always easy to decide in which cases a psychological and in which a physiological approach is indicated, for the individual cannot be divided into a body and a personality, since as a whole he functions as a psychobiological entity.

Psychoanalysis started within medicine as an attempt to cure hysterical symptoms by psychological means. Under the influence of Charcot's studies on hysteria and hypnosis, Freud and Breuer developed the method of cathartic hypnosis. They observed that patients under hypnosis could remember forgotten events intimately related to their symptoms. These memories recalled under hypnosis were accompanied by outbursts of emotion and were usually followed by a disappearance of the symptoms. Freud and Breuer called this process of emotional abreaction under hypnosis "catharsis" and their method "cathartic hypnosis." Historically the greatest significance of this discovery was that it demonstrated the existence of unconscious mental processes. Freud, however, soon gave up cathartic hypnosis and replaced it by free association. This technique supplied a more complete picture of the historical background of the symptoms and, apart from its therapeutic value, has yielded a deeper insight into human personality than was possible before. It is responsible for the fact that psychoanalysis, two decades after it started as a modest therapeutic device to alleviate hysteria, has developed a whole theory of personality.

Much of Freud's early work consisted in the demonstration of unconscious mental processes and their dynamic influence upon overt behavior and conscious mental activity. The concept of the "dynamic unconscious" is the cornerstone of the whole psychoanalytic system. Charcot's demonstration of the clinical effects of hypnotic suggestion and Bernheim's and Liébault's posthypnotic experiments provided Freud with the starting point for his investigation of unconscious processes. Posthypnotic experiments showed that persons after they have been roused from hypnosis may act on commands given them in their hypnotic state.

Freud's classical study of the trivial errors of everyday life such as slips of the tongue, misspelling, misreading or forgetting words, or forgetting to carry out such planned acts as mailing a letter, occurrences which happen occasionally to everyone when tired, in a hurry, or under emotional stress, has a primarily historical significance. He proved that these phenomena are determined by unconscious motivation. When a president of parliament erroneously declared a meeting closed when he intended to open it, he obviously had some good reason for having the meeting over with before it started. A person who carries a letter in his pocket for days has some definite, though unconscious, reason for not mailing it. From these trivial errors of everyday life Freud demonstrated in simple and convincing fashion the dynamic power of unconscious motivation. Whereas hypnotic phenomena are unusual and often appear artificial, these ordinary experiences were familiar to everyone.

The reader who today studies Freud's monograph on the errors of everyday life is impressed by its careful and elaborate arguments and occasional polemical tone. He may even feel that Freud's contentions are self-evident and do not require such circumstantial proof; but he forgets that when these ideas were first formulated in 1912, they met the resistance of preconceived notions promulgated by the academic psychology as well as by the "common sense" of those days. The change in attitude since that time shows to what extent the concept of the unconscious has influenced all modern thinking. It has defined the limitations of the rational and conscious part of personality and has become so fundamental to the mental attitude of the twentieth century that without it much of modern life is unintelligible. It is not an exaggeration to compare this change with that which the Copernican system effected four hundred years ago. The theory of the unconscious involves a new and definite break with the anthropocentric attitude toward the external world. The system of Copernicus destroyed anthropocentricity in the spatial cosmological sense, but man remained anthropocentric in a psychological sense. The rationalistic philosophers of the seventeenth and eighteenth centuries made the thinking mind the center in the universe. Descartes taught that nothing is certain except one's own thoughts, and this doctrine led in direct line to Kant's consistently anthropocentric thesis: The external world, as we see it, is dependent on the mind and its categories, which are themselves absolute and belong to the unchangeable structure of the mind. Psychoanalysis has deflated the Kantian categories by explaining them as products of the adjustment to the physical environment. The infant's mental processes are subject neither to the logical nor to the moral categories of Kant and, what is more important, even in the adult's unconscious personality there are mental processes which are not subject to the laws of logic. These processes, manifest for example in dreams, do not follow the law of causality, but only that of temporal sequence, and are not bound by such axioms as that the same thing cannot be at the same time in two different places. Briefly, rational thinking as well as moral feelings and prescriptions are products of the adjustment of the organism to its environment, but they do not entirely determine our thinking and behavior, and a dynamically powerful portion of mental life is neither rational nor moral, is adjusted neither to the external world nor to the demands of the community. The rationally adjusted part of every personality is in continual conflict with its rationally unadjusted depths. Repression is the means by which the disturbing influence of unadjusted tendencies is excluded from consciousness and becomes unconscious. Mental disturbances, such as psychoneuroses and psychoses, can be understood as intensive and overt manifestations of the unadjusted unconscious attitudes of the personality.

This view of human nature is now generally understood and accepted like the theories of evolution or the planetary systems and have become an integral part of modern thought. The emotional consequence of this modified perspective is that man now definitely feels himself to be only a small part of the universe. Because his belief in the absoluteness of his rational thinking has been broken, even this last claim to a special position in the world has lost its foundation. Rational thinking can no longer be regarded as unapproachable by scientific research, but must be thought of as a product of adjustment to the world. It is functional like the flight of birds or the swimming of fish. Our logical thinking is no more the only possible form of thought than flying is the only possible form of locomotion.

The scientific consequence of this new perspective is that psychology is related to biology. Thinking is one of the functions of the biological system, one means of orientation in the external world. The mental apparatus can be understood as a biological system such as the circulatory system, which in all its details is adjusted to the hydrodynamic problems which it has to solve. Similarly, the functions of the mind can be understood as adjustments to the problem of orientation in the environment. No teleological philosophy is involved in this view.

Thus separated from philosophy, psychoanalytic psychology becomes a mechanical, or better, a dynamic science and describes the functions of the mind as mechanisms or dynamisms. It studies psychological development in all phases of adjustment and follows the changes from the unorganized, unsystematic, diffused manifestations of the infant's mind to the complicated system of the adult ego. It explains pathological mental phenomena as due to the incomplete mastery of early periods and can determine, to a large extent, which phases of development were unsuccessfully resolved and to which phases certain types of mentally disturbed individuals remain fixed.

This genetic and dynamic approach to the understanding of mental disturbances can be considered a decisive step in psychopathology. The psychodynamic approach makes possible the intelligent and systematic influencing of pathological mental processes, that is to say, a causally oriented psychotherapy.

Psychotic and neurotic symptoms can be understood on the

basis of conflict between the infantile survivals and the adult development of the personality. The chief difference between a neurosis and a psychosis is the extent to which the repressed unadjusted mental content breaks through into consciousness after overcoming the resistance of the repressive forces. This outbreak of repressed content is most complete in psychoses. In the end-phases of schizophrenia, for example, the impression is made that the ego has given up all resistance and is dominated entirely by hallucinations. In a psychosis even the earliest adjustment of the ego, the capacity to subordinate imagination to the evidence of sense perceptions, breaks down, and the consequence is a loss of orientation to the world. The later achievements, such as aesthetic and moral restrictions and inhibitions, also disappear in psychoses. A psychosis can thus be considered as an attempted though never wholly successful flight from reality and, more particularly, from adult existence to childhood, to a happier time, when reality did not yet disturb the rule of fantasy. This flight may be temporary or permanent.

In the different forms of psychoneurosis the conflict between the adjusted and the more primitive attitudes is more obvious, since neither of them gains a decisive victory. If the end-phases of a psychosis are compared to a silent battlefield after all the soldiers on one side have been killed, a psychoneurosis is a battle still in progress, for psychoneurotic symptoms are partly manifestations of repressed tendencies and partly reactions of the ego against these tendencies. In psychoneuroses the conscious ego still has the upper hand, although it does not succeed entirely in repressing the unconscious tendencies. The important fact which shows the partial control of the ego is that the unconscious mental content can appear in consciousness only in distorted forms. These distortions are compromises between two antagonistic forces, the repressed and repressing forces. In the distorted form the unconscious content can appear in consciousness without hurting the conscious personality.

Psychoneurosis and psychosis can be considered as different stages of the same mental process, the outbreak of the unconscious, repressed, primitive part of the personality. In a psychosis the process goes much further, for the difference between conscious and unconscious disappears to a large degree and the unconscious dominates the whole personality, whereas in a neurosis the principal achievement of the later ego-development, the acceptance of reality, remains more or less intact, and the unconscious tendencies penetrate the ego only in isolated symptoms, which are like foreign bodies embedded in normal tissue.

Apart from these results in psychopathology, one type of dynamic manifestation of repressed mental force has a special significance for medicine: that in which unconscious psychic tendencies disturb the functions of the vegetative organs. The investigation of this field requires close co-operation between the medical specialties and psychoanalysis.

The discoveries of psychoanalysis in mental pathology have become integral parts of modern medical thinking, just as the fundamental notions of the unconscious and repression have penetrated contemporary thought. The theory that infantile attitudes become fixed and the discovery that psychoneurotics and psychotics regress to early patterns of thinking and feeling are today basic concepts of psychiatry. Psychic mechanisms like rationalization and projection, which are now understood as means of solving the conflict between the conscious ego and the wishes and tendencies unacceptable to it, are not only familiar to psychiatry, but current in general thought and conversation. The young medical student is often not aware of their origin in the psychodynamic system of Sigmund Freud.

In addition to the explanation of the apparently senseless

mental processes of the psychoneurotic and the insane, psychoanalysis has become the psychology of all kinds of irrational phenomena, such as casual slips and errors of everyday life, fantasy, and especially dreams. It has shown that the apparent irrationality of all these phenomena is due to the fact that our mature rational thinking has outgrown the more primitive stages represented in dream life. If, however, we relearn the mental language of our childhood, we can grasp the psychological meaning of our dreams.

From all this it must be apparent that not only the content but also the methods of psychoanalysis are essentially different from those of the natural sciences, including all branches of medicine except psychiatry. It is a subject which cannot be expressed in terms of time and space but which operates with psychological causality, motivation, and goals. In the following chapter the nature of the psychoanalytic method will be discussed.

BIBLIOGRAPHY

ALEXANDER, F.: "Sigmund Freud, 1856–1939." *Arch. Neurol. & Psychiat.*, 43:575, 1940.
———: *The Medical Value of Psychoanalysis.* New York, W. W. Norton & Company, Inc., 1936.
BREUER, J., and FREUD, S.: *Studies in Hysteria.* Nervous and Mental Disease Monograph Series No. 61. New York, Nervous and Mental Disease Publishing Company, 1936.
BRILL, A. A.: *Fundamental Conceptions of Psychoanalysis.* London, George Allen & Unwin, Ltd., 1922.
CHARCOT, J. M.: *Leçons du mardi à la Salpêtrière.* Paris, Bureau du Progrès Médical, 1889–1892.
ENGLISH, O. S., and PEARSON, G. H.: *Emotional Problems of Living: Avoiding the Neurotic Pattern.* New York, W. W. Norton & Company, Inc., 1945.

FREUD, S.: "Charcot," in *Collected Papers*, I. London, Hogarth Press, 1924, p. 9.

————: *A General Introduction to Psychoanalysis*. New York, Boni & Liveright, 1920.

————: *The Interpretation of Dreams*. New York, The Macmillan Company, 1913.

————: *New Introductory Lectures on Psychoanalysis*. New York, W. W. Norton & Company, Inc., 1933.

————: *The Problem of Lay-Analysis*. New York, Brentano's, 1927.

————: *Psychopathology of Everyday Life*. New York, The Macmillan Company, 1914.

HENDRICK, I.: *Facts and Theories of Psychoanalysis*. New York, Alfred A. Knopf, 1934.

WITTELS, F.: *Sigmund Freud*. London, George Allen & Unwin, Ltd., 1924.

Chapter II

The Nature of Psychological Understanding

1. COMMON SENSE

To UNDERSTAND personality requires methods in many respects basically different from those employed in the natural sciences. Every empirical science consists in the refinement and systematic development of the methods of observation used in everyday life. In any science we can use only the senses and reasoning faculties we actually possess, although we can increase their exactness and minimize their defects. Psychoanalysis, unlike earlier psychological methods, has merely refined and systematized the usual methods of understanding mental situations—the methods of common sense. Common sense is, however, a complex faculty. Its chief instrument is identification, a way of putting oneself in another's situation. If one observes another's movements, facial expression, tone of voice, and content of speech, some idea may be gained of what is going on in his mind. This understanding is possible because the object observed is a being similar to the observer. Both are human personalities. This similarity between observer and observed is essential and obtains only in psychology.

In physical phenomena, e.g., the behavior of two spheres in motion on a table, knowledge is limited by sight, and it is impossible to predict the next step without previous experience of rolling spheres under similar conditions. With persons, behavior can be interpreted by introspection. Another's motives can be understood from one's own reactions in similar situations.

The importance of introspection as an aid in interpreting human behavior cannot be overemphasized; it constitutes the basic difference between psychology and the natural sciences. All psychological methods which fail to recognize and exploit this unique advantage of psychology must have a limited value for the study of human personality. Experimental psychology and behaviorism have imitated the methods of experimental science but have either neglected to use and develop the natural faculty of understanding mental processes or, as in the case of behaviorism, have refused to use this faculty. Prescientific man interpreted inanimate nature psychologically and saw the wrath of God behind thunder and punishment in lightning. Behaviorism makes the opposite error of refusing to analyze the psychic background of living beings. Animism attributed personality to inanimate nature, but behaviorism wishes to rob even human beings of their personality. It is both an amusing and a depressing sight to observe how behaviorism stubbornly deprives itself of one source of knowledge and restricts itself to the observation of the so-called external behavior. Are not words also objective facts? And when you hear words, how can you prevent them from conveying knowledge of another's psychic processes?

 Of course this common-sense understanding of other individuals' mental situations is an unreliable method. But is not the task of every science to improve on natural faculties of observation? Is not unaided optical observation also unreliable? Was it not necessary to add to it by scales and magnifying pointers of physical instruments and microscopes?

2. SOURCES OF ERROR IN PSYCHOLOGICAL OBSERVATION

It is now time to describe more concretely what is meant by the natural faculty of understanding the mentality of others. Let us cite an example.

A common soldier attacks an officer and is asked why he did it. He explains that his superior has treated him unjustly for a long time and has humiliated him until he finally lost control of himself. His position is then clear, because everyone has experienced similar feelings. To say that the soldier attacked his superior because the latter treated him unjustly and that the soldier's resentment finally became stronger than his fear of punishment is a causal theory based on perception and introspection. It is based on common-sense psychology, which is used in understanding others. This faculty, possessed in varying degrees by everyone, is the basis of psychoanalysis, just as the optical and acoustic perceptions are the basis of physics. However, science begins with the refinement and development of untrained methods and faculties. It is obvious that common sense in psychology is an inadequate method and contains several sources of error.

The *first* and most important of these is deliberate deception. The common soldier in the case referred to will not tell all his motives for attacking his superior. He will give a story which puts himself in a good light. If you are an expert in human nature—what in Germany they call a good *Menschenkenner*—you may guess his real motives, but there is no evidence as to whether you are right or not.

A *second* source of error is self-deception. Even if the soldier wants to describe his actual mental condition he may be unable to do so because he does not know all his own motives. He deceives not only his hearer but also himself, and by his story he tries to put himself in a good light not only in others' eyes but also in his own. In mentioning this second source of error I am referring to repression, one of the basic discoveries of psychoanalysis. Repression excludes from consciousness desires and motives disturbing to the harmony and self-esteem of the conscious ego.

A _third_ possibility of error comes from great individual differences. The soldier may be so different psychologically from his hearer that the latter cannot understand his motives. Identification is possible between human beings, since both are human, but differences of sex, race, nationality, and social tastes obscure their common ground and introduce new sources of error. Men understand each other better than they do women, and women understand each other better than they do men. We understand those who share Western civilization better than we do Orientals. The greater the difference between two minds, the greater the difficulty in mutual understanding.

The difficulties adults experience in understanding young children, savages, psychotics, and neurotics are due to the differences in the level of their mentality.

A _fourth_ source of error is that the observer may have blind spots due to his own repressions. He has motives which he excludes from his own consciousness and does not want to admit to himself, and will not, therefore, be able to detect in others. Introspection is often lacking in untrained observers because it is blocked in certain situations by repression. The dynamic importance of one's own repressions as an obstacle to understanding others can be appreciated only if we realize that the uniformity and harmony of our conscious ego are guaranteed by repressions. To become an adult it is necessary to forget the infantile way of thinking. The attraction of infantile mental life is great, since it is subject in a much higher degree to the pleasure principle than is adult mentality, which has had to adjust itself to reality. It is characteristic of infantile mentality that it does not accept facts at variance with its wishes and needs. The recognition of a strange and by no means always benign external reality is a problem which the child has to solve in his later development. The most important means of overcoming infantile thinking and wishes is repression, by which the ego excludes from consciousness the disturbing survivals of its infantile existence. Through repression these infantile remnants come to form the unconscious part of the personality. The difficulty in understanding children, savages, and the insane is thus based not only on the differences between their mentality and ours, but also on repressed forces within ourselves. In order to become a normal adult, the primitive part of one's personality must be forgotten, or rather subjugated, and therefore the primitive mental processes of others and one's own dreams which are survivals of infantile personality are difficult to comprehend. In mental pathology science has to overcome the difficulties presented by repression.

The enumeration of so many sources of error might discourage confidence in the possibility of any scientific psychology. Some of these difficulties appear insurmountable; this explains why psychology has so long failed to evolve a method of eliminating or diminishing error. Psychological understanding, beyond common sense, has hardly been a science, but is rather the possession of a few geniuses, the great *Menschenkenner,* authors, novelists, and dramatists. They have been able to overcome some of the difficulties in understanding the real motives of others in spite of the universal tendency to self-deception, and the differences of age, race, and sex. Geniuses are able to do this because their own repressions are less highly developed.

3. ELIMINATION OF THE SOURCES OF ERROR

Certain discoveries in method have enabled psychology to become a science of personality. All scientific developments follow such discoveries. Anatomy began with the introduction of dissection, histology with the microscope, bacteriology with methods of growing cultures. Psychology, as an empirical science of personality, began with the discovery of the method of free association by Freud.

All sources of error are not eliminated by free association, but they are sufficiently reduced to meet the requirements of science. The patient is required to report everything that occurs to him during the analytic session and to verbalize everything that occurs to him in sequence without modification or omission. He is asked to assume a passive attitude toward his own trains of thought and dispense with all conscious control over his mental processes. This simple procedure seems at first to be a rather trivial device and it is not easy to appreciate its value, but the methods of percussion and auscultation also appear unpretentious and trivial, and it is only the interpretation of small acoustic deviations that make them so important for medicine.

The individual's resistance to giving a full account of his mental state is reduced in psychoanalysis by the fact that he is a patient. Only a sick person who hopes that his symptoms may be cured by following the physician's advice is willing to give such an intimate picture of his personality as is required by the method of free association. As the patient yields to spontaneous trains of thought ideas soon emerge which are usually put aside and forced from the focus of attention. This uncontrolled manner of thinking eliminates, or at least diminishes, conscious control, and an unknown part of the personality becomes manifest. All kinds of disagreeable and irrational notions and images appear which controlled thinking interrupts and blocks. Under analysis the patient gradually learns to overcome his natural reluctance to abandon his conventional façade and becomes entirely frank, displaying himself in a kind of mental nudity not only to the analyst, but, what is equally novel, to himself. The patient's desire to be cured thus supplies an indispensable factor in efficient psychological investigation, for it alone guarantees a willingness for unreserved self-revelation.

The only other situation which meets this requirement is a didactic analysis in which a student of analysis subjects himself to the same procedure in order to learn analytic technique. In this case it is not the hope of cure but the wish to learn the method by studying oneself that guarantees frankness. Without co-operation between the observer and the observed, analysis, in fact psychology, is impossible. In physics the willingness of inanimate objects to be studied is not necessary, but in psychoanalysis the analyst is absolutely dependent on this willingness.

The problem of repression has been met by analytic technique, which reduces the conscious control of mental processes. Spontaneous trains of thought are more influenced by repressed mental forces than ordinary thinking. They are not consciously controlled and hence appear more irrational, as in daydreams and states of drowsiness. Long and patient observation has led to a technique of interpretation which allows the psychoanalyst to reconstruct the unconscious tendencies which determine the sequence and content of these spontaneous trains of thought. In this way he is able to gain deeper insight into the structure of the personality and to understand motives and emotional connections which are normally covered up by the controlling and selective conscious ego.

The differences between observer and observed make the

difficulties in identification, and therefore common-sense understanding, in some cases almost insurmountable. The mentally ill often revert to primitive, infantile forms of thought. Long analysis, with frequent interviews over a period of months, is a means by which this difficulty can be overcome. If you travel in a foreign country you are at first quite unable to understand the mentality of the inhabitants, even though you may understand their language. Their facial expressions and their reaction patterns are unfamiliar. But in time you sense their reactions without being able to tell how or why, and gradually you orient yourself psychologically. The same thing happens in the course of a long psychoanalysis. Even an eccentric neurotic personality becomes familiar through prolonged and patient observation.[1]

Finally, the observer's own repressions must be eliminated if psychoanalysis is to prove a reliable form of investigation. To overcome this difficulty the observer has to be analyzed himself to overcome his repressions and learn to understand the unconscious elements in his personality and thus become sensitive to them in others. Let us take the previous example of the soldier who attacked his superior officer. An observer of this scene who represses his own tyrannical disposition could naturally miss the sadistic note in the officer and blame the underling. The former's attitude would appear natural to him; the latter's subversive and reprehensible. To reverse this situation he would be forced to reckon with his own domineering propensities, which would cause internal conflict.

The didactic analysis (training analysis) which every trained analyst undergoes serves to overcome this kind of error. It increases the analyst's knowledge of his own personality and enables him to allow for the disturbing influence of his own

---

[1] With the gradual advancement of psychoanalytic knowledge, the length of time necessary for such an understanding of neurotic personalities is becoming shorter.

character. The International Psychoanalytic Association as well as the American Psychoanalytic Association has for many years made it obligatory for every psychoanalyst to undergo analysis before undertaking to analyze others. Just as astronomy discounts the "personal equation," so psychoanalysis cannot be accurate and comprehensive without insight into those subjective peculiarities which may interfere with observation.

We have enumerated four sources of error inherent in ordinary psychological observation which psychoanalytic technique has learned to avoid. The patient's unwillingness to reveal himself to the analyst is offset by his desire to be cured; the inability of the individual to give a full account of his mental state is overcome by the method of free association; the differences between the observer and the observed are minimized by long and systematic observation; and the investigator's blind spots are reduced by didactic analysis. By these four devices psychoanalysis has succeeded in refining the ordinary capacity to understand the mental processes of others and in developing a scientific method which can be learned and controlled objectively by the serious student.

The efficacy of this method has been demonstrated by the improved insight into psychoses and neuroses which ordinary understanding, and even the genius of the great authors, has failed to achieve. The seemingly unintelligible, irrational and senseless behavior of the insane, the eccentricity and irrationality of the psychoneurotic's symptoms and dreams can now be explained and described in intelligible language.

4. CONCLUSIONS

The significance of psychoanalysis for medicine resides in the following two achievements: (1) With a technique adapted to psychological phenomena, it has developed a consistent and empirically founded theory of personality serviceable as a basis for the understanding and treatment of mental disturbances. (2) It has illustrated the fact that living beings are psychobiological entities, by investigating in detail the interrelation of physiological and psychological processes. The greater part of these investigations must, however, be left to the future for completion.

BIBLIOGRAPHY

ALEXANDER, F.: *The Medical Value of Psychoanalysis.* New York, W. W. Norton & Company, Inc., 1936.

————: "Psychoanalysis and Medicine," in *The Harvey Lectures, 1930–1931.* Baltimore, Williams & Wilkins Company, 1931, p. 88.

FRENCH, T. M.: "A Clinical Approach to the Dynamics of Behavior," in *Personality and the Behavior Disorders,* Vol. I. J. McV. Hunt, Ed. New York, The Ronald Press Company, 1944, p. 255.

HARTMANN, H.: *Die Grundlagen der Psychoanalyse.* Leipzig, Georg Thieme Verlag, 1927.

Chapter III

The Basic Principles of Psychodynamics

1. FUNDAMENTAL POSTULATES

EVERY SCIENTIFIC theory operates with certain underlying assumptions. They are not always explicitly stated, but are assumed and sometimes overlooked even by theoreticians. The more complex the field, the more important it is to clarify these basic postulates. Advances in knowledge, as for example in the theory of relativity, come from the re-evaluation of basic assumptions. Psychology, perhaps more than any other science, requires a clarification of its tacit assumptions. It differs from other sciences in that both its methods and its objects are psychological, such as feelings, motives, strivings, and thoughts. The psychologist, therefore, is confronted with the seemingly unsolvable problem of cutting a knife with a knife.

PSYCHOLOGY IS A VALID SCIENCE

The first assumption made by every psychologist is that minds can study minds. The only exception is the behaviorist, who observes only the outward manifestations of the inner life and does not deserve, strictly speaking, to be called a psychologist. In the preceding chapter the transformation of common-sense psychology into a scientific method by psychoanalysis was described.

PSYCHOLOGY IS A BIOLOGICAL SCIENCE

The second assumption underlying the following discussion is that the process of life can be studied both by the somatic investigation of the physical manifestations and by the psychological investigation of the psychological manifestations of the organism. This dual approach is possible because the human organism not only functions mechanically but is also aware of its emotions, needs, and wishes and can communicate them in speech. An automobile climbing a hill has no sensation of effort or fatigue, nor does it experience a wish to reach the top. In this it is unlike a man, and this obvious difference makes all comparisons between machines and living organisms not only inadequate but in many respects misleading.

Man can describe his sensations to others. Verbal communication is therefore the most important instrument of psychology. Whenever this method cannot be employed, as in animal psychology or in the study of small children, the results are at best inferential. It is equally difficult to understand a person who cannot talk one's language.

The somatic and psychological analyses of life are two approaches to the same thing. The former describes the operations of the body, the latter its inner experiences. Inner experiences have their own principles of causality, which can be either formulated in logical syllogisms or stated in terms of recurrent emotional connections which might be called emotional syllogisms. An example of the former is: "I need food —I can have it only for money—therefore I must get money," a formula which covers the greater part of behavior in contemporary civilization.

An example of an emotional syllogism would be: "He hurt me—therefore I want to hurt him." This is not a logical sequence but is a common emotional syllogism of wide applicability.

Logical and emotional sequences are both considered here as ways of adapting the organism to its environment and of preserving its existence. The functions of the mind are as truly biological as locomotion and breathing and are adaptive mechanisms which sometime in the future will probably be described in terms of physics and chemistry. In the present state of our knowledge, however, the psychological approach gives a more detailed insight into these complex biological functions.

2. THE PRINCIPLE OF STABILITY (FREUD-FECHNER)

Life consists in a continuous cycle of supply and output of energy. Energy is consumed and must be regularly replaced, and this requires a fresh supply from the environment. In the higher animals, the primary function of the cerebrospinal and autonomic nervous system is to maintain this dynamic equilibrium, which is upset both by external stimuli and by the process of living itself.

Disturbances of equilibrium appear psychologically in the form of needs and wishes which seek gratification and serve as the motive of voluntary behavior. A basic tendency of the organism is to keep these psychological tensions at a constant level. Freud borrowed this principle from Fechner and called it the "principle of stability." Its physiological counterpart was first recognized by Claude Bernard and formulated by Cannon in his principle of "homeostasis," the tendency of living organisms to preserve internal conditions like temperature and the concentration of body fluids at a constant level. The principles of stability and homeostasis are identical, one describing it in psychological, the other in physiological terms.

The psychoanalytic theory of the ego is that its function is to implement the principle of stability. The ego is the governing head of the organism and is doubly perceptive. By *internal* sensory perceptions it registers internal disturbances of the physicochemical equilibrium, perceiving them as needs and sensations. Through *external* sensory perceptions it registers the environmental conditions upon which the gratification of its needs depends. It has also *integrative* and *executive* functions. It is the center of motor control, and by confronting its internal with its external perceptions it can integrate them and gratify subjective needs as much as is possible under given external conditions (*co-ordinated goal-directed voluntary behavior*). A further function of the ego is protection from excessive external stimuli.

The principle of stability does not distinguish the quality of different instincts, drives, or emotions, though it applies to all of them, whether they represent such fundamental needs as hunger and sex or more complex impulses like curiosity and creativity, conflict and revenge, or complex emotional tendencies which find expression in such processes as weeping, laughing, or sighing.

It is evident that the principle of stability is identical with the so-called instinct of self-preservation, but is a more precise and useful formulation of the same thing—namely, that the organism strives to preserve those optimal internal conditions under which the process of life is possible.

3. THE PRINCIPLE OF ECONOMY OR INERTIA

Every organism is born with automatic functions, the unconditioned reflexes, which are useful for maintaining life or, more precisely, for maintaining those constant conditions within the organism which are necessary for life. All internal vegetative functions such as digestion, the circulation of the blood, breathing, and excretion are examples of useful automatic mechanisms. They do not require conscious effort and, with the exception of certain alimentary and excretory functions, belong to the hereditary equipment of the organism. Other functions, most of which regulate the relation of the organism to its environment, must be learned through trial, error, and repetition. Behavior patterns which prove adequate in maintaining biological and psychological homeostasis are repeated until they become automatic and are performed with minimum effort. This whole process is called learning. It consists of two phases: (1) groping experimentation through trial and error and (2) repetition of the adequate behavior patterns which have been found useful by trial and error. Learning aims ultimately at the gratification of need with the least expenditure of energy. Through repetition useful behavior patterns become automatic and effortless. Next to the principle of stability the most common and basic tendency of the organism is to replace adjustments requiring effort inherent in experimentation by effortless automatic behavior. This general tendency—as we will see later—is of great importance for psychology.

Thus learning is based on two dynamic principles: (1) the principle of stability, which compels the organisms to find by experimentation behavior patterns suitable for reducing internal tensions experienced as needs and wishes by gratifying them; (2) the economy principle, consisting in the repetition of suitable behavior patterns, which thereby become automatic and effortless. This second phase of learning merely consolidates the newly acquired learning by repetition. The stability principle expresses merely the tendency of the organism to maintain constant optimal conditions for life, and alone it is not sufficient to describe animal behavior.

This tendency toward stability is further defined by the principle of inertia—namely, that the organism tends to perform the functions necessary for maintenance of constant conditions with minimum expenditure of energy. This energy-saving tendency we shall call interchangeably the "principle of economy" or the "inertia principle." To a large degree, though not completely, it corresponds to the so-called "repetition compulsion." [1] These two principles together are the most universal dynamic principles of life.

The advantage to the organism of the principle of economy is obvious. It permits the saving of energy which adaptation to the environment requires. The energy saved by automatic behavior can be utilized to meet novel situations which require strenuous groping experimentation.

It is important, however, to realize certain disadvantages in automatic behavior. Conditions change, and owing to growth the organism itself changes. Changed conditions require fresh adaptation. The adult cannot, like an infant, satisfy his needs by relying upon maternal help. He must learn independence and become active instead of passive. He must walk and eat and ultimately satisfy many other needs on his own. Growth requires continuous learning. The principle of inertia impels the organism to cling to automatic behavior which was satisfactory in the past but which is no longer adequate. This indolence was recognized by Freud who called it *fixation*. He also discovered that when conditions become difficult and novel or threatening situations present themselves, earlier patterns of behavior tend to reassert themselves. This disposition, which he called *regression,* has proved one of the fundamental factors in psychopathology. In a later chapter the significance of both fixation and regression will be discussed in more detail.

Changing conditions require *flexible behavior* or, in other

1 See discussion of the repetition compulsion on page 40.

words, rapid *ad hoc* responses which are suitable at the moment but might be inappropriate in another situation. The capacity for sudden shifts of conduct belongs to the most highly developed functions of the personality, which will be discussed later as the integrative functions of the ego. It rests on the ability to learn from past experiences through memory and to exercise reason in abstraction and differentiation. By memory and reason man is able not only to continue behaving in ways he has found useful but to change as actual situations require. Life is thus a continuous struggle between the organism's tendency to retain old patterns on the principle of inertia and the challenge of growth and changed circumstances to adopt new ones.

The principles of stability and inertia can explain only those biological phenomena which consist in the preservation of life by useful adaptive responses. Another principle, that of surplus energy, is required for understanding growth and propagation.

COMMENTS

The recognition of the fundamental tendency to save energy appears in Freud's writings explicitly in his theory of wit. He explains laughter as the abreaction of the pleasurable sensation when the effort to repress becomes suddenly unnecessary. This occurs when a witty remark permits the expression of a repressed tendency. One laughs off the saved energy which was used for repression.

A similar idea is implied in his view of "primary" and "secondary" mental processes. The primary processes can be studied best in dreams. They are not yet adjusted to reality, nor do they conform to logic, the internal representative of reality. The secondary processes are what might be called reality-adjusted thought processes. The mind tends to revert to the primary processes but must overcome this tendency in order to fulfill its function of preserving life. The adjustment of thought to reality requires greater effort than the primary processes, which follow the pleasure principle. In dreams and fantasy there is regression to the primary processes along the path of least resistance.

Freud's "repetition compulsion" is also closely related to the inertia principle. However, as Fenichel correctly points out, repetition compulsion refers really to different psychodynamic phenomena. He enumerates three categories of repetitions: (1) Periodicity of instincts rooted in periodicity of their physical sources. ("Every kind of hunger is ended by satiety, and satiety after a certain time gives way to hunger.") (2) Repetitions due to the tendency of the repressed to find an outlet. These are most pronounced in the so-called neurosis of destiny (fate neurosis). (3) Repetitions of traumatic events for the purpose of achieving a belated mastery. The best-known example is repetitive dreams of traumatic neurotics in which they conjure up the traumatic event which they could not face; such dreams represent an effort at belated mastery of a traumatic situation.

The first and second categories are essentially the same and are the manifestation of what I call the inertia principle. Once a behavior pattern has been found which is suitable for the gratification of subjective needs, it is repeated until it becomes automatic. It is repeated because it follows the direction of least resistance—in other words, because it requires less output of energy. The third category is the manifestation of the homeostatic principle, the main executor of which is the ego. The ego reacts to every invasion of the organism by excessive stimuli with an effort to reduce these stimuli to a constant level. It continues in its efforts as long as it does not accomplish this task. The traumatic dreams are manifestations of this relentless struggle of the ego to master a situation in which it has failed in the past. According to this view Freud's repetition compulsion can be further reduced to two different psychodynamic principles: (1) the inertia principle and (2) the principle of stability.

The principle of economy was formulated explicitly by Ernst Mach, who described it in his study of the development of scientific knowledge. His main point is that thought is adapted gradually to reality, as illustrated by the evolution from magic to science. This gradual adaptation is counteracted by the inertia of habitual ideas. When a generalization is made which fits certain facts, it is stubbornly held until contradictory evidence compels its revision. The natural tendency is to adhere to what has already been achieved. Revision requires effort; old formulas can be repeated without a fresh investment of energy. Mach did not know that the adaptation of instincts follows the same principle as that of thought. The Freudian concept of "fixation" as adherence to proved forms of instinctual gratification, if pursued consistently, includes the principle of inertia. Mach also pointed to the tendency of science to reduce knowledge to the fewest possible principles and called this the "economy of science."

4. GROWTH AND PROPAGATION AS MANIFESTATIONS OF THE PRINCIPLE OF SURPLUS ENERGY

EROTIC PHENOMENA

Every organism undergoes a biologically predetermined course of development. Mammals develop uniformly until birth and are subject to relatively few external influences. After birth, however, the influence of the external environment becomes more important. Nevertheless the principal phases of postnatal development are also predetermined. In the human being the completion of the myelinization of the nervous pathways occurs in a certain phase; co-ordination in grabbing, walking, speaking, etc., occurs in a more or less uniform way; the intellect begins to function at approximately the same age in all; the maturation of the sex glands and the termination of skeletal growth takes place similarly in everyone; and senescence, though with variations, sets in at approximately the same period in all cases.

The progression from birth to maturity can be viewed as a series of steps toward the mastery of functions which make the human being independent of its parents. Man first learns to masticate food and focus his eyes; then to co-ordinate movements which make grabbing possible. He then learns to walk, speak, and take a reasoned view of the world, and finally achieves maturity in his sexual development. The child, however, clearly resists his own progress toward maturity and clings to acquired adjustments in accordance with the principle of inertia. Whenever he is tired of the arduous task of constant readaptation or is confronted with new and difficult situations, he tends to fall back on earlier modes of behavior. Particularly successful previous adjustments serve as fixation points to which he regresses in times of emotional stress.

This resistance to growing up is a most conspicuous trait in all children, but it is only one aspect of the total picture. Growth, of course, is biologically predetermined, and the organism has no alternative than to accept it as an unalterable fact and adjust itself to it. There are, however, many psychological factors as impressive as inertia and regression which point toward growth and independence. Everything which the child learns is acquired originally through spontaneous playful experiment. Activities such as the moving of the limbs, focusing the eyes, and experiments in walking are not at first utilitarian but merely pleasurable. The young colt exuberantly racing in the meadow illustrates spontaneous pleasurable exertion. It is true that by these playful exercises the organism prepares itself for the serious struggle for life which begins when parental care is outgrown and the organism is thrown on its own resources. In learning spontaneously and playfully to master the body, however, no such practical foresight governs the behavior. The child plays and exercises its voluntary body functions merely for the sake of the pleasure derived from these activities. The hands grab for the sake of grabbing and not to obtain food, the eyes focus for the sensation of seeing, and the legs are used in walking and running because this is enjoyable. One of the fundamental discoveries of Freud was that these playful exercises, along with the mature manifestation of sexuality, belong to the same category which he called "erotic." This was the rediscovery of a fact known intuitively to the ancient Greeks. The Greek god, Eros, was the god of both love and play and was represented appropriately by a child.

Erotic phenomena do not follow the principle of inertia. They are designed not to save energy but to expend it spontaneously. They are creative and progressive and serve as the dynamic motor power behind growth and propagation. They do not represent automatic repetitions or utilitarian adjustments but lead the organism toward new ventures and experiments. The practical utilization of the faculties which the organism has acquired by pleasurable experiment is a secondary step. The faculties must first be acquired separately before they can become integrated in a sensible manner for adaptive purposes. The energy spent in this lavish experimental and playful manner is surplus energy, not used for preserving homeostatic stability or survival. Its discharge, however, is one specific manifestation of the homeostatic principle. Excess of unused energy disturbs homeostatic equilibrium and must therefore be discharged. The origin of this surplus energy is the next question to be considered.

5. THE VECTOR ANALYSIS OF THE LIFE PROCESS

From the point of view of energy, life can be viewed as a relationship between three vectors: (1) the intake of energy in the nutritive substances and oxygen; (2) their partial retention for use in growth; and (3) the expenditure of energy to maintain existence, its loss in waste, in heat, and in erotic playful activities. In the mature organism the erotic activities assume the form of propagation. This occurs first in puberty as a new kind of eliminating function: the production of germ cells. Propagation may be understood as growth beyond the limits of the individual biological unit. It follows the pattern of propagation in monocellular organisms. The process of growth has a natural limit when the cell reaches maturity. Thereafter reproduction occurs through the division of the cell. When a biological unit reaches a certain size addition of substance and energy becomes impossible because its capacity to organize living matter has reached its limit. Individual growth then stops and propagation serves as a means of releasing surplus. Otherwise the homeostatic equilibrium would be disturbed.

Energy which is not needed to maintain life in equilibrium is called here surplus energy. This is the source of all sexual activity. In the infant, whose needs are satisfied by adults, the incorporating and retentive vectors outweigh the elimination. Hence the rapid growth. In spite of retention in the form of growth there is still much surplus energy neither stored nor used to maintain existence. The residuum is released in erotic activities. This explains the preponderance of erotic over self-preservative behavior in the child. When the child expends energy erotically he discovers at play new uses for his organs and exercises them until mastery is achieved and their different functions become integrated in a utilitarian fashion for independent existence. Erotic play for the sake of pleasure is the first phase, and the utilization of the functions acquired during erotic play is the second. This may appear paradoxical, but the prolonged dependence of the child upon the parents permits him the luxury of playful erotic activities. The gradual automatization of the adaptive utilitarian functions liberates energy which can be used in the child for erotic play and in the adult in sublimated creative activities and biological propagation. Thus the energy-saving principle and the creative use of surplus energy are interwoven and combine to maintain life and permit propagation. Repetition makes useful functions automatic and saves energy which can be used for growth and procreation.[2]

COMMENTS

The concept of surplus energy as the source of sexuality has been formulated in somewhat different terms in Ferenczi's *Thalassa.* He writes:

"One of the most gallant tasks of physiology would be the demonstration of those organic processes which make possible the summation of single eroticisms into genital eroticism. According to the hypotheses outlined above, whenever an organ fails to indulge its pleasure tendencies directly but renounces these in favor of the organism as a whole, substances may be secreted from this organ or qualitative innervations be shifted to other organs and eventually to the genital, it being the task of the latter to equalize in the gratificatory act the free-floating pleasure tensions of all the organs." [3]

To Ferenczi sexuality appeared as a discharge of "all those

---

[2] See further discussion of this concept of sexuality as a manifestation of surplus energy on pages 75–80.

[3] S. Ferenczi, *Thalassa: A Theory of Genitality.* Albany, The Psychoanalytic Quarterly Press, 1938.

accumulated amounts of unpleasure which, side-tracked during the utility functioning of the organs, were left undealt with, undisposed of. In ejaculation all those autotomic tendencies (tendency to get rid of a part of the body) are summated, the carrying out of which was neglected by utility functioning." [4] Every organ has its own individuality, its physiology of pleasure in contrast to its physiology of function. The summation of those excitations which have no utility constitutes genital sexuality, which releases accumulated, unused energy. The view stated in the previous chapter agrees with Ferenczi's theory in many respects.

Freud on more than one occasion raised the question whether sexuality was not merely quantitative in character. He writes in his *Three Contributions:* ". . . sexual excitation arises as an accessory to a long series of internal processes when the intensity of these processes has exceeded certain quantitative limits." [5]

Later he made a similar statement in his *Instincts and Their Vicissitudes:* "Are we to suppose that the different instincts which operate upon the mind but of which the origin is somatic are also distinguished by different qualities and act in the mental life in a manner qualitatively different? This supposition does not seem to be justified; we are much more likely to find the simpler assumption sufficient—namely, that the instincts are all qualitatively alike and owe the effect they produce only to the quantities of excitation accompanying them, or perhaps further to certain functions of this quantity. The difference in the mental effects produced by different instincts may be traced to the difference in their sources. In any event, it is only in a later connection that we

[4] *Loc. cit.*
[5] S. Freud, *Three Contributions to the Theory of Sex.* New York, Nervous and Mental Disease Publishing Company, 1930.

shall be able to make plain what the problem of the quality of instincts signifies." [6]

Still later, however, after he formulated his dual instinct theory (life versus death instinct) he was more and more inclined to attribute to sexuality a specific quality.

French came to conclusions similar to my views. He discarded the qualitative distinction between destructive and erotic drives and tried to explain the differences from quantitative factors. According to his view, "it is no longer necessary to regard erotic and destructive impulses as manifestations of two separate and antagonistic drives." He concluded that too intense desires make the ego's integrative task more difficult but that hope encourages integration. With hope the ego is able to endure the temporary frustrations always required in co-ordinating different desires into a rational behavior pattern. If hope disappears, intense desires may become dissociated from an integrated pattern and be released in rage. The surplus energy left over from other activities is discharged in erotic behavior. This part of French's theory is identical with Ferenczi's and with my own that erotism implies surplus. The essence of my view is that the important contrast is not between erotic and aggressive impulses, for the latter also can be discharged erotically, but between erotic and purposeful integrated behavior. The same impulse can be expressed as a constituent part of a utilitarian pattern or erotically, when the impulse is not subordinated or co-ordinated to other impulses in the self-preserving interest of the whole organism.

The strongest argument for the view that sexuality should be defined as a specific, quantitatively and not qualitatively determined, mode of discharge of any excitation within the

[6] S. Freud, "Instincts and Their Vicissitudes," *Collected Papers*, IV, p. 60. London, Hogarth Press, 1934.

organism comes from the study of perversions. In perversions any emotional tension, if strong enough, becomes the psychological content of sexual excitation: hostile feelings in sadism, guilt feelings in masochism, curiosity in scoptophilia, pride in exhibitionism. The spontaneity and generosity of mature love is an example of the sexuality of the healthy mature organism. All sexual emotions have nonsexual equivalents. It is not their quality but the degree of tension involved and the mode of discharge which makes them sexual. Linguistic usage registers this fact by employing the same word for nonsexual and sexual love.

The views proposed here are nearer to Freud's earlier notions of sexuality.

6. THE DIFFERENT FORMS OF EROTIC BEHAVIOR

ORAL EROTICISM

The psychological characteristics of the consecutive phases of human development can be understood in the context of the general view just presented. The psychological trends of the growing organism in each phase of its growth reflect the underlying biological processes. The infant's existence at first centers in the accumulation and retention of energy. Its main occupation is growing. The infant's early existence is characterized by its rapid growth and helpless dependency. These are expressed in the dominant preoccupation with nutrition and desire to be taken care of. The so-called oral phase as described by Freud and other early psychoanalytic writers includes the pleasure sensation in the oral zone caused by sucking and a form of oral play (thumb-sucking), and dependent, passive, receptive, and demanding attitudes toward the mother.

As we have seen, many bodily functions can yield erotic

pleasure and can be exercised for their own sake without any consideration for the self-preservative needs of the total organism. Thumb-sucking is a playful, erotic practice of the incorporative function independent of its utilitarian aspect —the incorporation of food. It manifests a surplus excitation beyond that caused by hunger. Its homeostatic value consists merely in freeing the organism of surplus excitation.

The first to suspect that thumb-sucking is related to sexual pleasure was not a psychoanalyst. Lindner, a Hungarian pediatrician, suggested the sexual nature of thumb-sucking in a remarkable article published at a time when infantile sexuality was as yet unrecognized. Lindner observed older children who indulged in this habit and reported their sensations. He noticed that thumb-sucking often coincided with masturbation and concluded that it must have some relation to sexuality. This article would have remained unnoticed if Freud had not unearthed it to substantiate his own views. He had, however, discovered the sexual nature of thumb-sucking independently.

The pleasure felt in nursing is closely related to certain emotional attitudes. The main feeling is probably security resulting from relief from the unpleasant tension caused by hunger. This, together with the sense of being cared for, becomes linked with the act of incorporation and with pleasure located in the mouth's mucous membrane. Originally these oral sensations have a passive connotation. The mammary gland has erectile tissue and squirts milk into the child's mouth. It is appropriate to call this whole complex of emotions and localized pleasure oral receptive or oral incorporative.

There is, however, another emotional attitude connected with oral assimilation. When the flow of milk is insufficient, the child bites. It tries to take by force what it has not passively received. An aggressive oral attitude can thus be distinguished from an earlier receptive one (Abraham). Another characteristic emotional link with oral activity is envy. This early oral tendency is a possessive one and can be observed in the child's envious reaction when another sibling takes his place at the mother's breast (sibling rivalry). In some cultures like that of Bali, this envy is deliberately encouraged by deliberately tantalizing the older child in exposing him to the nursing of the younger one; this is a regular feature of the Balinese cultural pattern (Margaret Mead).

ANAL EROTICISM

The excremental functions also yield pleasurable sensations. The child's coprophilic interests and activities evidence a supercharge which exceeds the requirement to eliminate waste. The child discovers that the other end of the intestinal tract can supply pleasure similar to that which he has known from suckling. This is caused by the pressure of a solid body on the mucous membrane of the anus and by the retention of the fecal mass. The pleasure obtained from anal retention is the chief obstacle in training children to regulate excretion. When interrupted by parental insistence on regulated and controlled evacuation, the child rebels.

Psychoanalytic observation of children and adult neurotics has shown that anal retentiveness is connected with stubbornness, independence, and possessiveness. The child experiences pleasure in withholding the products of his body to which no one but himself has any access. Possessiveness, stubbornness, and a sense of independence are linked with this. Its connection with possessiveness is best seen in the emotional relationship between money and excrement. Expressions like "filthy with money," "filthy lucre," the Roman proverb *pecunia non olet* ("money does not stink"), the ass in the fable which produced gold coins instead of feces, John Bull sitting on his money bag, the word *possedere* (from *sedere,* to sit) are a few of many examples which reveal the intimate unconscious link between money and feces. This is not surprising when one realizes that excrement is the child's first possession. In order to persuade him to part with it at regular intervals, the mother offers inducements like praise or candy or other tokens of affection. It is therefore the first currency which the child can exchange for other values.

The relation of anal eroticism to independence is recognized instinctively by calling the child's chamberpot the throne, his symbol of authority. The intimate relation between anal retentiveness, the sense of independence, and its exaggeration, stubbornness, is based on the fact that sphincter control is one of the first functions which the child masters. He retains or surrenders the products of his body at will and resists or yields to adult pressure. It is noteworthy that drastic interference with the child's oral gratifications encourages anal retentive attitudes which compensate for the inhibited oral gratifications.

Abraham distinguished two anal phases, one dominated by retentive, the other by eliminative pleasure. Whether these follow chronologically is questionable. It is certain, however, that not only retention but also expulsion is pleasurable and that the feelings connected with expulsion are quite different from those of retention. The retentive pleasure is connected with a sense of independence and possessiveness; the expulsion of excrement is associated with pride in what is, indeed, the child's first accomplishment. It is usual to consider these eroticisms as belonging to the second or anal-erotic phase of instinctual development. It is difficult to substantiate the theory that an oral phase precedes the anal phase, for it is certain that they overlap. The emotional life of the child centers in interest in both nutrition and excretion, and his eroticism follows a similar path.

The fact that the child's toilet training brings the excremental function into the foreground may explain the view that the anal phase follows the oral phase. After weaning, toilet training is the second serious systematic interference with the child's basic biological functions. These interferences are particularly drastic in our era of clock feeding and insistence upon early toilet training (Benedek, Karl Menninger). Earlier oral deprivations occasioned attacks of rage and stimulated oral aggression in biting. Frustration is now experienced in excretion, and it evokes sadistic aggression. This becomes erotic when surplus energy is suddenly discharged. Hurting for its own sake, merely for discharging accumulated rage, is erotic aggression and is called sadism. In contrast to aggression designed to eliminate obstacles interfering with subjective needs, sadism, like all erotic phenomena, releases pleasurable aggression for its own sake. The early connection between sadism and excretion led to the concept of anal sadism, the primary motive of which is to hurt the object of hostility by soiling it.

OTHER EARLY TYPES OF EROTICISM

Along with the development of oral and anal interests the child engages in various other types of erotic play. He discovers gradually the uses of his limbs and eyes and exercises them for a considerable period playfully and with erotic pleasure but not for useful purpose. These activities may be called muscular and visual or scoptophilic eroticism.

The original concept of erogenous zones in the mucous membranes of the mouth and rectum assumes a different meaning when we realize that a great many functions of the body may be sources of erotic pleasure.

PHALLIC EROTICISM AND THE OEDIPUS COMPLEX

As soon as the child achieves a certain degree of independence, other types of behavior and erotic gratification become increasingly pronounced. These have been called phallic because they involve urination and masturbation. Their emotional complements are competitiveness, assertiveness, pleasure in achievement and ambition (Jones). This is a period of testing various faculties of body and mind in play. Learning through identification with the attitudes of adults is an important feature of this phase of life. It is difficult to define precisely the beginning and end of this period, but in most children it reaches its peak in the fifth or sixth year. Most of what was originally known of this period was reconstructed from the reports of adult neurotics. The rapidly growing observations of child analysts have, however, confirmed this reconstruction in all details. The aggressive impulses assume at this time a more co-ordinated and personal form. In early infancy the child reacts to frustration with rage, whether it is caused by the interference of the adults or by impersonal means—for example, a chair which obstructs the child in reaching for an object. This rage is expressed in un-co-ordinated muscular activity. In the phallic period hostility is directed more purposefully and competitively. Love is still dependent, possessive, and demanding as in the oral and anal phases, but it anticipates certain features of later sexual feelings. The development of erotic drives does not run a course precisely parallel with the rest of either physical or mental growth; sexual impulses outstrip the rest. This discrepancy is clearly observable in the typical emotional constellation of this age, the Oedipus complex, a mixture of love, jealousy, inferiority, and guilt occasioned by the child's possessive sexual attraction to the parent of the opposite sex. The origins of guilt will be dealt with later in

SALVE REGINA
COLLEGE LIBRARY

connection with the development of the ego. Much of this period of life is later obscured by what Freud has called infantile amnesia. This extends over the first six years of life and permits only isolated and fragmentary recollections to survive. The amnesia is due to repression, the nature of which will be discussed in the next chapter. Here it need only be said that the repressions are due to discrepancy between instinctual and ego development. The child's personality has to meet both psychosexual tension and aggressive impulses which he can neither relieve nor control by genital and muscular activity. This uneven development of instinct, intellect, and genitality explains the child's emotional conflicts. Childhood is the most vulnerable phase of human development. Bad educational or traumatic experiences of any kind which may increase this conflict exert a pathogenic influence upon later life.

Along with Oedipus rivalry, sibling rivalry attains a new importance. Siblings in the pregenital phase rival each other for the mother's love; in the phallic period they try to outdo each other more actively. The little boy who once envied his little sister's or brother's privileges as a baby now begins to compete for the right to stay up later in the evening, to leave home unaccompanied, to know and do what the older members of the family know and do. In contrast to the early regressive type of sibling rivalry this may be called a progressive type of rivalry.

The repression of the conflicting feelings of the Oedipus period accompanies the gradual disappearance of the child's earlier sexual curiosity. This is replaced by curiosity about the surrounding world, which is encouraged and developed by education. This period of latency is assumed to start about the sixth year and lasts until puberty.

GENITAL IMPULSES

In puberty the organism undergoes endocrinological changes and the sexual impulses assume a more adult form. The organism is now reaching its mature state and the sexual glands begin to function. After maturation the child becomes biologically adult and able to produce its kind. The emotional developments consist primarily in the struggle of the adolescent to adjust himself to his new biological status. Competition becomes the central emotional issue, motivated by insecurity in the newly achieved maturity. The adolescent, though biologically in full possession of his faculties, has still to prove himself. Measuring up to others is the natural way of overcoming his sense of inferiority. Adolescent competitiveness, the tendency to show off, and other characteristic defenses against insecurity distinguish this period of life. The sexual impulses are competitive and at first have a psychological content similar to those in the phallic phase. Only when maturity has been fully accepted and the young male and female feel secure does mature love appear as a new feature in the emotional structure. In adolescence the sexual object serves primarily to increase self-confidence, as a proving ground for the ego. In maturity love assumes for the first time a generous, giving quality, the evidence of strength and energy which the mature organism no longer requires for its own maintenance. This type of love is what Freud called genital sexuality.

It is obvious that even the small child is tender and generous in the love it displays toward its family, its dolls, and its pets. Close observation, however, reveals that this affection is based on identification with its objects. The child loves others as an indirect way of loving itself. In adult love a new component enters, corresponding to the state of saturation, the urge to give of itself abundantly. It is best represented in Greek mythology by the goddess Ceres, with her over-flowing horn of plenty.

In psychoanalytic literature the attempt was made by Freud and Ferenczi to explain genital sexuality as the summation and integration (amphimixis) of pregenital impulses. According to Ferenczi, genital sexuality is a mixture of anal and urethral impulses with their expulsive and retentive characteristics. This view overlooks the fact that with maturation the dynamic equilibrium of the organism has changed. The production of sperm cells is a novel event, and that self-giving attachment reaches beyond the previous impulses of the developing organism, the main concern of which is the completion of its own growth. The dependence and possessiveness implied in oral receptivity reflect psychologically the biological condition of early infancy. Competitiveness is the mark of adolescence, but the capacity for genuine love characterizes maturity. The cup is full and overflows. Genitality cannot be explained merely as the summation of pregenital impulses. In maturity a new factor is added: the impulse to give, which is a new derivative of elimination on the pregenital level. In pregenital phases elimination was equivalent merely to elimination of waste products.

The difference between pregenital relationships and the genital attitude is well expressed in the notion of narcissism (self-love) as distinguished from the love of objects outside the self (object love). In all pregenital attitudes the narcissistic attitude prevails. The infant is highly narcissistic, and its interests in the external world are completely subordinated to its self-interest. Later, through identification with external objects, the child's interest is gradually but increasingly invested in outside objects, but love which is independent of identification appears only in maturity.

BIBLIOGRAPHY

ABRAHAM, K.: "A Short Study of the Development of the Libido, Viewed in the Light of Mental Disorders," in *Selected Papers*. London, Hogarth Press, 1927, p. 418.

———: "Character Formation on the Genital Level of Libido," in *Selected Papers*. London, Hogarth Press, 1927, p. 407.

———: "Contributions to the Theory of the Anal Character," in *Selected Papers*. London, Hogarth Press, 1927, p. 370.

———: "The First Pregenital Stage of the Libido," in *Selected Papers*. London, Hogarth Press, 1927, p. 248.

———: "The Influence of Oral Erotism on Character Formation," in *Selected Papers*. London, Hogarth Press, 1927, p. 393.

———: "The Narcissistic Evaluation of Excretory Processes in Dream and Neuroses," in *Selected Papers*. London, Hogarth Press, 1927, p. 318.

———: "Restrictions and Transformations of Scoptophilia in Psychoneuroses; With Remarks on Analogous Phenomena in Folk Psychology," in *Selected Papers*. London, Hogarth Press, 1927, p. 169.

———: "The Spending of Money in Anxiety States," in *Selected Papers*. London, Hogarth Press, 1927, p. 299.

ALEXANDER, F.: "General Principles, Objectives, and Preliminary Results" (The Influence of Psychologic Factors upon Gastrointestinal Disturbances: A symposium), *Psychoanalyt. Quart.*, 3: 501, 1934.

———: "The Logic of Emotions and Its Dynamic Background," *Internat. J. Psycho-Analysis*, 16:399, 1935.

———: *Our Age of Unreason*. Philadelphia, J. B. Lippincott Company, 1942, Part Two.

BENEDEK, T.: "Adaptation to Reality in Early Infancy," *Psychoanalyt. Quart.*, 7:200, 1938.

BERNARD, C.: *Leçons de physiologie expérimentale appliquée à la médicine*. Paris, J.-B. Bailliere, 1855.

BRILL, A. A.: "Anal Eroticism and Character," *J. Abnorm. Psychol.*, 7:196, 1912.

CANNON, W. B.: *The Wisdom of the Body*. New York, W. W. Norton & Company, Inc., 1932.

FECHNER, G. T.: *Einige Ideen zur Schoepfungs- und Entwickelungsgeschichte der Organismen*. Leipzig, Druck und Verlag von Breitkopf und Haertel, 1873.

FENICHEL, O.: "The Drive to Amass Wealth," *Psychoanalyt. Quart.*, 7:69, 1938.

————: "The Pregenital Antecedents of the Oedipus Complex," *Internat. J. Psycho-Analysis*, 12:141, 1931.

FERENCZI, S.: "Composite Formations of Erotic and Character Traits," in *Further Contributions to the Theory and Technique of Psychoanalysis*. London, Hogarth Press, 1926, p. 257.

————: "The Ontogenesis of the Interest in Money," in *Contributions to Psychoanalysis*. Boston, Richard G. Badger, 1916, p. 269.

————: "Pecunia Olet," in *Further Contributions to the Theory and Technique of Psychoanalysis*. London, Hogarth Press, 1926, p. 362.

————: *Thalassa: A Theory of Genitality*. Albany, The Psychoanalytic Quarterly, Inc., 1938.

FRENCH, T. M.: "Goal, Mechanism and Integrative Field," *Psychosom. Med.*, 3:226, 1941.

————: "The Integration of Social Behavior," *Psychoanalyt. Quart.*, 14:149, 1945.

FREUD, S.: *Beyond the Pleasure Principle*. London, Hogarth Press, 1922.

————: "Character and Anal Erotism," in *Collected Papers*, II. London, Hogarth Press, 1924, p. 45.

————: *The Ego and the Id*. London, Hogarth Press, 1927.

————: *A General Introduction to Psychoanalysis*. New York, Boni & Liveright, Inc., 1920.

————: "The Infantile Genital Organization of the Libido," in *Collected Papers*, II. London, Hogarth Press, 1924, p. 244.

————: "Instincts and Their Vicissitudes," in *Collected Papers*, IV. London, Hogarth Press, 1934, p. 60.

————: "On the Transformation of Instincts with Especial Reference to Anal Erotism," in *Collected Papers*, II. London, Hogarth Press, 1924, p. 164.

————: "The Passing of the Oedipus Complex," in *Collected Papers*, II. London, Hogarth Press, 1924, p. 269.

————: "Repression," in *Collected Papers*, IV. London, Hogarth Press, 1925, p. 84.

————: *Three Contributions to the Theory of Sex*. Nervous and Mental Disease Monograph Series No. 7. New York, Nervous and Mental Disease Publishing Company, 1930.

JONES, E.: "Anal-erotic Character Traits," in *Papers on Psychoanalysis*, 4th Edition. Baltimore, William Wood & Company, 1938, p. 531.

————: "Hate and Anal Erotism in the Obsessional Neurosis," in *Papers on Psychoanalysis*, 2nd Edition. Baltimore, William Wood & Company, 1919, p. 540.

————: "The Phallic Phase," in *Papers on Psychoanalysis*, 4th Edition. Baltimore, William Wood & Company, 1938, p. 571.

————: "Urethralerotik und Ehrgeiz," *Internat. Ztschr. f. Psychoanal.*, 3:156, 1915.

KLUCKHOHN, C., and MURRAY, H. A.: "Outline of a Conception of Personality," in *Personality*, C. Kluckhohn and H. A. Murray, Ed. Cambridge, Harvard University Press, 1948.

KUBIE, L.: "Instincts and Homoeostasis." *Psychosom. Med.*, 10:15, 1948.

LEVY, D. M.: *Studies in Sibling Rivalry*. New York, American Orthopsychiatric Association, 1937.

LEWIN, B. D.: "Kotschmieren, Menses und weibliches Ueber-Ich," *Internat. Ztschr. f. Psychoanal.*, 16:43, 1930.

LINDNER, L.: "Das Saugen an den Fingern, Lippen, etc. bei den Kindern," *Jahrbuch fuer Kinderheilkunde und Physische Erziehung*, Neue Folge, 14:68, 1879.

MACH, E.: *Die Analyse der Empfindungen und das Verhaeltnis des Physischen zum Psychischen*. Jena, G. Fischer, 1900.

————: *Die Mechanik in ihrer Entwickelung*. Leipzig, F. A. Brockhaus, 1883.

————: *Die Principien der Waermelehre*. Leipzig, J. A. Barth, 1896.

MASSERMAN, J. H.: *Principles of Dynamic Psychiatry*. Philadelphia, W. B. Saunders Company, 1946.

MENNINGER, K. A.: *Love against Hate*. New York, Harcourt, Brace and Company, Inc., 1942.

RADO, S.: "Die Wege der Naturforschung im Lichte der Psychoanalyse," in *Almanach fuer das Jahr 1929*. Wien, Internationaler Psychoanalytischer Verlag, p. 62.

ROHEIM, G.: "Heiliges Geld in Melanesien," *Internat. Ztschr. f. Psychoanal.*, 9:384, 1923.

SADGER, J.: "Ueber Urethralerotik," *Jahrbuch f. Psychoanalytische u. Pathologische Forschungen*, 2:409, 1910.

SAUL, L.: *Emotional Maturity*. Philadelphia, J. B. Lippincott Company, 1947.

STERBA, R.: *Introduction to the Psychoanalytic Theory of the Libido*. Nervous and Mental Disease Monograph Series No. 68. New York, Nervous and Mental Disease Publishing Company, 1942.

Chapter IV

The Concept of Sexuality

1. EARLY FREUDIAN VIEWS

WHEN FREUD first formulated his ideas on the instinctual constitution of personality he observed the customary distinction between the instinct of self-preservation and the sexual instinct which serves racial preservation. This distinction, however, soon led to theoretical difficulties. As soon as he recognized that sexual libido exists in infancy before the organism is either biologically or psychologically equipped for propagation, he had to extend his view of sexuality beyond those phenomena which are related to race preservation. He therefore termed sexual also all early pleasurable excitations which did not aid self-preservation, such as thumb-sucking, coprophilic behavior, and, of course, infantile masturbation. The theoretical difficulty in retaining the original distinction between the instinct of self-preservation and sexuality lay in the fact that early oral, anal, urethral, and muscular eroticism are closely connected with nutrition, excretion, grabbing, and locomotion, which become ultimately connected with self-preservation. Furthermore, the emotional accompaniments of infantile sexuality are self-centered and narcissistic. The first object of love is the self, and this makes the distinction between self-preservation and sexuality contradictory. The distinction between narcissistic libido and object libido drew attention to the fact that love may be directed toward the self or toward other objects, but it did not solve the problem. So-called pregenital sexual pleasure was experienced in self-preservative, mainly vegetative functions; and narcissism, a form of libido, was selfish and self-assertive and aimed at self-preservation. According to this view nearly all self-preservative functions were included in libido except aggression, and even this assumes a sexual connotation in the form of sadism. Jung proposed a solution to this dilemma by abandoning Freud's dualism and attributing everything to *libido*. This view was similar to Bergson's theory of *"elan vital"* and to the notions of German vitalists like Driesch. Freud, however, maintained his dualism to the end in spite of these theoretical difficulties and continued to distinguish between self-preservative and sexual instincts. He regarded aggressive hostile impulses as ego instincts distinct from sexuality.

It cannot be denied that the psychoanalytic theory of instincts remained confused for a long time. Until 1920, when Freud revised his views on instincts, his theory was never stated simply and clearly. The expressions *libido, ego drives, narcissism,* and *aggression* had been used vaguely, and it was impossible to make sharp distinctions or precise definitions. There was no answer to the question, "Of what does the self-preservative instinct consist?" except that it was made up of hostile and destructive impulses. All other self-preserving manifestations of the organism were called libidinous. The greatest difficulty, however, was that in sadism aggressive and destructive behavior possessed all the earmarks of sexuality. Furthermore, when destructiveness was turned against the self and became suicidal, it appeared paradoxically that aggression, which *ex hypothesi* was self-preservative, may end in destroying the self.

2. THE THEORY OF LIFE AND DEATH INSTINCTS

In order to overcome these inconsistencies while preserving a dualistic view of instincts, Freud proposed his theory of the instincts of life and death. According to this view, the erotic drive is a binding force, the fundamental manifestation of which is the anabolic phase of metabolism. The destructive death instinct, on the contrary, is a disintegrative force operative biologically in biochemical katabolism. Freud assumed that these two tendencies are always mixed in their psychological manifestations. This view, though hypothetical, seemed to agree with the observed facts better than the old distinction between ego-instincts and the sexual instinct, which did not adequately reckon with such antithetic impulses as love and hate and creativity and destructiveness. The earlier distinction between the instincts of self-preservation and racial preservation differentiated not two separate instincts but two different manifestations of the same, viz., love directed toward different objects. The erotic instinct in its narcissistic phase is self-preservative, but when it involves other objects than the self, it preserves the race. The distinction between destructive and erotic tendencies is, however, basic.

3. A CRITICAL DISCUSSION OF THE THEORY OF LIFE AND DEATH INSTINCTS

The theory of the death instinct was no longer an attempt to describe the instinctual forces but was rather a philosophical abstraction. Freud had distinguished between two conflicting tendencies—a constructive, unifying trend resulting in the development of cells into complex organisms and an opposite disintegrative force leading to death. According to this theory, the organism is born with a life potential which is gradually exhausted and counteracted by the disruptive death instinct. Freud considered both instincts expressions of a repetition compulsion which, in his view, is a basic characteristic of life and consists of a disposition to revert to a previous state. The death instinct inclines to revert to the original inorganic state; the life instinct attempts to re-establish the more complex state of organization that existed before cell division. Cell division or the separation of the germ plasm from the soma plasm is a sudden step in the direction toward death: it is a process of disintegration. The first part of the life curve toward maturation is a slow re-establishment of the complex mature state which existed before soma and germ plasm were separated. The germ plasm during the integrative process of growth rebuilds the complex multicellular organism. This constructive tendency is the life instinct.

This view is fundamentally a *vector theory* and depends upon a metabolic conception of life as a process consisting of continuous anabolic construction and katabolic disruption of the complex biomolecules.

The description of life as the result of construction and disintegration is well established in contemporary biology. Freud's new theory as a vector concept but without philosophical elaboration provides a useful orientation. Its difficulty lies in regarding the disintegrating factor as a death instinct.

Further observation shows that the disintegrating tendency is nothing but the separatistic, or in Freudian terms narcissistic, self-assertion of the constituent parts. In such highly organized structures as the bodies of vertebrates the constituent parts die as soon as their connection with the body is severed. The far-reaching specialization of the cells and their interdependence makes individual life for them impossible. Death is merely the inevitable result but not necessarily the aim of this disruptive tendency. Freud considered his theory of instincts generally valid and also applicable to social organization. In society, however, it is obvious that the disruptive tendency of the units is not suicidal but a crude expression of the wish of the constituent units to live as individuals. For example, the Austro-Hungarian Empire did not dissolve through a suicidal act, because empires are not individuals and have no suicidal tendencies. Disruption was due to the nationalism of the Czech, Rumanian, and Serbian minorities who wanted to live separately and independently.

The disintegration of social groups can best be understood from a particularistic tendency of the constituent parts rather than from a universal death instinct. The reasoning which led Freud to the assumption of a death instinct runs approximately as follows: Biological units, cells, or human beings originally compete with each other and lead a disordered existence. When faced by a common enemy, their destructive tendencies unite against it. This allows the unifying erotic tendency, which is always present, to effect a coalition of the originally independent units. Up to this point there is no need to assume an innate death instinct, only outward-directed antagonistic tendencies between the units against each other. The assumption of a death instinct becomes relevant only if applied to the organization of the cell itself, which is a complex organization of biomolecules. Freud, indeed, consistently applied his death instinct to the biomolecules as the result of a destructive attitude of the biomolecules toward each other. This internal disruptive force is called the death instinct, since it aims at the disintegration of the cell, the most elementary of all biological units.

This view presupposes an earlier state in which the bio-molecules had been independent in competition and conflict with each other until some external pressure mobilized their aggression against a common foe. At this point they united by eros. Eventually, however, they become disrupted by the force of the disruptive tendency, the death instinct: in death organic matter again disintegrates into inorganic. Carried out consistently, this theory becomes metaphysical and identifies molecular attractions and repulsions with love and hate in the Strindbergian sense.[1] The validity of this concept is obviously beyond proof and its usefulness for biology questionable.

It would appear that this dualistic view would be more applicable to social organization than to the development of cells, for the former can be observed in statu nascendi. The formation of a cell from the inorganic state is a wholly unknown process. The development of multicellular from monocellular organisms is little understood. The formation of social groups, however, can be observed and even experimentally effected. An unorganized mass faced by a common foe will quickly organize, divide labor, and co-operate spontaneously. Some may defend the left flank, others the right, while others will provide supplies for the defenders. A leader may be chosen to organize the group. This process can be considered dynamically as an adaptation of the members of the group to a common task. The psychology involved has been well described by Freud as the spontaneous identification of individuals with each other under the pressure of common circumstances. The choice of a leader indicates the emergence of a dependent attitude in the face of danger. Another important psychodynamic principle in group formation is the sacrifice of self-interest, for consideration for

[1] Strindberg considered the chemical affinity and repulsion between molecules to be the same force which appears as love and hate in humans.

the interest of the other group members with whom he cooperates becomes a condition of each one's own security. If, under external pressure, an organized group persists, it will gain cohesiveness. The identification of the members with each other becomes more and more important as a cohesive force, as is clearly seen in nationalism. Moreover, through division of labor the individual members become to some degree dependent on each other. When, however, the pressure eases, individuality again asserts itself and may disrupt the organization, because originally only external necessity made its members renounce their personal freedom. This disruption is encouraged by the fact that no social group observes strict equality; some enjoy privileges which the others must sacrifice for the sake of co-operation. It is therefore natural that when there is no longer need for strict co-operation, the disruptive, selfish interests of individuals will again predominate. These are basic factors in sociodynamics of which the playroom and history supply abundant illustrations.

It is evident, then, that no death instinct is needed to explain social disintegration. Social organization can be understood in terms of the adaptation of individuals to an external situation. Only the members' self-preservative tendency and their identification with each other need be assumed for its understanding. Individualism and the disinclination of each member to sacrifice his sovereignty are dynamic forces no different from the instinct of self-preservation, and are rather derivatives of it. In no existing group do the individual members completely abandon their individuality. Disintegration of social groups is due to this individualism, not to any self-destructive instinct.

The cohesion of a group is probably based at first on mere self-preservation. This cohesion gradually increases by the identification of the group members with each other, their instinctive attachment to each other, and their dependence on their leader. With increasing interdependence, the tendency toward individual self-preservation becomes socialized. Clan spirit, tribal spirit, and nationalism express this cohesion through identification.

The application of elementary principles of sociodynamics to the formation of multicellular organisms might prove a fruitful working hypothesis. It would break with the widespread belief that complex systems can be understood only from principles prevailing in simpler ones, and that the study of social phenomena would profit from the application of biological principles rather than the reverse. Discussion of this point would, however, lead to theoretical considerations which are outside the scope of this discussion. Enough examples of both methods are available. Herbert Spencer in his *Study of Sociology* explained biological facts from the facts of sociology. Astronomical principles dealing with the more complex but visible planetary bodies have proved useful for an understanding of invisible atomic structures. Principles of chemistry have also shed light on problems of physics. Social organization takes place before our eyes and is in many respects better known than the biological dynamics of cells. It would not be surprising if an understanding of the dynamics of social groups would shed light upon the organization of multicellular organisms.

A few further remarks will illustrate more clearly the disadvantages of identifying the disintegrating factor in the Freudian theory of instincts as a death instinct rather than as the individualistic tendency of each biological unit. These remarks require an anticipation of the theory of neurosis which will be discussed in greater detail in a later chapter.

The theory of the death instinct was applied mainly to psychoneuroses and psychoses. It was assumed that since only two fundamental drives exist, one component of each neurotic symptom must be the death instinct. This view was developed most consistently by Karl Menninger, in whose theory every neurosis and psychosis must be considered in the last analysis as a partial suicide.

The study of neuroses, however, does not substantiate this conclusion in the least. What is found is a disintegration of complex emotional adaptations, and regression to earlier and simpler forms of gratification. When an individual cannot gratify his emotional needs on an adult level, he regresses to a more infantile and dependent attitude; but this can hardly be described as a partial suicide. There is protest against adult independence and an insistence upon being loved and cared for, if necessary at the sacrifice of others. This regression creates new emotional problems. Shame may develop and express the tension between the regressive behavior and adult standards, which are not wholly relinquished. To relieve this shame and sense of inferiority, other neurotic attitudes may develop, such as a disparaging and critical attitude toward others. Megalomanic self-esteem is another form of morbid defense.

The regression to an extremely self-centered attitude may cause feelings not only of inferiority but also of guilt and anxiety, which the individual seeks to evade through self-punishment. The analysis of such masochistic manifestations shows that they are subordinate to the infantile wish to be loved and aim at eliminating guilt which might otherwise block the wish to enjoy consideration at the expense of others. The dynamic nucleus of neuroses is regression to an earlier form of adaptation. This regression creates internal conflict, because the total personality does not participate in it. This discrepancy between it and more mature requirements is expressed in feelings either of inferiority or of guilt. The complex symptoms of a neurosis represent an unsuccessful attempt to eliminate the secondary conflicts caused by regressive gratifications, for example, by the wish to be loved by an all-powerful person, and to achieve security through dependence on that person. This is a common factor in neurosis but is not self-destructive. It is, on the contrary, a striking example of the life instinct in the Freudian sense. It is a wish to live, though on a more primitive level, and appears only when mature adjustment collapses because of the ego's inadequate integrative powers. The psychodynamic analysis of neurotic regressions shows clearly that a differentiation between life and death instincts is of little use for understanding psychopathological phenomena. Neuroses do not occur through a disturbance in the equilibrium of the two opposing basic instincts of life and death, but through conflict between the complex emotional adaptation of maturity and the more primitive patterns of childhood. These complex adaptive patterns can best be understood as hierarchal organizations in which partial functions and tendencies are subservient to a dominant goal (French).

This can best be demonstrated by concrete examples. A young man studies a profession to earn his living. His scientific desire to know something about his field is subordinate to his utilitarian wish for a career. In the course of his studies he may develop a deep attachment to one of his teachers and thus gratify a wish to be guided and to be dependent upon him. This dependent tendency, however, like his scientific curiosity, remains subordinate to his wish for a career. The gratification of the dependent attitude serves his dominant purpose of advancing his career, since he uses his teacher's help toward this advancement. While preparing for his profession, he may also become so fascinated by some aspect of his studies that he sacrifices his professional goal to his scientific curiosity. This may become so strong as to interfere with his career, and he may neglect all practical considerations and fail on the practical economic level. In order to satisfy his scientific curiosity he has ignored his obligation as an adult to support himself. He fails in his career and may never be able to realize his scientific ambitions. In this case creative enthusiasm assumes larger proportions than are practicable and is therefore not integrated with the need for survival.

A healthy compromise in the solution of the same problem is exemplified by the scientist who subordinates other interests to his scientific curiosity, but also provides for himself. He may teach in order to earn his living although his dominant aim remains the gratification of his scientific curiosity by research.

Another pattern obtains in the practical man who is devoted to his career. He capitalizes on his interests in order to earn his living and create a position in the world. The gratification of scientific curiosity is the scientist's dominant goal and other needs are subordinate to this.

The student who aims at a career but develops an excessive dependent love and admiration for his teacher may be deflected from his goal by this personal attachment. His filial loyalty may lead him to sacrifice his own interests to it and so miss his original mark. Here again a normally subordinate tendency may become dominant. Students naturally admire their teachers, but when this admiration becomes dominant it ceases to be mature and cloaks the neurotic desire for dependence at any cost.

All neuroses can be understood as disintegrations in which a single tendency, which has been a useful element in an adaptive pattern, emancipates itself and seeks isolated gratification in an impractical and disadvantageous manner which is incompatible with the patient's social situation and age.

Suicide is an extreme example of an isolated tendency run wild. Aggressive impulses which are subordinate to other goals like self-defense may disintegrate and seek self-destructive gratification if all other outlets are banned.

This may suffice to show that neuroses cannot be explained as conflicts between two basic instincts, those of life and death. The most common neurotic conflict arises from the refusal to accept maturity with all its effort and responsibilities and from the wish to resort to earlier, more dependent ways. The complex structure of the neurosis can best be understood as an attempt to resolve internal conflicts which arise as the unavoidable results of partial regressions. The total personality does not participate in the regression but remains partially on an adult level; this explains the conflict caused by partial regressions.

We conclude that the valuable element in Freud's theory of life and death instincts is the recognition of two dynamic vectors in life, one constructive and integrative, the other disintegrative. These two opposing vectors are, however, not manifestations of two contrary instincts. Biological units of a similar kind organize under the pressure of external danger and survive by combining resources and dividing responsibilities. The originally independent units, however, follow the principle of inertia and never give up their individual identity completely. Whenever the need for co-operation diminishes, the individualistic tendency of the units revives and the group disintegrates. When the interdependence of the units, through differentiation and division of labor, becomes as great as it does in multicellular organisms, the individual units lose their capacity for independent existence and disintegration necessarily leads to the death of the cells. This occurs in higher animals, whose cells cannot survive the disintegration of the organism. In social groups disintegration does not necessarily lead to the death of the members. Death consequently is not the aim of the disintegrating process but is occasionally its unavoidable result. It occurs only in biological systems in which the independent existence of the units becomes impossible through radical division and specialization of functions. It is important to remember that the integration and the disintegration of groups manifest the same dynamic force, the tendency of their members toward self-preservation. In order to survive, the units form an organized group, but only under external pressure. To regain their individual existence they may free themselves from the group whenever the need for group life relaxes. All groups are not equally successful, for different organizations have greater or lesser cohesion and stability.

The development of personality also consists in a progressive integrative process. The child is born with certain faculties and develops others through experience. Sense perception and muscular motility must be co-ordinated in useful behavior patterns. The child's dependence upon the mother, which persists longer in the human species than in most animals, delays co-ordination. Faculties and impulses subsist longer in elementary disorder and seek erotic gratification without regard to the needs of the organism as a whole. This is possible because for a considerable period the child is not required to use his faculties to gratify his vital needs. Personality development can well be conceived as the formation of dynamic patterns in which different functions are co-ordinated and afford the child increasing independence of adults. The main factor in this process, the progressive adaptation of individual needs to external conditions, is implied in Freud's concept of the transition from the pleasure to the reality principle, which will be discussed later. In the development of personality the early phases are characterized by a lack of integration. During this period the individual faculties become strengthened in play so that they may later become useful elements in the integrated functioning of the total personality. As in social organization, individual tendencies which later become integral parts of behavior patterns always retain some of their original independence. Whenever life presents insuperable obstacles to the gratification of needs, there may be reversion to earlier, less complex behavior patterns suitable to the more dependent phase of childhood. This may be described as a failure of the integrative functions. Because these regressive patterns are immature, they appear morbid and conflict with those portions of the personality which have not disintegrated. The individual tendencies emancipated from useful patterns seek individual goals no longer subordinate to those of the total organism.

A simple example of this is a patient, thirty-five years old, married, and the father of two children, who had led a stable existence as long as he worked under a fatherly friend of his family who gave him much moral support. When, at the instigation of his ambitious wife, he was promoted to a more responsible position in which he could not lean on anyone, he broke down. He had not arrived at an emotional maturity which permitted independent responsibility. His promotion placed him in a situation for which he was emotionally unprepared. The first result, therefore, was that he began to lean more heavily on his wife. Since she lacked motherly dispositions and protested against these increased demands of her husband, friction developed. After a period of marked strain the woman divorced her husband, who reacted by resorting to drink. This is a typical alcoholic history. Psychodynamically his drinking afforded regressive gratification of dependent cravings which had previously been satisfied by his reliance on his superiors in a manner compatible with his social and marital situation. His dependent relationship to his superior preserved his emotional equilibrium and was therefore useful in his work. This adjustment broke down as soon as he was called upon to bear more responsibility than he could. Then the dependence, which had had a useful function, detached and sought more primitive gratification in drinking. This became a goal in itself dissociated from other needs and thus threatened the patient's welfare.

The integration of separate functions in the total organism is adaptive and contributes to survival. It can ultimately be explained from the principle of stability. It is not, however, sexuality. The building stones of the integration consist, however, originally in erotic play, the manifestation of surplus energy which is gradually disciplined to aid survival.

What Freud called the death instinct is disintegration of mature behavior into its elementary parts. This takes place whenever the integrative functions fail in situations beyond the organism's adaptive capacity. The regression involves the principle of inertia, which encourages automatic repetition of old patterns even when novel effort is required. What Freud called the death instinct is a tendency not toward death, but toward old and worn patterns of life.

4. A PSYCHOSOMATIC VIEW OF SEXUALITY

We shall now attempt to review the considerations which led Freud to extend the concept of sexuality beyond procreation and to complement them with the fundamental dynamic principles stated in the previous chapter.

The different forms of erotic pleasure experienced by infants are similar to those of adult perversions. They are without doubt sexual in nature, although they do not contribute to the preservation of the race. Many functions and many parts of the body can yield erotic pleasure. The lips and mouth, the anal mucous membrane, the skin, can all produce erotic sensations when stimulated and can lead to excitation of the genitals. A child can experience erection through thumb-sucking. Equally significant is the fact that all intense emotions can be the psychological content of sexual excitation, the craving for love and care, love of others and the desire for bodily contact, the sadistic impulse to hurt and destroy, the masochistic inclination to suffer pain and humiliation, scoptophilic curiosity, and the exhibition of one's body in order to become the center of attention. These wide variations indicate that the sexual impulse does not have one specific content but that any emotion can become sexualized. On the basis of these observations Freud originally concluded that sexuality is not dependent on a special emotional quality, but must have a quantitative basis. Unfortunately he did not elaborate this irrefutable contention. In his latest theory of instincts, the theory of life and death instincts, he assumed that sex had a constructive or unifying quality. He was therefore forced to explain sadism, which is obviously neither unifying nor constructive, as a mixture of the life and death instincts. In his view all actual psychological tendencies are mixed.

Ferenczi maintained in his ingenious biopsychological speculations that the organism expresses sexually all tensions which it cannot or need not co-ordinate for useful purposes. This is essentially the equivalent of the view I later elaborated —that sexuality discharges any surplus excitation, regardless of its quality.

The correctness of this view can best be demonstrated in the most elementary form of propagation, cell division in the monocellular organism. When the organism reaches the limits of its growth, it can no longer increase and must divide. Surplus organic matter which cannot be integrated in a single biological unit is eliminated and becomes a new organism. This is the basic factor in racial preservation; all other forms, such as asymmetrical division in multicellular organisms, are derivations and modifications of it. Propagation results from surplus energy generated by growth. The psychological equivalent of propagation is love.

Adult perversions based on infantile eroticism discharge

surplus excitation which cannot be drained through other channels. The study of perversions confirms the view that erotic phenomena are manifestations of surplus excitation which cannot be integrated in the personality. Sexual sadists are incapable of expressing their aggressive feelings and their desires to dominate others by ordinary means. Mostly they are very timid, inhibited persons. Their aggressive and hostile impulses originate in early experiences but are inhibited in normal expression and can be relieved only by a short-circuit type of discharge in their sexual activity. Masochists conceal large amounts of accumulated guilt and a consequent need for punitive suffering. They also often display in human relationships an exaggerated egotism contrasting sharply with their sexual behavior. Sexual suffering compensates for their self-centered attitude in nonsexual human relations. It is instructive that when the masochistic sexual outlet is blocked, their need for nonsexual suffering increases and produces a kind of moral masochism. Sexual and moral masochism are related to each other like fluid in communicating tubes: when the level rises in one, it sinks in the other. Much the same thing can be observed in sexual exhibitionists, who are notoriously inhibited in asserting and expressing themselves freely in speech and gesture. They are more than normally modest and shy and the compulsive exhibition of their genitals is a sudden discharge of suppressed desire to impress others. Voyeurs are also extremely inhibited in all nonsexual forms of curiosity and inquisitiveness. The urge to observe has not become integrated for utilitarian purposes of the total organism but has retained its original erotic character. The sexual perversions of adults are fixations and regressions to the pregenital erotic interests of infancy and childhood. A more detailed discussion of them is reserved for a later chapter. They have been mentioned here only as illustrations of the principle of surplus as the basis of all erotic phenomena.

It has been mentioned before that infantile sexuality can also be explained on the principle of surplus. To summarize briefly what has already been stated about pregenital sexuality, all voluntary functions of the body are practiced originally in a playful, erotic manner during some phase of early development. At different periods of growth different functions take the lead. In the earliest, nutrition and excretion are in the foreground. Suckling movements practiced for the pleasure they yield indicate a surplus excitation beyond hunger. Coprophilic activities also have no useful physiological aim and attest to surplus excitation in the field of excretory functions. These again are surplus excitations of retentive and eliminating nature. All voluntary muscular activities in early life are practiced playfully and for no practical purpose. Later the intellect functions erotically, especially in curiosity, and represents surplus energy not yet requisite to survival. In early forms of curiosity, seeing and knowing are aims in themselves. Later they supply motivation for scientific interests in pure research. In puberty competition is the central issue and is an aim in itself. To prove oneself becomes a highly eroticized aim but serves as yet no useful purpose in the struggle for existence.

The genito-urinary tract in the course of maturation gradually assumes the function of draining surplus excitation. Phylogenetically in the cloacal state there was one common organ for elimination both of waste products and of germ cells; later it became divided into a urinary and a genital portion, but its function remains—that is to say, all excitations which are not utilized for the purpose of self-preservation are drained by it. In the early phases of life, sexual excitation is pregenital and often extragenital and can be relieved locally, in the mouth, anus, etc. Gradually more and more of the erotic excitations are discharged through the genito-urinary tract. *Every gratification intrinsically has an erotic character, which is satisfaction of a tendency for its own sake and not subservient to the needs of the total organism.* Free-floating impulses to assimilate, retain, or eliminate assume an erotic character when their gratification serves only to relieve surplus tension. Every surplus excitation which the organism cannot use for its own preservation is erotic and most of it is drained through the genito-urinary tract.

Incorporative tendency in the form of hunger is not considered an erotic phenomenon. However, its surplus manifestation in the form of thumb-sucking is called oral eroticism. Curiosity, which is requisite to orientation in the environment, is not erotic but becomes so when looking and knowing are isolated aims. Voyeurism is curiosity which serves no useful purpose, but only pleasure. Rage or destructiveness which is not defensive or necessary in obtaining the necessities of life becomes sadistic and erotic. Sadism is destructiveness for its own sake. Whenever surplus tensions accumulate beyond the limits of usefulness they are released in erotic forms. During development, impulses originally erotic become increasingly useful in maintaining life and so lose their erotic quality. The cruelty of little children, which is originally erotic in character, becomes useful aggressiveness in later life.

As Freud and later Ferenczi have shown, mature genitality combines early erotic elements which are revealed in activities preparatory to the genital act, e.g., looking, touching, overpowering, and seduction by exposure. Although these partial experiences of eroticism are subordinate to the major goal of reproduction they still retain some degree of independence. If disintegration takes place, owing to traumatic experiences, they may as perversions again become isolated as sexual goals in themselves. Genital sexuality, however, cannot be reduced altogether to a summation and mixture of pregenital trends. In genitality a new component appears, the tendency to give.

The infant releases energy in un-co-ordinated motor discharge, in heat production, and in excretion. In the genital phase release is accompanied by the desire to give and results, physiologically, in reproduction. In involution the manifestations of surplus energy diminish, growth and propagation cease, and the psychology of involution has in some respects resemblance to the earlier phases of life.

The fact that most sexual tensions, both pregenital and genital, are discharged in orgasm through the genito-urinary system confirms the surplus theory of sexuality. The genito-urinary system is anatomically and physiologically the specific organ through which both waste products and germ cells are discharged. *It is a system through which surplus material and surplus excitation not used in the co-ordinated self-preservative activities of the organism are drained.* Before maturity it releases the excess of incorporating, eliminating, and retentive impulses which are not utilized for growth. When the limit of individual growth is reached, it releases the creative energies physiologically in germ cells, and emotionally in mature love.

BIBLIOGRAPHY

ALEXANDER, F.: *The Medical Value of Psychoanalysis.* New York, W. W. Norton & Company, Inc., 1936.
———: "The Need for Punishment and the Death-Instinct," *Internat. J. Psycho-Analysis,* 10:256, 1929.
———: *Our Age of Unreason.* Philadelphia, J. B. Lippincott Company, 1942.
———: *The Psychoanalysis of the Total Personality.* Nervous and Mental Disease Monograph Series No. 52. New York, Nervous and Mental Disease Publishing Company, 1929.

————: "Psychoanalysis Revised," *Psychoanalyt. Quart.*, 9:1, 1940.

FENICHEL, O.: "Zur Kritik des Todestriebes," *Imago*, 21:458, 1935.

FERENCZI, S.: *Thalassa, A Theory of Genitality*. Albany, The Psychoanalytic Quarterly Press, 1938.

FREUD, S.: *Beyond the Pleasure Principle*. London, Hogarth Press, 1922.

————: "The Economic Problem in Masochism," in *Collected Papers*, II. London, Hogarth Press, 1924, p. 255.

————: *The Ego and the Id*. London, Hogarth Press, 1927.

————: *A General Introduction to Psychoanalysis*. New York, Boni & Liveright, Inc., 1920.

————: "Instincts and Their Vicissitudes," in *Collected Papers*, IV. London, Hogarth Press, 1925, p. 60.

————: *Three Contributions to the Theory of Sex*. Nervous and Mental Disease Monograph Series No. 7. New York, Nervous and Mental Disease Publishing Company, 1930.

MENNINGER, K. A.: *Man against Himself*. New York, Harcourt, Brace and Company, Inc., 1938.

WEISS, E.: "Ueber eine noch nicht beschriebene Phase der Entwicklung zur heterosexuellen Liebe," *Internat. Ztschr. f. Psychoanal.*, 11:429, 1925.

Chapter V

The Functions of the Ego
and Its Failures

1. THE STRUCTURAL THEORY OF THE MENTAL
APPARATUS

IT WAS NOT until 1921, some thirty years after his first publications on psychoanalysis, that Freud proposed a comprehensive theory of the structure and function of the mind. He
distinguished three structurally different parts: (1) the id,[1]
or the inherited reservoir of chaotic, instinctual impulses as
yet unharmonized with each other or with the facts of external reality; (2) the ego, or the integrating part of the personality, which modifies, selects, controls, and co-ordinates
the tendencies of the id and excludes or modifies those in conflict with external reality; (3) the superego, the mind's latest
development, which embodies the code of society. This code
is dependent upon the social environment and varies in different cultural milieus. Through identification with adults this
code is gradually incorporated into the personality and becomes a part of it.

In an earlier work I proposed a distinction between the

1 On account of its impersonal quality.

unconscious superego and the conscious ego-ideal. The latter contains values accepted in later life which govern conduct. The superego is acquired early and remains unconscious, functions automatically, and is not easily changed by later corrective influences. It can be compared to a complex set of conditioned reflexes. This distinction was accepted by many psychoanalysts, but I question today whether such a rigid structural distinction is possible. In the normal individual most of the early regulations are slowly modified by later influences. The difficulty of making schematic distinctions between the different portions of the personality will be discussed later. It is obvious that Freud regarded this structural theory as a means of approximate orientation. It should therefore not be pressed in detail (Hartmann, Kris, Lowenstein).

It appears more convenient to distinguish different functions of the mind than to divide it into air-tight compartments. To consider the three parts as structurally well defined may lead involuntarily to the assumption of corresponding anatomical structures in the brain. This means a stricter anatomical localization of brain functions than is justified by actual knowledge. Although functions of the brain can be precisely differentiated, their corresponding anatomy is much vaguer and there is overlapping, especially in the highest centers. The notion of the id, as originally defined, is problematical. Strictly speaking, a completely unorganized, inherited mass of instinctual urges is not found even at birth. The organism has even then a considerable amount of reflex co-ordination. The co-ordinating functions attributed to the ego have not yet come into play and are acquired by learning. Learning, however, starts immediately with birth, and it is therefore difficult to see at what period the sharp distinction between an unorganized id and an organized ego obtains. The ego is obviously the product of development and adaptation. This is a continuous process which begins at birth, so that the distinction between id and ego should be conceived as fluid continuum rather than as rigid dichotomy. Thomas French's recent studies have shown that in dream life, which is primitive and more closely related to id than to ego functions, there is a large amount of integration. More or less highly organized mental functions can be recognized, but a sharp distinction between a completely organized and a completely disorganized portion of the mind is impossible.

It is customary to consider the functions of the superego as early internalized reactions which become largely automatic and unconscious and so no longer susceptible to modification by external influences. Here again it is advisable to distinguish between more and less automatic emotional reactions and behavior rather than between a completely automatic superego and a conscious, more flexible ego. The superego develops through the child's identification with its parents' attitudes, opinions, and judgments, which is one of the most important factors in the learning processes. The ego learns correct behavior through identification with others who have mastered it. By repetition this behavior becomes automatic and habitual. Expressed structurally, parental attitudes are taken over by the personality, one part of which assumes the same attitude toward the rest as the parents did previously toward the child. This identification with the parents and incorporation of their images conditions adjustment to the social environment. One part of the personality accepts the code and becomes its internal representative. This part Freud called the superego. It is important to realize that the total personality does not make a social adjustment, or, more precisely, asocial attitudes survive in everyone, even in normal persons. There is continuous conflict, even in normal persons, between the earlier unadjusted instinctual tendencies and the restrictive influence of the superego.

The existence of the superego explains how in every form of civilization there is a disciplinary force in individuals which is indispensable for social order. If there were no internal code like that imposed by the superego or conscience, social order could be secured only by policing every citizen. Social behavior is by no means enforced only by fear of external punishment. Every well-adjusted individual possesses a sense of discipline which depends very little upon coercion. Psychological analysis has shown, however, that inner assent to social usage covers only a few fundamental regulations. Without fear of punishment the majority would behave less socially than they actually do, for the superego is in most people not a wholly adequate substitute for actual authority.

The only way to test which asocial dispositions are controlled by internal and which by external authority would be to abolish all punishment. A statistical investigation of the kinds of crime which increase under those circumstances and the criminal tendencies requiring no external control might indicate how far man is now adjusted to collective life. Psychoanalytic experience suggests that in contemporary civilization only cannibalism, actual incest, parricide and fratricide would not increase if all penalties were abolished. These asocial tendencies, though manifest in man's early development, are repressed so successfully that they no longer operate effectively. Special prohibitions against cannibalism which are necessary in some primitive civilizations are superfluous with us, for the impulse to eat other human beings has been deeply repressed at an early stage.

It may appear paradoxical that our knowledge of the higher integrative and co-ordinative functions of the ego has been acquired later than the understanding of the id's more primitive emotional patterns. Few systematic studies on the synthetic, adaptive, and cognitive functions of the ego have as yet been published in psychoanalytic literature. There are many reasons for this. First, psychoanalysis developed not merely a descriptive but also an explanatory type of psychopathology. It deals with irrational, primitive reaction patterns rather than with well-adjusted behavior. Scientific curiosity in human behavior was first aroused by its anomalies. In mental illness, in which more primitive, less well-adjusted mentality prevails, common understanding of human behavior is inadequate. Why should anyone be afraid in harmless situations like walking downtown or sitting in a restaurant, or be depressed and want to die for no obvious reason? This requires special explanation. Hence pathological material first attracted systematic scientific study.

Another reason why we have less knowledge of the conscious functions of the ego is that they lie too close at hand. We are constantly aware of our own egos. This is a commonplace of clinical experience. Patients often admit without much resistance objectionable tendencies which the psychoanalyst shows them are in their unconscious and outside their actual ego. Because these disapproved and repressed tendencies lie outside the actual personality their existence can be admitted and the patient comfort himself by saying: "These strange things are in my unconscious, but not in me. They are no part of my conscious personality." Real conflict arises only after the unconscious tendencies begin to penetrate the ego and the patient becomes aware of them as part of his own personality.

A third reason for the scantiness of our knowledge of the ego's functions is that they are more complicated than those of the id and include highly differentiated conditioned reflexes and reflex inhibitions. Recent advance in psychoanalysis permits a more precise definition of these than formerly, but much knowledge has still to be acquired. What we now know about the ego can be summarized as follows:

The ego is an apparatus which has two perceptive surfaces,

one directed inwardly toward the instinctive impulses and needs, the other directed toward external reality through sense perception. The integrative function of the ego is to confront internal perception with the results of sense perception and to harmonize subjective demands with external circumstances in such a way that the maximum satisfaction possible is achieved. In addition to its integrative function, the ego has an executive function which depends on its control of voluntary motor behavior. Through adaptive behavior, conditions within the organism are maintained in constant, homeostatic equilibrium. These three functions of the ego, external and internal perception, integration, and executive action, correspond to the afferent and efferent pathways in the brain and to the complex cellular architechtonics between its functional centers.

The conscious ego is the most plastic part of the mind, since at any moment it can adjust behavior to a given situation, in contrast to the more rigid reflex and automatic behavior. Automatic reactions respond to certain stimuli in a uniform manner and so cannot adjust themselves to sudden changes in the external situation, whereas the ego has the capacity of performing adjustments *ad hoc*.

The functioning of the whole mental apparatus can be described approximately as follows: Instinctual needs and tendencies tend to become conscious because the conscious ego controls the motor innervations on which their satisfaction is dependent. A large part of the instinctual demands becomes immediately conscious and is accepted or rejected after conscious deliberation. This involves an estimate of the external situation and a comparison of the inner demand with conflicting tendencies in consciousness. For example, in choosing between attending a lecture and going to a theater there is a conscious conflict which can be solved by a conscious judgment. One desire has to be relinquished because it is incompatible with another, more important, one. Conscious mental activity consists in a continual reconciliation between incompatible desires. Some must be temporarily checked, others modified, others subordinated to more important demands or reconciled with existing external conditions. Even a healthy person can effect these constant compromises well only under certain conditions. Anyone's adaptive capacity may fail under difficult conditions which exceed the mind's strength. Neuroses have been produced experimentally in animals by artificially creating situations with which the animal is unable to cope. Continued strain, as in war, has created acute neurotic disturbances in formerly healthy persons.

The major part of what we know about dynamic psychopathology today comes from the study of the breakdown of this adaptive functioning of the ego, which results in neuroses and psychoses. Only very recently has systematic study of the normal adaptive functions been undertaken (French). Since most of our knowledge of psychodynamics comes from pathological material, the major part of this book will be devoted to a study of the failures of ego functions. Whenever the ego fails in its integrative task it reverts to those defense measures which the infantile ego has used against impulses it could not harmonize with each other and relate effectively with the environment and which it therefore had to exclude from its scope. All of the ego's typical defense mechanisms are employed occasionally by normal persons, but they are used more extensively under neurotic and psychotic conditions. The understanding of psychopathological phenomena requires the knowledge of these defense mechanisms, which all originate in childhood because the integrative powers of the child's ego are very limited. Therefore it is necessary to become acquainted with the earlier forms of ego development.

2. DEVELOPMENT OF THE EGO FUNCTIONS

We have seen that the ego's basic function is to maintain constant conditions in the organism. It is the agent of the stability principle. Freud formulated this by saying that the ego's function is to keep the amount of excitation in the organism at a constant level. To accomplish this it has to ward off or reduce external stimuli and to relieve the pressure of needs, impulses, and wishes. The protection against excessive external stimuli is ensured primarily by the structure of the sense organs, which select certain stimuli or are sensitized only to certain physical stimuli of a specific quality. The protective function of the skin against changes in temperature and other physical stimuli is well known. The eye reacts only to optical stimuli of certain wave lengths; and a similar situation obtains in hearing, though the eyes can be closed, while the ears unfortunately cannot. In sleep external stimuli which intrude upon the waking state are excluded.

The reduction of internal stimuli to a constant level is a most complicated performance. The adaptive, integrative function of the ego consists in gratifying needs and releasing emotional tensions in such a way that the integrity of the ego is maintained. It is often necessary to endure pain or to engage in unpleasant, exhausting tasks to ensure the gratification of certain important needs. A scale of values must be developed by the ego and important desires subordinated or relinquished if they are in conflict with more important ones. A mountaineer may deliberately increase the effort of climbing by carrying a heavy knapsack, but on arrival he enjoys his stay at the mountaintop because he took food and clothing with him.

We are now concerned with understanding how this complex functioning of the ego is developed in the growing child. We shall first define this functioning more precisely and then try to reconstruct what we know about its growth. Before the integrative functions of the ego have developed, every impulse seeks gratification without regard to the needs of the total organism. If angered, the child will show temper by kicking, screaming, and indiscriminately hostile behavior. He later controls such outbursts because he has learned that he jeopardizes in that way the support and affection of his parents. The child may want to eat and play at the same time but finds that the two do not go together. The motivation of behavior controlled by isolated impulses seeking immediate gratification was called by Freud the pleasure-pain principle. He borrowed this notion from the seventeenth- and eighteenth-century "voluntarists," such as Hobbes and Helvetius, who took it from the Greek Epicureans.

Through playful experimentation and painful experiences the child, whose adaptive and integrative faculty is smaller than that of the adult, gradually learns to co-ordinate his impulses and relate them to the environment according to what Freud called the reality principle. It is, as he aptly expressed it, an improved pleasure-pain principle, gratifying needs, more effectively avoiding painful tensions created by frustrations and painful external stimuli like punishment. To act on the unmodified pleasure-pain principle would eventually cause the organism more pain than pleasure; in fact, the organism could not survive. The reality principle means carefully planned and co-ordinated behavior, which often requires voluntarily imposed restrictions and effort but ensures more gratification. It represents the best deal the organism is able to negotiate with reality under given conditions and therefore can be correctly called an improved pleasure principle. Naturally the reality principle is applied with varying degrees of success, and probably no organism achieves maximum efficiency. The integrative capacity of individuals varies, and the same individual's effectiveness may vary according to a variety of factors which we cannot evaluate precisely. The most important factor in applying the reality principle is learning through experience.

We have now reached a fairly adequate conception of the later phases of the process of learning how to co-ordinate and relate desires to external conditions. Freud formulated this in his writings about the transition from the pleasure-pain principle to the reality principle. We know the essentials of this process, though many details must be left for future investigation. Much of it was already a matter of common sense. As French has correctly observed, common sense and rational behavior are always with us and are taken for granted but not methodically described. To explain them appears an elaboration of the obvious.

In order to describe more precisely the operations of the reality principle, French has tried to analyze the mechanisms upon which it relies. He distinguishes between two kinds of wishes. One kind, such as hunger, pain, and fear, arises from unsatisfied needs. These produce tensions which, unless inhibited, are released in muscular activity like the thrashing about of a hungry infant. With this may be contrasted wishes stimulated by opportunities for satisfaction or memories of satisfactions. These arouse hopes of positive satisfaction. They aim at achieving, not escaping, something.

This distinction is important because of the different effect of needs and hopes upon the tension of unsatisfied desire. Unsatisfied needs cause unpleasant and painful tension, but hope tends to relieve it.

Increased need or conflict between incompatible needs may not increase the effectiveness of efforts toward satisfaction. Well-directed effort is more than mere relaxation of tension. In order to achieve, it is not enough merely to do something; it is necessary also to know what to do. To be of any use efforts must be guided by understanding of the problem to be solved.

If tension rises too high, understanding loses control. Ability to act on the reality principle depends on integrative capacity or, in other words, on an adequate plan to gratify needs and to resolve conflict between incompatible needs, and on the ego's ability to carry out such a plan. This latter is largely dependent upon the capacity for control of impulses demanding immediate gratification which would disturb the plan.

IDENTIFICATION

One fundamental process by which the ego acquires efficiency is identification with the parents, their attitudes, feelings, and thoughts. The ego can learn not only from its own trials and errors but also from the experiences of others. Identification leads ultimately, however, to increased independence. In assuming the attitudes of the parents the child dispenses gradually with their actual support and becomes self-sufficient. This can be illustrated by a common occurrence, the identification with a lost love object. The sense of loss is offset by recreating the lost person within the own personality. Marcusewicz [2] cites the case of a child who lost her kitten and declared that she herself was the kitten. She then began to crawl on her hands and feet like an animal and refused to eat at the table.

Identification is the basis of all learning which is not acquired independently by trial and error. It is the most important mechanism in the development of a mature ego but may serve also in some psychopathological processes as a defense. This will be discussed later, together with the other defense mechanisms of the ego (page 117).

Since the child's integrative faculties are acquired gradually by experience, the ego has for a time to defend itself against internal stimuli to which it cannot yield without up-

[2] After S. Freud, *Group Psychology and the Analysis of the Ego*, London, Hogarth Press, 1922.

setting its harmony or suffering pain from external causes. These defense measures have been carefully studied and will be discussed in Section 3 of this chapter. They have, for example, been more methodically treated than the adult's rational activities because they are inadequate and underlie all regressive behavior which is puzzling to the common sense.

SOME ASSUMPTIONS ABOUT THE EARLIEST PHASES OF EGO DEVELOPMENT

Our knowledge of the earliest phases of ego development is hypothetical rather than the result of direct observation. They can be observed in severely neurotic and especially in psychotic patients, who often revert to very primitive phases of ego development. Direct observations of children on the prespeech level permits only conjecture about what is going on in the child's mind. It should be remembered that verbal communication is the only really adequate method in psychological research and that without it first-hand knowledge is impossible. What can be stated with a fair degree of certainty about this early phase of ego development is therefore not comprehensive. We have reason to assume that one of the child's earliest applications of the reality principle consists in distinguishing his own person from his environment. From birth he is exposed to constant external and internal stimuli, in contrast to the prenatal state, in which he was protected and his biological needs automatically satisfied by the mother organism. After birth the child has to engage in various activities to maintain homeostatic conditions. Such activities as breathing and sucking are automatic, yet learning begins immediately after birth. In comparison with animals, the human organism is dependent upon the mother for a longer period, and its learning process is correspondingly longer and more thorough.

The organism is born with a certain hereditary equipment

to protect it from external stimuli. The gratification of internal needs, with the exception of breathing and nutrition, must, however, be learned. Even nutritional activities become modified after weaning, and the control of excretory functions must be learned. In an earlier chapter this and the gradual mastery of the voluntary muscles through the progressive co-ordination of originally erotic play has been described. Here we shall try to summarize what can reasonably be assumed about the first phases of the ego's reality-testing function.

There is reason to believe that originally no distinction is felt between the internal and external worlds. All stimuli and sensations belong to the same category, and differentiation between the ego and the external world is made only gradually as the ego progresses in its development. The first basis of differentiation, according to Freud, is that only pleasant sensations are assigned to the self, whether they originate from stimuli outside or inside the organism, and the rest is attributed to the external world. This is the basis of projection, a defense mechanism which will be described later.

It seems probable that the child can, at least temporarily, gratify his needs through hallucinatory reproduction of former satisfactory experiences. This is possible because adults eventually satisfy all his needs and he is required to do nothing for himself. With growing independence, however, fantasy must be replaced by greater activity to secure gratification of needs, and this involves a broader recognition of reality. Even the unpleasant features of reality must be recognized. The psychotic gives up his first adjustment to reality and reverts through hallucinations to a wishful distortion of sense perception. It must be assumed that patients who develop schizophrenia have not satisfactorily accomplished this first task, so that the distinction between ego and non-ego has never been firmly established in them. Only a tenuous relation to external reality can explain so radical a solution of mental conflicts.

We do not yet know precisely how hallucinatory gratification is given up and replaced by real satisfaction. As long as the child's needs are taken care of by the mother, the child is not compelled to care for himself. Imaginary gratification gives the child transitory satisfaction when the biological needs are not satisfied by the mother. This satisfaction is never complete, and when the child experiences tension he engages in un-co-ordinated activity. During this activity he accidentally discovers behavior patterns which are useful in gratifying biological needs. These are repeated because the child has connected them with relief from tension. By repetition they become stabilized and perfected. The value of imaginary satisfaction diminishes in proportion as the child becomes capable of finding real gratification. It is probable that thumb-sucking is discovered in this way and that after visual control and co-ordination of the skeletal muscular innervations are mastered, the possibility of grabbing and inserting objects in the mouth is discovered and prepares the way for more independent forms of eating.

The child must learn to acknowledge external reality; he must also acknowledge impulses involving painful experiences as arising within himself. The recognition of objectionable impulses is reversed in paranoid psychoses, in which these impulses are projected onto others. Naturally the capacity for controlling one's impulses develops only gradually, and the child's primary defense consists in repressing them. Repression and its psychodynamic sequelae are the most important processes for understanding the psychopathology of neuroses.

3. DEFENSE MECHANISMS OF THE EGO

a. REPRESSION

The ego's fundamental defense measure is repression. Freud assumed that repression is the normal reaction of the infantile ego, whose integrative capacity is extremely limited. Repression consists in excluding impulses and their ideational representations from consciousness. It always occurs when a wish, impulse, or idea would on becoming conscious cause unbearable conflict resulting in anxiety. Repression of a desire, in contrast to its conscious rejection, is an inhibition on a deeper level of the personality. The fact that it is unconscious saves the conscious personality painful conflict. The whole act takes place outside of consciousness. The rejection is automatic; otherwise the unacceptable mental content could not remain unconscious. It is a reflex inhibition following the principles of conditioned reflexes. It is obvious that such unconscious inhibition presupposes an unconscious inner perception which leads to automatic reflex inhibition.

Repression is based on a process which Freud called censorship. This censorship, which functions automatically in the face of unacceptable tendencies, is a primitive kind of unconscious judgment which excludes certain tendencies from consciousness and operates schematically, being incapable of subtle differentiation, and so reacts uniformly to certain emotional tensions regardless of their actual and sometimes important differences. It is therefore more like a conditioned reflex than like a deliberate judgment. To cite a common example, the repression of the first incestuously tinged sexual strivings of the child establishes a general pattern of sexual repression which persists in later life so that when sexuality emerges in adolescence a general timidity prevails. Although the sexual impulse has lost its openly incestuous character and is directed toward acceptable objects, it suffers from the intimidations of childhood. Since the superego lacks the capacity for making fine distinctions, it represses sexuality in general without being able to recognize that the object of striving is no longer the same as in childhood. This is described by reflexologists as the spreading of an inhibition. The shy and inhibited adolescent shows the result of this automatic restriction. In short, repression is always exaggerated and involves tendencies which the conscious ego would not reject if they became conscious. This automatic and oversevere inhibiting function is one of the most general causes of psychoneurotic disturbances. Many psychoneurotic symptoms are the result of unbearable tensions occasioned by exaggerated repression.

In Freud's original view repression operates in the following way: It starts with an inner perception of tension which tends to become conscious in order to stimulate the motor innervations necessary for its release. If the tendency conflicts with the code accepted in childhood and lodged in the superego, the conscious ego rejects it with fear, which is the motive of repression. In the terminology of the original structural theory, the ego acts on the cue given by the superego and rejects the condemned id-tendency and so produces repression. The fear of the superego felt by the ego is the signal which warns the latter to repress impulses of which the parents earlier disapproved.[3]

The ego is exposed to two directing forces: the assertion of individual needs by the id and their denial by the superego. The tendency of the ego is to compromise between the two forces by modifying them in a way compatible with the code of the superego. This process we call domestication or sublimation of the original, inherited, nonsocial demands. Sublimation is a modification of the original nonsocial tendencies and occurs in normal adjustment. It will be discussed

[3] See further discussion on page 100.

later. It has been generally assumed that neurotic and psychotic personalities possess a smaller capacity for sublimation than is necessary in view of their excessive repressions. These pathological personalities are led by their original tendencies, which they cannot follow through because, paradoxically enough, they have also developed a rigid code of behavior. They are both oversocial and nonsocial at the same time.

It has been stated before that repression is the infantile ego's characteristic method of dealing with those instinctual demands which bring the child into conflict with its environment. Everything repressed has been originally forbidden by the parents or thwarted by the impersonal unchangeable conditions of the environment. A common example is the child's repression of coprophilic tendencies under the influence of parental disapproval. The gratification of this tendency occasions parental rejection, and the child, who is completely dependent on his parents, reacts to rejection with anxiety, no matter whether it is expressed by corporal punishment or by the withdrawal of affection. Since the child's ego is incapable of controlling strong impulses, anything which he desires is immediately sought in action. The only way of controlling these impulses is to exclude them from consciousness. The child's ego cannot withstand temptation. The postponement of immediate gratification and the relinquishment of desires are accomplishments acquired painfully during growth. Lacking these, the child must repress forbidden impulses in order to keep out of trouble.

Although repression is an unconscious process, it leaves certain emotional phenomena of a defensive nature on the surface of consciousness. In the place of coprophilic tendencies, disgust appears. The desire to play with excrement disappears from consciousness, leaving a feeling of disgust. Pity is a similar protective countercharge (counter-cathexis) against original tendencies toward cruelty. The most primitive sense of justice is also a protective countercharge against the child's desire to have everything for himself, expressed in his envy of siblings. Another conscious manifestation of repression is anxiety, which appears whenever a tendency alien to the ego threatens to break through into consciousness.

In summary, repression is a measure by which impulses which cannot be integrated within the ego are excluded from it, since they would otherwise cause anxiety, guilt, and self-condemnation. The infantile ego has an insufficient capacity to resolve conflict by compromise, and its only recourse is to exclude the disturbing forces from consciousness.

In the last analysis repression is a primitive device of the ego to maintain its integrity. Since the child's integrative powers are weak, his ego can only exclude from consciousness impulses which it cannot control and harmonize. He has learned through identification with his parents and other adults standards of behavior which restrict his own desires in the interest of others. Punishment and the withdrawal of affection have taught him to accept these standards and to exclude disruptive impulses. This weakens the ego's dynamic resources but saves its unity. Tendencies alien to the ego are repressed because they cannot undergo necessary modification. The psychoanalytic study of neuroses and psychoses has shown that repressed psychological forces do not cease to exist. The ego must take defensive measures against them which drain the ego's dynamic resources and make it less able to exercise its adaptive function of grappling with external reality. It loses especially that surplus energy which is the source of creative activities, both sexual and social.

Excessive repression is one of the most important causes of neurosis. The repressed impulse occasionally breaks through the barriers of the ego and is expressed in overt behavior. Many of the defensive measures of the ego are directed against psychological content which has thus broken through the barrier of repression. Such revolutionary outbreaks appear as neurotic and psychotic symptoms or in neurotic behavior which is characterized by (a) its irrationality, (b) its lack of co-ordination with the rest of the personality, and (c) its repetitive nature. These will be discussed in the chapter on psychoneuroses and behavior disorders.[4]

b. ANXIETY

It is obvious from what has been said that the motor force of repression is anxiety aroused by certain impulses the gratification of which in the past has proved painful. Fear is aroused by the memory of painful past experiences. The temporal sequence is: (1) the perception of an impulse; (2) action to gratify this impulse; (3) resultant painful experiences (punishment, withdrawal of love, or pain caused by impersonal obstacles). Through repetition of this sequence fear becomes connected with the first link in the chain, the impulse itself. Originally there is a fear of the parental retribution or pain caused by impersonal obstacles; gradually this fear becomes internalized, and it is directed toward the first link in the chain—namely, the impulse which caused all the trouble. This fear is aroused not by external danger but by dangerous impulses within. Anxiety is internalized fear. The punishing agent also becomes internalized. The original fear of someone who punished gratification becomes a fear of conscience, that part of the personality which represents the parents. Anxiety is aroused not by an overt act but merely by the impulse to commit it. It is therefore obvious that anxiety is preventive, a warning signal to the ego that a dangerous impulse which in the past has caused trouble and pain is about to break through. This internalized fear may be felt as formless anxiety or may be connected with concrete expectations of suffering, or it may appear in feelings of guilt. Since it is an unconscious re-

[4] See Chapter IX, "Psychopathology," pages 205–206 and 238.

action to repressed tendencies, the anxiety is rationalized by secondary explanations which do not really account for it. It is sometimes not even recognized as a sense of guilt and appears as free-floating anxiety without any specific content, as a general state of panic.

In the study of male neurotics the content of this unconscious anxiety has been consistently found to be the fear of castration. In children, in compulsive obsessive neurotics, as well as in schizophrenics, this fear often appears openly without distortion; in other neurotics and in the dreams of both healthy and neurotic people it is expressed in more or less distorted forms. The ubiquity of the castration fear, its presence in normal children and neurotic adults, and particularly its widespread and various expressions in folklore, mythology, and fairy tales (e.g., Medusa, Samson and Delilah, Salome, Judith, the story of the seven-headed Hydra, Oedipus Rex, Struwwelpeter, Pinocchio, etc.) led Freud to give it a central significance as the earliest factor in repression. There is an extensive literature by Freud and others on this subject. The gist of his views, which have been supported by clinical evidence and direct observation on children, can be briefly summarized.

The first interpersonal conflict of the child develops in the triangular situation in the family (Oedipus complex). The mother is the primary object of dependent love in both sexes. In the boy this attachment assumes an incestuous sexual connotation between approximately the third and the sixth year as a kind of anachronistic anticipation of the genital desires. This is the phallic phase of the classical libido theory. Some boys may express directly the desire to marry their mother; others show only a great deal of instinctive sexual curiosity toward her. At the same time overt jealousy and hostility against the father appears in varying intensity. From the observation of children as well as adults it can be claimed with certainty that the hostility toward the father is connected with the recognition of the little boy's own physical inadequacy which provokes in him envy for the superior physical equipment of the father. The observation of the mature genitalia induces the desire to appropriate them and thus to be able to replace the father in relation to the mother (castration wish). This aggressive desire follows the primitive law of conscience, the *lex talionis*, "an eye for an eye and a tooth for a tooth," and leads to a fear of retaliation, which is one of the most important factors in developing castration fear. This fear is further reinforced by the discovery of the anatomical differences between girls and boys, which appears to the little boy as a proof that one may lose one's penis. Another common reinforcement of this fear lies in the frequent overt or veiled threats of parents at children's masturbation. In the past few generations such threats were very common.

The universality of castration fear in children suggested to Stärcke and myself the investigation of other early common experiences which may co-operate in producing the fear of castration. We came independently to the conclusion that there are such earlier experiences in which pleasure is abruptly terminated by the loss of something which the child considers a part of his own body. During weaning the child must give up the nipple or the bottle as a source of pleasure and later during toilet training he must give up the retention of feces as a source of erotic excitation. In both cases erotic pleasure is followed by the loss of something pleasurable, and this sequence is already deeply rooted in the child's mind before the Oedipus conflict arises. Early masturbation fantasies involving desire for the mother and jealousy and fear of the father arouse fear of losing the penis, the source of erotic pleasure. His loss of the nipple and the excreta which were sources of pleasure makes him apprehensive of losing the penis. Castration wishes, knowledge of the female anatomy, and actual castration threats further contribute to his anticipation of mutilation.

Freud considered castration fear the primary factor in the resolution of the Oedipus complex. It induces the boy to relinquish his sexual attachment to the mother and transfer it to other objects. This in turn permits a positive identification with the father as a person whom he wishes to emulate rather than replace. His goal is to become like his father by adopting his attitudes, opinions, and modes of behavior. Even in normal individuals, however, this process is neither smooth nor simple. The road from the phase of hostile competition to that of identification is long emotional development. Guilt feelings which reflect internalized castration fear develop as reactions to hostility and competitiveness and these prompt suffering and submissiveness. When guilt requires submissive obedience and this becomes erotized, it is masochistic in character and combines with passive feminine desires for the father (inverted Oedipus complex). These rouse shame and as a rule are overcompensated by exaggerated hostile impulses, which in turn rouse fresh fear and guilt and lead to renewed waves of masochistic female submissiveness. In neurotics this vicious circle is often the nuclear conflict and its resolution frequently requires long and arduous therapy.

The girl's emotional development is different from the boy's and has long puzzled investigators. Even today there is little agreement on the subject. The first object of attachment of both boys and girls is the mother. In the case of the girl it must be explained why she turns eventually from the mother toward the father. Freud assumed that the development of boys and girls at first runs a parallel course; both have the same dependent love for their mother. After the pregenital phases the orientation of both sexes becomes phallic or masculine; the girl's clitoris becomes the important erogenous zone. Phylogenetically the clitoris is a rudimentary penis, the anatomical expression of female bisexuality. Only after the little girl's hope that the clitoris will grow into a penis is disappointed is she forced to renounce her masculine aspirations and accept the more passive female role. Then she can turn to her father and compete with her mother.

These views of Freud have been challenged, among others, by Karen Horney, who derives the little girl's masculine strivings from the high estimate which current civilization puts on being a man and which is impressed early upon the female mind. Horney explains the little girl's attachment to her father by the simple fact that she is biologically and psychologically a woman in whom the passive and receptive wishes appropriate to her anatomy and physiology prevail.

Physiological and psychological bisexuality is, however, unquestionable in both men and women, although a prevalence of male characteristics in infants of both sexes is, so far as I know, not substantiated by biologists. The gradual emancipation of children of both sexes from the mother can be explained by their increasing biological independence. Moreover, the parents' instinctive emotional reactions toward their sons and daughters must be given much more consideration than was done in the past. The influence of parents upon their children's emotional development has been easy to overlook, but the inclination toward one or the other parent is largely determined by the parents' own attitudes toward their children. Nothing shows this more clearly than the study of homosexual boys and girls. It is easier for adults to attribute the origins of the Oedipus complex to the child than to admit their own contribution to its development.

c. OVERCOMPENSATION (REACTION FORMATION)

The most common defensive measure against repressed tendencies is the development of attitudes or character traits exactly opposite to those against which they serve as a bulwark. Thus repressed cruelty is kept unconscious by exaggerated compassion for the suffering of others. Early coprophilic tendencies lead to excessive cleanliness and disgust at dirt. Repressed hostility may be countered by extreme submissiveness and humility. Exhibitionism remains unconscious through shyness and insecurity, and inferiority may be covered by boastful, exhibitionistic behavior. Overcompensation and reaction formations are defense measures of the ego against repressed tendencies which remain unconscious as long as the overcompensatory attitudes or character trends are sufficient to keep them repressed. Repressed tendencies, however, sometimes break through the overcompensatory defenses and appear openly.

A middle-aged male patient came a half-hour late to his psychoanalytic interview. When asked the reason for his being late he said that while walking on the street he saw a truck driver unmercifully beating his horses, who struggled to pull a heavily loaded truck from the mire. "I could not move," said the patient. "I was compelled to watch the scene." Watching it for a while, he became very angry and attacked the driver, who then turned against him and threatened to whip him if he didn't mind his own business. An argument developed, and they were just about to come to blows when a policeman called in by one of the spectators in a quickly gathering crowd separated them. "Well," ended the patient, "this is the reason why I am late." I asked him to speak about his attitude toward animals. He emphasized that he was most compassionate with the bodily sufferings of men and animals and "couldn't even kill a fly." Then, after some hesitation, he said that this was not always true. As a child he caught flies, tore their wings out, and watched their helpless behavior. Gradually more and more cruelties committed against animals were remembered—for example, how he caught frogs, pushed straws in their bellies, and blew them up until

they exploded. This led in consecutive interviews to memories about hostility and cruelty against younger siblings and
weaker playmates when he was five years old.

Overcompensation as a means of suppressing alien tendencies is more acute when the unconscious tendencies threaten
to seek an outlet in behavior. A common example is the sudden feeling of emotional paralysis as a defense against fear at
a sudden upsurge of rage. In some situations an overly polite
and humble attitude may serve to keep aggressive feelings in
abeyance. When overcompensatory measures are more constant and become character traits they are called reaction
formations. Many social traits are at least partially compensatory defenses of the ego. In reaction formations, however,
identification with others and ambivalence toward them are
contributory. Pity, for example, presupposes a positive identification with a person toward whom one feels both hate
and love. If love were absent pity could not serve to keep hostile impulses in check.

Freud considered the principle of polarity to be one of
the most fundamental in personality. Emotional trends always appear in opposite pairs: love and hate, cruelty and
compassion, bravado and fear, humility and boastfulness, exhibitionism and voyeurism. This ubiquitous polarity was one
reason why Freud adhered so consistently to a dualistic view
of the instinctual life. Ego instincts and sex, erotic and hostile trends, and finally the life and death instincts became for
him the basic contrasting forces within the living organism.

Most of this apparent polarity can be explained without
philosophical assumptions concerning the ultimate quality
of psychic forces. The growing child is at first governed only
by biological forces and later becomes a part of social groups,
beginning with the family. Life in groups requires new adaptations; the original self-centered narcissism becomes fused with

attitudes toward others: dependence, hostility, envy, love, and identification. Moreover, the principle of surplus energy operates in the erotization both of certain activities and of social relations. Human attachments acquire a libidinous, erotic character, and object love replaces ego love. This shows that in addition to the amount of biological energy needed for adaptive purposes there is a surplus which is invested not in individual survival but in propagation. This surplus appears psychologically as love for others once the narcissistic needs are saturated.

This difference between love of self and love of others is the only genuine polarity in the personality. Many of the antitheses cited earlier, such as sadism and masochism, or exhibitionism and voyeurism, which appear in clinical material in pairs, can be explained by repression and overcompensation. The ego's defense against alien trends involves the use of such contrasting attitudes. There is no need to assume a mystical pre-existent polarity. In pity, for example, identification is used to block the wish to be cruel.

Clinically the most important polar phenomenon was observed by Bleuler and described as ambivalence: love and hatred directed toward the same person at the same time. Ambivalence, which is due to the dual orientation of man as an individual and as a member of society, is universal. In fact, the more one loves another, the more the narcissistic nucleus of the personality hates the loved object. Under normal conditions, however, one of these attitudes is deeply buried. This is intelligible, because there is perhaps no more perplexing situation than to hate whom you love or to love whom you hate. In morbid conditions, however, both parts of the ambivalent attitude may become conscious. An overconscientious mother who lived only for her children developed the obsessional idea that she would strangle them while they slept. She had obviously lost the ability to repress her hostile impulses which emerged as reactions to her excessive and compulsive maternal concern. In ordinary life the repressed hatred of a person one loves may break through when one feels betrayed by him. Love is then suddenly replaced by relentless hate. Murders inspired by passion are usually the outcome of ambivalence.

In normal persons repressed hostile feelings also emerge in dreams about the death of close friends or near relations. These are common manifestations of the ambivalence common to all human attachments. The antithesis between love of self and love of other objects explains why all love objects are enemies to the narcissistic core of the personality and may under certain conditions become objects of hate. The more one loves another the more love one takes away from oneself. Overcompensation of hate by love and vice versa illustrates this common polarity in personality which the ego uses to keep one component of ambivalent human relationships unconscious.

d. RATIONALIZATION

One of the most fundamental principles of psychodynamics is that all human acts are overdetermined and motivated by a number of conflicting motives. A philanthropist may give money for a cancer hospital because his wife died of cancer, because he wants to do something for the community from which his wealth originated, because he desires prominence, because he wants to relieve guilt feelings caused by ruthless business methods, and also because he wishes to satisfy an interest in humanity. The correct answer to such questions as "Why did you help your friend?" is not "I did it out of loyalty and not because I wanted to be superior to him," but "I helped him because of loyalty *and* because I wanted to be superior to him *and* because I felt under obligation to him *and* because I hoped that at some other time he might help me." Most likely there are still several other reasons. Not "either . . . or" but "both . . . and" is the formula for human acts.

Rationalization means selecting the most acceptable from a complex of mixed motives to explain behavior. This permits the repression of other alien motives. Since the selected motives are suitable to the act, the unacceptable ones may be overlooked or denied. It is by no means correct to define rationalization as the invention of necessarily nonexistent motives; it is usually an arbitrary selection which passes speciously for the whole.

Obviously rationalization is a powerful aid in repressing unacceptable motives and is probably the most common defense measure of the ego.

e. SUBSTITUTION AND DISPLACEMENT

Another common defense measure of the ego consists in displacing the object of an emotional attitude by another, thus saving the attitude. In displacement the tendency remains conscious and only its original goal remains unconscious. For example, a man who feels hostile toward a benefactor because he is competing with him in business may direct his hostility against another competitor to whom he owes nothing or against his wife, children, or dog. A reprimand in the office may cause a man to come home in an irritable mood and, without being aware of his hostility against his superior, find everything wrong with his wife, scold his children, and kick the dog. The objects of sexual feeling can also be displaced. Early sexual attractions to members of the family are transferred to persons outside the family. If the displacement is successful and the whole emotional charge redirected, repression is unnecessary because the alien tendency has found an acceptable outlet.

The expression "substitution" is often used synonymously

with "displacement." I find it advisable, however, to speak of "substitution" when the act but not necessarily the object is changed. For example, aggressive impulses felt toward a person may be relieved by violent physical exercise like wood chopping or other destructive but energy-consuming and useful acts which ultimately are subordinated to a constructive goal. The domination and exploitation of nature largely absorb in our civilization the aggressive impulses and the wish to dominate and exploit. Slaves are replaced by machines and conquest by the mastery of the forces of nature.

It is important to realize that displacement and substitution are not always the outcome of repression. They may simply result from frustration. If a desire cannot be gratified on account of external obstacles, even if it is not repressed, it may be exchanged for some other gratification. "A bird in the hand is worth two in the bush." The German saying is even more illustrative: "In der Not frisst der Teufel Fliegen" (in need, the devil eats flies). There is no doubt that every substitution and displacement represents a compromise; the second choice is accepted because the one really desired is repudiated internally or blocked by external obstacles. The substitutive value of one act for another is a quantitative problem which can be studied only by experimental methods. It is not known precisely how far and in what ways impulses can be modified and redirected. This problem must be subjected to the precise methods of experimental psychology. A particular form of substitution called sublimation will be discussed under the following heading.

f. SUBLIMATION

Certain forms of substitution are called sublimation. When a primitive urge is unacceptable to the ego and is modified so as to be socially acceptable, this is called sublimation. Aggressive sports are sublimations of destructive, competitive, and even homicidal impulses. Their aim is not to damage seriously but to exhibit greater skill than one's rival and to entertain the spectators by permitting them through identification to release their own hostile competitive impulses. In sports like boxing and wrestling the original desire to injure one's opponent is more obvious than in tennis, golf, or chess.

In our competitive civilization gambling may be considered as a sublimation of the urge to steal and is combined with sociability and hospitality. In its cruder, commercialized form, however, it is not socially valuable and therefore we do not call it sublimation.

It is a question whether modified expressions of pregenital erotism, such as smoking or chewing, which are substitutes for thumb-sucking, or collecting stamps or art objects, which replaces early coprophilic and anal-retentive tendencies, should be considered sublimations. Since often they have some social value, they belong in this category. From a psychodynamic point of view sublimation can be considered as a special form of substituting for a primitive impulse another related one more acceptable to society.

Of greater social importance than the civilized release of hostile and competitive and other pregenital impulses in games and sports are the substitutive expressions of mature sexuality. Like biological propagation, creative activities indicate surplus energy employed no longer selfishly but creatively. In sexual propagation a new organism is created; in artistic, literary, and scientific work some new object of art or scientific knowledge emerges. Creative activities are not subordinate to any other goal. This was expressed in Hippolyte Taine's principle of "l'art pour l'art." Scientific research also indicates a curiosity which is not subordinate to any utilitarian goal. The scientist's aim is to know something heretofore unknown, and the aim of his research is knowledge for its own sake. Art and science can serve useful purposes like education and technology, but even in this application the creative urge may outweigh the utilitarian interest.

Flying was originally invented not for commercial or military purposes, but merely to gratify the eternal dream of man to raise himself toward the skies—a deeply rooted longing which often appears in our dreams when we feel the sensation of levitation and skim easily over the surface of the earth as if we wore seven-league boots. The motive behind such dreams is the struggle of man for power and mastery, for freedom from natural forces which chain him to earth and reality.

As the artist gives creative expression to his fantasy from an internal creative urge, the scientist is motivated in his efforts by a creative curiosity to understand those puzzles which nature offers. The satisfaction of this curiosity is an aim in itself. Hippolyte Taine's concept of "l'art pour l'art" can be equally applied to science.

It is significant how often scientists compare the satisfaction which they derive from their activities with beauty in art. Baker quotes Haldane: "As a result of Faraday's work, you are able to listen to the wireless. But more than that, as a result of Faraday's work scientifically educated men and women have an altogether richer view of the world: for them apparently empty space is full of the most intricate and beautiful patterns. So Faraday gave the world not only fresh wealth but fresh beauty." [5]

Modern anthropology also supports this view. In a recent publication Roheim [6] showed that even agriculture, garden-

[5] J. B. S. Haldane, "The Biologist and Society," in *Science in the Changing World*. London, M. Adams, Ed. George Allen & Unwin, Ltd. 1933.

From John R. Baker. *Science and the Planned State*, New York, The Macmillan Company, 1945.

[6] Géza Roheim, *Origin and Function of Culture*, New York, Nervous and Mental Diseases Publishing Company, 1943.

ing, and cattle raising were not originally purposeful, but playful. They were at first hobbies but were secondarily exploited for economic purposes. Man, at play, inadvertently discovered their practical uses. Roheim shows that gardening can be traced to play and that it reproduces primitive fantasies of propagation; it originally served emotional rather than economic needs. Cattle raising also stems from totemistic rites—rites which are universal in the religious performances of the primitives. Domestic animals were first adopted as symbolic representations of the father and mother or of children, and only later was their practical usefulness discovered.

At present this nonutilitarian libidinous origin of the domestication of animals can still be observed in the habit of keeping dogs, which are often substitutes for children. The fact that Eskimos keep dogs for utilitarian purposes would hardly be considered as an argument against this view. Under certain conditions keeping dogs may prove useful.

In need or in danger practical considerations may prevail, but when hunger is satisfied and security obtained, human interest expands and becomes creative. Man produces artistically and scientifically by investing surplus energy no longer needed for self-preservation.

g. PROVOCATIVE BEHAVIOR

Another common defensive measure of the ego against alien motivations consists in provoking others to hostility against oneself. This justifies retaliation and releases hostility without recognition of its source in the self. Hostility appears as a natural response to the hostility of others. The man with a chip on his shoulder is a victim of his own provocative behavior.

h. PROJECTION

When the ego can no longer keep objectionable tendencies out of consciousness, more drastic defenses become necessary. One of these more radical measures is to attribute repressed tendencies or desires to others. Unjustifiable hostility may simply be attributed to someone else. If the hostility became conscious it would cause guilt and anxiety. To avoid this the whole situation may be distorted by saying, "I do not want to attack him; he wants to attack me." This defense mechanism, which is the basis of delusions of persecution, falsifies reality by attributing to someone an attitude which he does not have. Such distortion of reality becomes possible only when the ego renounces its contact with reality under the pressure of emotional need. In less extreme cases the attitudes of others may be grossly exaggerated, though not invented out of hand. Freud has correctly maintained that unconscious hostile impulses exist in everyone. The delusional paranoiac has therefore some basis for his projection. He treats the unconscious hostile impulses of others as if they were conscious. The exaggeration of unconscious hostile impulses in others is a common phenomenon of everyday life.

Not only repressed hostile impulses are projected. In erotomania conscious sexual inclinations are attributed to others: "Not only do I love him; he also loves me."

Anything repressed may be projected on others. "I am not cowardly, indiscreet, inquisitive, dishonest, etc., but he is." Personal sins are reflected in an exaggerated form in the faults of others.

In the chapter on psychopathology, projection will be discussed in more detail because it plays an important role in some neuroses and particularly in the schizophrenic psychoses. Projection occurs when the ego can no longer repress an alien tendency and therefore cannot deny its existence; its only recourse is to misplace it and to attribute it to the outside world. The person who is aware of these tendencies but is unable to repress them must deny that they are a part of his own ego. As we have pointed out before, the differentiation between one's own ego and external reality is one of the first accomplishments in the individual's development. In projection this is lost and the person's mental content which cannot be assimilated is attributed to external reality. Under the pressure of strong and unacceptable emotions, normal persons may resort to projection in order to preserve the integrity of their own ego. This occurs, however, only occasionally and is corrected when the emotional tension diminishes. A normal person seldom completely falsifies the external world but selects suitable occasions which suit his emotional needs. Projection is only one step away from provocative behavior. In provocative behavior there is a strong sense of reality so that the behavior of others cannot be completely distorted but must be manipulated to fit the subject's needs. Such a person makes other people angry and hostile in order to justify his claim that they are attacking him and he, poor victim, is only acting in self-defense. In paranoid projection the person is less bound by a sense of reality and arbitrarily misinterprets obvious facts.

i. TURNING FEELINGS TOWARD ONESELF

Another important defense mechanism is the release of alien impulses by turning them against oneself. This, like projection, takes place when the repressive measures fail. For example, if an unconscious hostile impulse toward a loved object cannot be repressed, it may, because it is unacceptable to the ego, be turned inward upon the self. To avoid conflict the hostile impulse is shifted from one object to another. The admission, "I hate him," is unacceptable to the ego and is replaced by the statement, "I hate myself." The reason for this reversal of sentiment is guilt created by the hostile feeling toward a beloved person. Turning these feelings inward both relieves the guilt feelings and releases the hostile impulse.

Erotic impulses can also be diverted from another person to oneself. The reaction to frustration and repudiation in love leads to a compensatory increase of narcissism.

A parvenu who had vainly tried to be accepted socially met by chance in a railway compartment an intellectual leader of modest means. He began the conversation with the offering of an expensive cigar. The gentleman politely refused his offer and took out his own modest-priced cigar. The parvenu correctly interpreted this as a rebuff and thus expressed his feeling:

"I do not understand you, sir. You smoke those cheap cigars. Look at me; I smoke the best cigars money can buy and wear clothes made by the best tailor in town. I have the best box at the opera house, drive the best horses, and have the most beautiful mistress in town. In short, I give myself all affection and respect, because no one else gives them to me."

Turning hostile impulses against oneself plays an important role in depressions; inverting love to oneself is an important mechanism in schizophrenia, especially in the megalomanic syndrome.

j. IDENTIFICATION AS DEFENSE

We have shown how identification operates in the healthy growth of the ego and in the learning process by which the ego acquires functional efficiency. Accepted standards and principles of behavior are adopted by the child's superego through identification with parental attitudes. This is a slow process and in healthy development leads to assimilation of the parental attitudes in the ego. In this way the ego becomes transformed, and there is no very sharp division between ego and superego. In morbid development, however, the superego remains a foreign body within the personality.

Under traumatic conditions, when the developing ego is exposed to greater emotional stress than it can handle, identification may be used as a defensive measure. Identification as a means of replacing a suddenly interrupted object relationship has been discussed before. In depression and melancholia the person whom the patient has loved and lost may be re-created in his own personality. To compensate an unbearable loss the bereaved identifies himself with his lost love. Because the identification is rapid and not the result of a gradual assimilation of parental attitudes and because this type of identification incorporates another person *in toto,* it is often called introjection. The introject remains a foreign body within the ego, which regards it with the same ambivalence which it entertained toward its original love object. This is why a hostile and destructive attitude toward the object is transformed into self-destruction.

Another defensive identification has been discovered by Anna Freud: identification with a threatening opponent as a means of allaying anxiety. By assuming the opponent's qualities by introjection, anxiety is mastered. The little boy who has undergone dental treatment suggests playing dentist with his sister. He will be the dentist and his little sister the patient. Not only children but adults, when brutally oppressed, may revert to this primitive defense mechanism. Persons who have survived imprisonment in Nazi concentration camps have given vivid descriptions of prisoners who acted toward their fellow-prisoners with the same brutality which they themselves suffered at the hands of their Nazi torturers.

k. GUILT FEELINGS AND MASOCHISTIC DEFENSE

The precise knowledge of guilt feelings has been acquired from the study of psychoneuroses in which they have a central etiological significance. In psychoneuroses guilt feelings and the emotions which arouse them appear in an exaggerated form which makes them more easily investigated. Neurotic processes are only quantitatively different from normal ones. There are not two different forms of psychodynamics, one valid for the healthy, the other for the neurotic, mind. The study of psychoneuroses has given us an opening wedge to the understanding of the same dynamic principles which underlie all forms of human behavior.

The origin of guilt feelings is found in the child-parent relationship. If the child does something which has previously evoked parental disapproval and punishment, he reacts to it with the fear of punishment. He has atoned for his guilt by being punished and a good relationship with the parents is re-established. It is immaterial whether the punishment is corporal or verbal or administered in withholding affection; its result is insecurity and suffering. This sequence of events is repeated: misbehavior—anxiety—punishment and atonement—which leads to forgiveness. The expectation of punishment leads to the need for punishment because only thus can the anxiety caused by unruly behavior be reduced. After parental attitudes have been incorporated in the conscience (superego) the whole process is internalized. Not only do acts which were once punished by the parents cause anxiety, but every impulse to commit such acts. This fear of one's conscience is what is called the sense of guilt. Since it is no longer external authority but conscience which induces fear and demands punishment to relieve anxiety and remorse, the guilty person must either inflict punishment on himself or induce others to punish him.

This need for punishment is one of the most constant findings in psychoneuroses. Patients of this type inflict punishment on themselves through their symptoms; this is required to relieve the guilt caused by their repressed wishes. The notion that suffering can relieve guilt is one of the basic phenomena of our social life. Many religious practices such as flagellation and penitence, as well as our whole penal code, are based on it. Theoretically at least the criminal can return to society after he has served his sentence, since he has paid in full for his transgression. One of the most common defense mechanisms is based on this deeply rooted emotional syllogism, that suffering atones for guilt. According to this peculiar equation conscience accepts suffering as a currency by which its claims can be satisfied. After suffering, the ego's defense against alien tendencies is diminished. In terms of the structural theory this can be expressed allegorically by saying that the ego bribes the superego through suffering to lessen its dependence upon the latter. Through suffering the superego's claims are satisfied and its vigilance against repressed tendencies is relaxed. This explains why persons who have been subjected to intense suffering feel that their turn has come to do what they want and that they can therefore disregard convention. The common recidivism of criminals who have been severely punished is largely explicable on this basis. The social conscience is relaxed by unjustly severe punishment, and the hardened criminal develops. Through self-inflicted or provoked suffering the ego is able to accept and give in to ego-alien tendencies without conflict. This mechanism has a central significance in depressions and in manic-depressive conditions. Our knowledge of guilt feelings was derived primarily from the psychoanalytic study of these disturbances.

In this connection masochism deserves special consideration. Any strong emotional tension may be erotized so that its discharge becomes an end in itself and sexually pleasurable. This occurs when there is surplus tension which cannot be released in pursuing the integrated goals of the total organism. In masochism an excessive need for punishment occasioned by guilt is erotized and discharged with erotic gratification. Suffering becomes an erotic aim in itself and no longer merely serves the purpose of relieving guilt.

The source of this strange phenomenon is the reality principle. In adjusting itself to the unalterable facts of the environment, the ego learns that certain gratifications require suffering. Satisfaction comes with sweat and labor. A well-adjusted person endures pain when necessary but would gladly avoid it. He tills the earth, mines minerals, and exposes himself to the dangers of the sea in order to secure his existence and increase his comfort. In sharp contrast to this rational adaptive behavior, pain in masochism is not a means but an end in itself, the erotic distortion of the reality principle. It is the sexual release of excess excitation caused by guilt.

From this we obtain a deeper understanding of guilt and punishment. In using punishment to educate children and restrain criminals man has imitated the natural process of adjustment to reality. Because the world is not constructed to meet our subjective needs and wishes, we must struggle against its unalterable facts and carve out an existence for ourselves. We must yield to facts and accept pain and strain as an unavoidable part of life. The fact should not be overlooked that punishing a child involves a primitive emotional response to the child's behavior. This has its uses, however, since it is motivated constructively to help him socialize his behavior. In the formation of the superego the ego adjusts to a code just as it adjusts to other unalterable facts. Once this occurs, the ego submits to the code incorporated in the superego as it formerly submitted to the parents. Masochism appears only when self-inflicted suffering becomes an erotic aim and loses its adaptive value. Self-punishment itself is a primitive defense measure to relieve the ego of guilt. When it becomes erotized in masochism it not only relieves guilt but becomes an erotic goal. Because of this double function it is one of the most difficult defense mechanisms to treat therapeutically.

Comments

The same facts have been somewhat differently described by Freud, who distinguished three forms of masochism—erogenous, female, and moral masochism. The first is a form of sexual excitation, the second the expression of femininity, and the third a mode of behavior.

In applying his dual-instinct theory to the problem of masochism, Freud explained erogenous masochism as a residue of the death instinct which has not issued in destructive impulse but remains confined within the organism. The mixture of this residual death instinct with eros he called erogenous masochism. Female masochism in his view is essentially identical with erogenous masochism. Moral masochism is connected with unconscious guilt feelings which are expressed in the need for suffering. Freud explains this as a combination of the ego's masochism and the superego's sadism, which is turned against the ego. This sadism is the result of secondarily introverted destructive impulses.

The dual-instinct theory requires this complex theoretical explanation of masochism. It replaced Freud's original view that all impulses might cause sexual excitation and be relieved sexually when they had reached a certain degree of intensity. Clinical observation of masochism as a form of sexual excitation can be explained on this basis without the assumption of a primary death instinct. Moral masochism is a defense measure of the ego against guilt. It is based on the child's notion that guilt can be relieved through suffering.

Parental punishment of the child's transgressions supplies the universal foundation for this pattern. The fact that women's masochistic fantasies can be traced to Oedipus guilt confirms the view that such fantasies fuse sexual desire with the need for suffering which serves as a defense against guilt feelings resulting from oedipal fantasies. This is most obvious in fantasies of rape by women who shift the responsibility for their desires to the brutal attacker, thus relieving their own conscience and satisfying their sexual interests at the same time by assuming the role of the innocent victim. The projection of guilt permits gratification of sexual desire on the condition that it is accompanied by suffering. In men masochistic suffering eliminates the guilt which otherwise would block sexual gratification. One masochistic male patient had to be spanked playfully by his sexual partner before intercourse. After this his potency was undisturbed and he could fully enjoy the sexual act. He paid in advance for his pleasure. The more passive role of women in the sexual act explains why this masochistic type of defense is more common in women than in men.

In moral masochism the same need for punishment is not erotized but only serves to relieve the guilty conscience. It is a nonerotized defense of the ego against guilt aroused by alien tendencies. When the need for punishment is erotized moral masochism is transformed into sexual perversion.

l. DEFENSES AGAINST INFERIORITY FEELINGS AND THEIR RELATIONSHIP TO GUILT FEELINGS

In the older psychoanalytic literature it was customary to deal with inferiority feelings and guilt feelings as more or less parallel manifestations of tension between the actual self and the ideal self, between what one is and what one would like to be, between what one actually does and feels and what one ought to do or feel. On closer examination, however, a fundamental difference between guilt feelings and inferiority feelings becomes evident. In fact, these two types of reaction are dynamic antagonists, comparable in physiology with sympathetic and parasympathetic innervations or with extensor and contractor muscles. The emotional syllogisms which underlie guilt feelings and inferiority feelings are quite different. The psychological content of guilt feelings can be verbalized about as follows: "I am no good. What I want to do or what I have done is mean and objectionable. I deserve contempt and punishment." In contrast, the emotional content of inferiority feelings is: "I am weak, I am not as strong, as clever, as efficient as the other fellow. I am ashamed on account of my weakness." In inferiority feelings, the self-condemnation is the result, not of wrongdoing, but of a shameful recognition of weakness. Accordingly, inferiority feelings stimulate competition and aggression. The only way to eradicate them is to show one's superiority in competition. Guilt feelings, on the contrary, inhibit competition. They are reactions to hostile, aggressive impulses. To get rid of guilt feelings, one must renounce competition. This defense measure alone is usually not enough. Guilt feelings require the opposite of the competitive attitude, namely subordination, self-debasement, and even punishment. From inferiority feelings one tries to free oneself by ambitious competition—by trying to get revenge on the one who has no other fault than being stronger than one's self. From guilt feelings one frees oneself by submission and by avoidance of hostile aggressive behavior.

The objection might be raised that this distinction between inferiority and guilt feelings is artificial and hair-splitting; that in both cases one accuses oneself of some kind of deficiency. In the case of inferiority feelings one says to oneself, "Are you not ashamed that your friend is stronger than you and licked you?" In the case of guilt feelings: "Are you

not ashamed that you steal candy?" In both cases the same expression is used—"Are you not ashamed?" Closer inquiry
shows, however, that the use of language is somewhat loose,
that the expression "shame" has a different connotation in
the two uses. Shame for being licked by one's friend stimu-
lates hostile competition and ambition, or leads to an attempt to depreciate the friend, whereas guilt for stealing has
a paralyzing effect. The first type of shame can be eliminated
by licking one's friend, that is to say, by aggressive behavior.
The second type of shame can be eliminated only by atonement or future avoidance of stealing, that is to say, by an
inhibition of the guilt-producing impulse. The difference between guilt feelings and inferiority feelings is clearly seen in
the expression: "It is better to be a knave than a fool." For being a knave one may feel guilty; for being a fool one feels
ashamed.

If doubt still remains that we deal here with two entirely
different emotions, a brief reference to a clinical example
will demonstrate the antithetical dynamic effect of these two
forms of self-criticism. The structure of many neuroses consists precisely in the conflict into which the coexistence of
strong inferiority and guilt feelings brings the patient, because
these two reactions require opposite kinds of behavior for
their relief.

> In a case of chronic alcoholism this conflict became evident
> shortly after the beginning of the analysis. A middle-aged
> man, the second of three brothers, showed from the begin-
> ning of his remembered life an extremely pronounced self-
> consciousness connected with vivid sensations of inferiority.
> He always compared himself unfavorably with his brothers
> and others, had great ambitions in competitive sports, but
> had no confidence in himself. In the course of years he de-
> veloped an extremely modest and submissive personality. His
> ambitions to compete and excel remained restricted to fan-

tasy. He was a retiring type, non-conspicuous, conformist, always polite, avoiding contradiction, with the tendency to minimize his abilities. This overt attitude of modesty and submissiveness put him under extreme pressure, however, and created intense inferiority feelings in him. These became tormenting, especially in relation to his chief. The patient would never contradict his chief, would follow his suggestions and accept blame while talking with him; but after he left the office he was filled with self-contempt and would tell himself, "You should have answered. You should have said 'no.' You should have demonstrated to him that he was not right. You are no good and you never will be any good." This self-depreciatory attitude usually became so unbearable that he would have the urge to drink. Alcohol dissipated his sense of weakness and inefficiency. As soon as the alcohol began to take effect, his spirit lifted; he felt courageous and strong. Apart from the effect of the drug, the act of drinking itself had for him the significance of a rebellious act. He secretly enjoyed the feeling that in the middle of the day during office hours he escaped his duties and indulged in a forbidden activity. In this alcoholic mood he would also indulge in promiscuous sexuality in a spirit of rebellion against limitations imposed upon him by social standards and by the voice of his conscience. Obviously these alcoholic and sexual escapades relieved his sense of inferiority because under the influence of alcohol he dared to commit offenses he would never have ventured without alcohol.

But as soon as he escaped the pangs of inferiority feelings he ran into a new conflict, that of guilt. The most instructive part of this observation pertains to the second phase of his alcoholic spells. When the effect of the alcohol began to wear off, he began to feel guilty—guilty and not inferior. Now, after he had committed forbidden sexual and nonsocial acts in order to show his independence and thus escaped his inferiority feelings, his conscience began to work and make itself felt in the form of remorse. To get rid of this remorse he again had to turn to alcohol, which before had served to rid him of his inferiority feelings. An ingenious physician whom I analyzed used to call the superego the alcohol-soluble portion of the human personality. In the case described, the alcohol dissolved both types of reactions, inferiority feelings and the sense of guilt. The emotional sequence was unmistakable: First there was a sense of extreme inferiority and self-contempt because of his submissiveness; then as a reaction to this he indulged in aggressive uninhibited behavior; and finally as a reaction to the latter he developed a sense of guilt in the form of remorse. While he was the victim of guilt feelings he would make up his mind never to drink again and never to indulge in illicit sex relations. While tormented by inferiority feelings his attitude became just the contrary: "Why not drink? Why not do forbidden things? Only a weakling gives in to every external or internal pressure!"

This vicious circle caused by the antithetic effect of inferiority and guilt feelings gives the dynamic clue for the understanding of many criminal careers. In the little boy, the intensely ambitious and competitive hostile attitude toward brothers and father provokes guilt feelings and fear of retaliation. Under the pressure of guilt feelings and fear he abandons his competitive attitude and adopts a submissive role by means of which the inhibited and intimidated boy tries to gain the love of his dangerous and powerful competitors. This submissive attitude now creates intense inferiority feelings, hurts the male pride, and leads to aggressive criminal behavior by means of which a tough, independent, stubborn, unyielding attitude is demonstrated and every dependence denied. This attitude becomes a new source of guilt feelings that lead to new inhibitions which again cause inferiority feelings and again stimulate aggressive behavior. Here the antithetical effect of guilt feelings and inferiority feelings becomes obvious. In order to escape inferiority feelings the neurotic criminal is driven to commit acts which give him the appearance of toughness and power. But this behavior which seeks to avoid the Scylla of inferiority feelings drives him into the Charybdis of guilt feelings. Under the influence of guilt feelings he commits blunders which often lead to his apprehension. Hence, there is no such thing as the perfect crime.

Inferiority feelings are the sign of a deeper instinctual conflict than is indicated by guilt feelings, which stem from the later structural differentiation within the personality. The deepest source of inferiority feelings is the childhood conflict between the progressive wish to grow up and be like the adults on the one hand and the regressive longing for the early dependent forms of existence on the other. Whenever this regressive wish makes itself felt, the ego, which identifies itself with the progressive attitude, reacts to it with a sense of inferiority. This conflict asserts itself strongly when the first phallic cravings develop around the Oedipus period. These longings are not only the conflict with the oral dependent attitude of the child but are further intensified by a feeling of frustration arising from the discrepancy between instinctual cravings and somatic maturation, between the wish and the possibility of its realization. Accordingly inferiority feelings are pre-social phenomena, whereas guilt feelings are the result of efforts at social adjustment. It is noteworthy that under the pressure of guilty conscience a person may become so inhibited and be driven back so far toward a help-seeking attitude that his dependence becomes incompatible with his pride. To remedy this narcissistic injury he may take recourse to extreme forms of independent and aggressive behavior. In this way excessive social inhibitions may become the very source of non-social behavior.

m. CONVERSION

The first ego defense which was discussed by Freud consists in the release of an alien tendency by certain innervations in the voluntary neuromuscular and sensory systems. It plays a most important role in conversion hysteria. In conversion symptoms both the alien tendency and its rejection are expressed either in the voluntary muscles or in the sensory organs. The most common examples are hysterical paralyses, contractures, spasms and convulsions, hysterical laughter or weeping, and certain anesthesias and paresthesias of the skin or of specific organs, as in hysterical blindness and deafness. It is characteristic of conversion phenomena that the motives behind the innervations are completely unconscious. The impulse to strike, scratch, bite, or swallow and to inhibit hearing or seeing does not appear in consciousness but is expressed by appropriate innervation or more often by the inhibition of voluntary muscles. In the sensory field also the patient is unaware of his refusal to see or hear; only the physiological results are manifest in blindness or deafness. In the hysterical convulsions of Charcot's grand attacks, the underlying desire for sexual intercourse is unconscious although the patient's convulsive movements openly indicate it. Conversion symptoms will be further discussed in the chapter on psychopathology.

n. REGRESSION

Regression has already been discussed as one of the common manifestations of the inertia principle. It is essentially the same phenomenon as Freud's "repetition compulsion," a tendency of the organism to re-establish an earlier situation.[7] In the course of adaptation, behavior patterns which have

[7] Repetition compulsion also includes other psychodynamic phenomena. See discussion on page 40.

proved useful are repeated, become automatic, and thus consume less energy. Since the organism's fundamental tendency is to preserve homeostatic equilibrium with the least possible expenditure of energy, it clings tenaciously to successful automatisms. When conditions change and the automatic adaptive reactions no longer serve to maintain stable conditions, the organism is forced to replace them with new modes of behavior tested through trial and error. Acquired mechanisms are apt to break down under emotional stress, fatigue, the sudden impact of external stimuli, or rapid change in external conditions. Regression to earlier behavior patterns can be observed, and with it the disintegration of set behavior patterns, which resolve into their constituent parts. All new behavior is learned by modifying older automatic patterns. Regressive behavior is characterized by a return to the original elements out of which adjusted behavior has been constructed. For example, a crowd in a panic may run aimlessly, screaming and crying for help, like children expecting to be rescued by adults. Each of these partial reactions, running or calling for help, may be a useful action in itself but is no longer co-ordinated in a reasonable pattern. Adjusted behavior in dangerous situations would require first reliance upon one's own resources to the utmost and then a demand for help as it is needed.

Regression also occurs when a mature sexual adjustment breaks down. After failure in a love relationship there is often a return in fantasy to earlier objects of sexual desire, like members of the family. This may induce neurosis because such regressive fantasies create conflict and can be expressed only in neurotic symptoms.

Regression operates in all psychopathological manifestations, though it is one of the most ineffective of the ego's defenses against demands which it cannot satisfy in a mature, acceptable form. Regression always means abandoning realistic efforts to achieve adequate gratification. It is most frequently a retreat from reality into fantasy. In fantasy, the way for regressive gratification is wide open for the return to points of fixation, to patterns which were once satisfactory but in the meantime have been outgrown.

Like other defenses of the ego, regression can be observed under certain conditions in healthy individuals. It has an important function in games, sports, rest, and recreation. The business man who plays cards or golf after a strenuous day in the office behaves in a sense like a child. He competes innocuously and finds gratification in physical or mental accomplishments which have no significance in his daily struggle for existence. Such regressive gratifications provide relief from the strains of adjusted co-ordinated behavior and involve giving in temporarily to the regressive trends latent in everybody. Tension is relaxed and vigor for the serious tasks of life is restored.

Sleep and dreams are the most common regressive manifestations and belong to the basic rhythm of life. In sleep the organism withdraws all interest from external reality and reproduces its state of oblivion before birth. The embryonic positions adopted by persons asleep indicate sleep's regressive nature. Metabolism during sleep also approximates that of infancy. Dreaming is a return to infantile forms of thought. The recreational value of sleep is based precisely on this regressive feature.

A Clinical Example of Various Ego Defenses

Since most of the ego defenses we have described can be most clearly observed when the ego fails in its integrative functions, they can be best illustrated by clinical examples of neurotic behavior. The following demonstrates a number of these mechanisms.

A twenty-three-year-old businessman came for consultation about a severe depression which had developed shortly after he was promoted to a responsible position. His father had died four years earlier and left him and his mother completely without resources. At the instigation of his mother he turned to a rich uncle for employment. The latter turned him down and declared that he did not believe in giving employment to relatives. In this distressing situation he tried to find a job on his own and was employed in his present position. His employer became fond of him and gave him the opportunity to advance. After four years of faithful service he was promoted to the position of head of the entire business, for which he had worked steadily and ambitiously. In his first consultation he described his condition as tense and depressed. He was critical of himself and experienced suicidal impulses. What he considered most strange was that he could not stand the presence of his employer without becoming extremely embarrassed and uneasy. He was always somewhat shy and inclined to be excessively polite and compliant, but he had recently become markedly servile toward his chief. He could not look him in the eye, blushed when he talked to him, and whenever his chief entered the room he felt impelled to rise and be of service. At the same time he felt inadequate to fill his independent and responsible position. When his chief offered him a larger salary appropriate to his new position he refused to accept it. He realized how strange this was because improving his financial status had been an important issue with him since he had begun his career in business.

After a few interviews he told me a short dream in which his rich uncle had caught cold, developed pneumonia, and died. The details are here unimportant, but the main plot gives us an insight into the most important psychodynamic factors responsible for his condition. In the dream he replaced his employer by his uncle. Actually his death wish was directed against his chief and benefactor, not against the uncle who no longer played any part in his life. This death wish was unacceptable to his ego. When asked what he thought about his uncle's death he said that he "wouldn't give a hoot" if his uncle died. "He is a mean person who deserted me when I needed his help and for whom I feel no affection whatever." Further discussion revealed that his employer had called up the office on the preceding day saying that he would not be in on account of a cold. The patient even remembered the fleeting thought that his chief might develop pneumonia and die.

Confronting this dream with the patient's symptoms and situation in life, it was not difficult to reconstruct the unconscious conflict. This ambitious young man had achieved everything he could in his present position when he was made head of the office. From this point on the only possible advancement would have been to take the place of the chief executive, his benevolent employer. When his employer phoned about his cold it precipitated the unconscious hope that he might die so that the patient could take over the whole business. This death wish was unacceptable to his ego, since he was deeply obligated to the man whose death he unconsciously desired. He felt gratitude and affection toward him, but his ambition demanded his death. In his dream he resolved the conflict by displacing the death wish to his uncle, who was a person whom he could justifiably hate. His symptoms were also explicable from his conflict situation. His depression was due to turning his hostility toward his superior against himself. His depression began when his hostile competitive and ambitious feelings could no longer be repressed because he was near his goal of taking the business away from his employer. His depression was an orgy of criticism and punishment of himself. It released his hostile impulses, which could no longer be kept fully repressed. Once they appeared in the open their object had to be changed. He could no longer deny their existence. Instead of attacking his employer, however, he attacked himself.

His guilty behavior in the presence of his employer, his

inability to face him, can now be explained from his conflict. This case illustrates the existence of unconscious guilt feelings and shows how a person may feel guilty and behave as if he were guilty although he does not know why. The patient had committed no offense but reacted to his unconscious death wish and hostility to his employer as if he had openly carried them out.

His exaggerated humble and servile attitude also illustrates the mechanism described as overcompensation. In his unconscious he wanted to be the head of the business, but he behaved like a servant. His hostile impulses were offset by his eagerness to be of service. His refusal to accept a raise in salary was an overcompensatory defense against his grasping attitude.

Another symptom was his constant fear that he would lose his position because his chief would find out how little he deserved it. This is an example of projection, for he attributed to his chief his own wish to get rid of him.

During this period the patient had become extremely dependent upon his mother. He shunned company, and by his depressed behavior he unconsciously but effectively appealed to maternal sympathy. He ceased to be an ambitious, self-supporting person, his mother's mainstay, and assumed the role of a helpless child. This narcissistic regression evoked past guilt feelings and revived an early conflict. As a child he had wished to supplant his father. This conflict was revived in his agitated depression. Because the earlier problem remained unsolved, he failed in his later adjustments and regressed to a pre-oedipal phase. He refused not only an increase in salary but was about to give up his job and become completely dependent upon his mother. He was rescued from this regression only by psychoanalytic treatment. He substituted an extremely dependent relationship with his physician for his dependence on his mother and thus could carry on in his job until gradually his conflicts were resolved and he could continue his career effectively.

BIBLIOGRAPHY

ABRAHAM, K.: "Manifestations of the Female Castration Complex," in *Selected Papers*. London, Hogarth Press, 1927, p. 338.

ALEXANDER, F.: "The Castration Complex in the Formation of Character," *Internat. J. Psycho-Analysis*, 4:11, 1923.

————: "Concerning the Genesis of the Castration Complex," *Psychoanalyt. Rev.*, 22:49, 1935.

————: "Fundamental Concepts of Psychosomatic Research: Psychogenesis, Conversion, Specificity," *Psychosom. Med.*, 5:205, 1943.

————: *The Medical Value of Psychoanalysis*. New York, W. W. Norton & Company, Inc., 1936.

————: "The Need for Punishment and the Death Instinct," *Internat. J. Psycho-Analysis*, 10:256, 1929.

————: *The Psychoanalysis of the Total Personality*. Nervous and Mental Disease Monograph Series No. 52. New York, Nervous and Mental Disease Publishing Company, 1929.

————: "Psychoanalysis Revised," *Psychoanalyt. Quart.*, 9:1, 1940.

————: "Remarks about the Relation of Inferiority Feelings to Guilt Feelings," *Internat. J. Psycho-Analysis*, 19:41, 1938.

————: "The Role of the Scientist in Society." Presented at the Meetings of the American Orthopsychiatric Association, Cincinnati, February 17, 1947.

BAKER, J. R.: *Science and the Planned State*. New York, The Macmillan Company, 1945.

BERNFELD, S.: "Bemerkungen ueber Sublimierung," *Imago*, 8:333, 1922.

————: "Zur Sublimierungstheorie," *Imago*, 17:399, 1931.

BOSSELMAN, B.: "Role of Transference in Treatment of Patient with Conversion Hysteria," *Psychosom. Med.*, 8:347, 1946.

BREUER, J., and FREUD, S.: *Studies in Hysteria*. Nervous and Mental Disease Monograph Series No. 61. New York, Nervous and Mental Disease Publishing Company, 1936.

DEUTSCH, H.: *Psychoanalyse der weiblichen Sexualfunktionen.*

Wien, Internationaler Psychoanalytischer Verlag, 1925.

DEUTSCH, H.: *Psychology of Women,* Volumes I and II. New York, Grune & Stratton, Inc., 1944, 1945.

FEDERN, P.: "Narcissism in the Structure of the Ego," *Internat. J. Psycho-Analysis,* 9:401, 1928.

FENICHEL, O.: "Die Identifizierung," *Internat. Ztschr. f. Psychoanal.,* 12:309, 1926.

————: *The Psychoanalytic Theory of Neurosis.* New York, W. W. Norton & Company, Inc., 1945.

FERENCZI, S.: "An Attempted Explanation of Some Hysterical Stigmata," in *Further Contributions to the Theory and Technique of Psycho-Analysis.* London, Hogarth Press, 1926, p. 110.

————: " 'Materialization' in Globus Hystericus," in *Further Contributions to the Theory and Technique of Psycho-Analysis.* London, Hogarth Press, 1926, p. 104.

————: "The Phenomena of Hysterical Materialization," in *Further Contributions to the Theory and Technique of Psycho-Analysis.* London, Hogarth Press, 1926, p. 89.

————: "Stages in the Development of the Sense of Reality," in *Contributions to Psycho-Analysis.* Boston, Richard G. Badger, 1916, p. 181.

————: "Transitory Symptom-Constructions during the Analysis," in *Contributions to Psycho-Analysis.* Boston, Richard G. Badger, 1916, p. 164.

FRENCH, T. M.: "A Clinical Study of Learning in the Course of a Psychoanalytic Treatment," *Psychoanalyt. Quart.,* 5:148, 1936.

————: "Defense and Synthesis in the Function of the Ego," *Psychoanalyt. Quart.,* 7:537, 1938.

————: "Goal, Mechanism and Integrative Field," *Psychosom. Med.,* 3:226, 1941.

————: "Reality and the Unconscious," *Psychoanalyt. Quart.,* 6:23, 1937.

FREUD, A.: *The Ego and the Mechanisms of Defence.* London, Hogarth Press, 1937.

FREUD, S.: "The Aetiology of Hysteria," in *Collected Papers,* I. London, Hogarth Press, 1924, p. 183.

FREUD, S.: "A Case of Paranoia Running Counter to the Psycho-Analytical Theory of the Disease," in *Collected Papers*, II. London, Hogarth Press, 1924, p. 150.

———: " 'Civilized' Sexual Morality and Modern Nervousness," in *Collected Papers*, II. London, Hogarth Press, 1924, p. 76.

———: *The Ego and the Id*. London, Hogarth Press, 1927.

———: "Fragment of an Analysis of a Case of Hysteria," in *Collected Papers*, III. London, Hogarth Press, 1925, p. 13.

———: *A General Introduction to Psychoanalysis*. New York, Boni & Liveright, Inc., 1920.

———: "General Remarks on Hysterical Attacks," in *Collected Papers*, II. London, Hogarth Press, 1924, p. 100.

———: *Group Psychology and the Analysis of the Ego*. London, Hogarth Press, 1922.

———: "Hysterical Phantasies and Their Relation to Bisexuality," in *Collected Papers*, II. London, Hogarth Press, 1924, p. 51.

———: *Inhibitions, Symptoms and Anxiety*. London, Hogarth Press, 1936.

———: "Medusa's Head," *Internat. J. Psycho-Analysis*, 22:69, 1941.

———: "Mourning and Melancholia," in *Collected Papers*, IV. London, Hogarth Press, 1925, p. 152.

———: "Negation," *Internat. J. Psycho-Analysis*, 6:367, 1925.

———: "On Narcissism: An Introduction," in *Collected Papers*, IV. London, Hogarth Press, 1925, p. 30.

———: "On the Psychical Mechanism of Hysterical Phenomena," in *Collected Papers*, I. London, Hogarth Press, 1924, p. 24.

———: "On the Transformation of Instincts with Special Reference to Anal Erotism," in *Collected Papers*, II. London, Hogarth Press, 1924, p. 164.

———: "The Passing of the Oedipus Complex," in *Collected Papers*, II. London, Hogarth Press, 1924, p. 269.

———: "Psycho-Analytic Notes upon an Autobiographical Account of a Case of Paranoia (Dementia Paranoides)," in *Collected Papers*, III. London, Hogarth Press, 1925, p. 387.

———: "Repression," in *Collected Papers*, IV. London, Hogarth Press, 1925, p. 84.

————: *Selected Papers on Hysteria.* Nervous and Mental Disease Monograph Series No. 4. New York, Nervous and Mental Disease Publishing Company, 1909.

————: "Some Points in a Comparative Study of Organic and Hysterical Paralyses," in *Collected Papers,* I. London, Hogarth Press, 1924, p. 42.

————: *Three Contributions to the Theory of Sex.* Nervous and Mental Disease Monograph Series No. 7. New York, Nervous and Mental Disease Publishing Company, 1930.

————: "Ueber Psychoanalyse" (Vierte Vorlesung, 1909), in *Gesammelte Schriften,* IV. Leipzig, Internationaler Psychoanalytischer Verlag, 1924, p. 387.

————: "The Unconscious," in *Collected Papers,* IV. London, Hogarth Press, 1925, p. 98.

HARTMANN, H., KRIS, E., and LOEWENSTEIN, R. M.: "Comments on the Formation of Psychic Structure," in *Psychoanalytic Study of the Child,* II, 1946. New York, International Universities Press, Inc., 1947, p. 11.

HORNEY, K.: *The Neurotic Personality of Our Time.* New York, W. W. Norton & Company, Inc., 1937.

————: *New Ways in Psychoanalysis.* New York, W. W. Norton & Company, Inc., 1940.

————: "On the Genesis of the Castration Complex in Women," *Internat. J. Psycho-Analysis,* 5:50, 1924.

————: "The Problem of Feminine Masochism," *Psychoanalyt. Rev.,* 22:241, 1935.

JONES, E.: "Love and Morality. A Study in Character Types." *Internat. J. Psycho-Analysis,* 18:1, 1937.

————: "Rationalization in Everyday Life," in *Papers on Psychoanalysis,* 1st Edition. New York, William Wood & Company, 1913, p. 1.

KRETSCHMER, E.: *Physique and Character.* New York, Harcourt, Brace and Company, Inc., 1925.

LAMPL-DE GROOT, J.: "The Evolution of the Oedipus Complex in Women." *Internat. J. Psycho-Analysis,* 9:332, 1928.

LEE, H. B.: "A Critique of the Theory of Sublimation," *Psychiatry,* 2:239, 1939.

LEE, H. B.: "The Cultural Lag in Aesthetics," *J. Aesthetics & Art Criticism*, 6:120, 1947.

———: "On the Esthetic States of the Mind," *Psychiatry*, 10:281, 1947.

———: "Poetry Production as a Supplemental Emergency Defense against Anxiety," *Psychoanalyt. Quart.*, 7:232, 1938.

———: "A Theory Concerning Free Creation in the Inventive Arts," *Psychiatry*, 3:229, 1940.

MASSERMAN, J. H.: *Principles of Dynamic Psychiatry*. Philadelphia, W. B. Saunders Company, 1946.

MENNINGER, K. A.: *Love against Hate*. New York, Harcourt, Brace and Company, Inc., 1942.

REIK, T.: *Gestaendniszwang und Strafbeduerfnis. Probleme der Psychoanalyse und der Kriminologie*. Leipzig, Internationaler Psychoanalytischer Verlag, 1925.

———: *Masochism in Modern Man*. New York, Farrar & Rinehart, 1941.

ROHEIM, G.: *The Origin and Function of Culture*. Nervous and Mental Disease Monograph Series No. 69. New York, Nervous and Mental Disease Monographs, 1943.

SAUL, L.: *Emotional Maturity*. Philadelphia, J. B. Lippincott Company, 1947.

SHELDON, W. H., and STEVENS, S. S.: *The Varieties of Temperament*. New York, Harper & Brothers, 1942.

SHELDON, W. H., STEVENS, S. S., and TUCKER, W. B.: *The Varieties of Human Physique*. New York, Harper & Brothers, 1940.

STAERCKE, A.: "The Castration Complex," *Internat. J. Psycho-Analysis*, 2:179, 1921.

STORCH, A.: *The Primitive Archaic Forms of Inner Experiences and Thought in Schizophrenia*. Nervous and Mental Disease Monograph Series No. 36. New York, Nervous and Mental Disease Publishing Company, 1924.

WEISS, E.: "Projection, Extrajection, and Objectivation," *Psychoanalyt. Quart.*, 16:357, 1947.

Chapter VI

Sociological Considerations[1]

1. SPECIFIC CULTURAL INFLUENCES

THE PROBLEM of personality development requires consideration of the social environment. The development of the personality is determined by two sets of factors: (1) the inherited equipment and (2) the molding influence of the environment. The latter can be roughly subdivided into the influence of the first environment of the child, the family, and the social setting. Every family has its individual features and must be considered as a whole. It is useless to discuss a mother's influence upon one child apart from her attitude toward her husband and the other children. These facts present a complex emotional interrelation between all members of the family. Maternal rejection of a child may be more damaging if supported by the father's attitude and less so if compensated for by the father's attention and care. These characteristics of each family have unquestionably a decisive influence upon the child's development.

---

[1] In this chapter the specific contributions of psychoanalysis to social theory are not treated, but only the sociological factors which influence personality development.

In addition to these, there are family attitudes typical of different cultures and determined by the social structure. The mentality of a typical German or Japanese family is quite different from that of an American family. Parental attitudes, educational principles and aims, are peculiar to each culture.

These common features produce national qualities. We speak of a western type of mind in contrast to oriental mentality. With the exception of the extreme representatives of the racial theory who try to explain all such differences by racial constitution, most people believe in the importance of the formative influence of the cultural milieu upon personality. The scientific analysis of the relative significance of constitutional and environmental factors contributing to personality formation awaits future study.

The psychoanalytic study of individual cases has impressed us with the influence of the emotional experiences of childhood upon the development of personality. The main contribution of psychoanalysis has been to demonstrate the formative influence of early emotional experiences in the family relationships upon character and mental disturbances. It is important to emphasize that the variety of emotional influences in early family life is not great but stems from a few fundamental and universal emotional patterns. The child's dependence on the mother is perhaps the most powerful emotional factor and leads to his possessiveness toward the mother with its resultant jealousies, hostilities, and fears toward siblings and adult rivals. In conflict with this stand the progressive tendencies arising from primitive sexual desires and curiosity and resulting in all kinds of identification with adults. The psychoanalytic study of these emotional relationships has been so fruitful that they temporarily obscured the constitutional differences between children which are unquestionably responsible for at least some of the differences between people. There is no reason to doubt that races and individuals differing in hereditary equipment differ from each other as much as an Arabian race horse differs from a Mecklenburger, or a retriever from a St. Bernard or dachshund.

The lay mind was only too ready to explain national differences on a racial basis. One hears of the temperamental Latin, the commercial Greek or Jew, and the thrifty Scot. Freud mentioned the anal erotic qualities of the Swiss. Are these, however, truly racial characteristics and due to heredity? In contrast to animals, culture is transmitted among men by tradition, customs, ideologies, and institutions, and these must be given special consideration. Are the Swiss thrifty, neat, and orderly because these traits are inherited from their Swiss ancestors or because their cultural conditions and traditions encourage such habits? Even without careful scientific investigation one is inclined to attribute a powerful influence to cultural factors. Common personality traits are found among people belonging to the same cultural group independent of race. We can rightly speak of the characteristics of the peasant which are not shared by the mercantile class, regardless of race. The Russian kulak, the Hungarian and French peasant, and the American farmer have surprisingly many personality traits in common. This country is a living example of the strength of the cultural factor. Immigrants are rapidly Americanized, and the process is usually complete in the second or third generation. Only those who live in isolated racial groups retain many of their original customs and ideologies.

The question of the depth of cultural influences upon the formation of personality is still open. Are the psychological differences between men due primarily to the different distribution of the genes in their parental cells, to their early specific emotional experiences in the family, or to different cultural influences? It is obvious that cultural factors alone cannot explain the great variety of personalities emerging from the same group, but that they can be held responsible only for trends in character common to all members of the group. The more subtle individual differences must be due to constitution and early family influences.

The scientific analysis of this problem leads to a distinction of different categories of personality features. We shall have to differentiate between characteristics which are common to all members of the same cultural group—for example, peasants or soldiers—and then between characteristics which are common to all individuals with a similar heredity—for example, all Finns—whether they are peasants or university professors. The more subtle characteristics are highly individual and distinguish one member of the same cultural or racial group from another. Some of these personality traits may be considered less changeable and more fundamental than others which are more superficial and flexible. The characteristics transmitted by heredity are the most fundamental and least changeable. It is more difficult to estimate how deeply the structure of a family or the general characteristics of culture act upon individuals. Since custom determines so elementary a thing as the method of nursing, it cannot be considered as more superficial than the influence of a neurotic marital situation in a family. Such considerations illustrate the complexity of the problem and the difficulty of isolating cultural influences upon personality formation from experiences due to particular circumstances within families.

Personality is ultimately the result of both heredity and the specific family constellation and cultural environment. As yet no scientific method has been evolved to determine the relative significance of these different factors. Not even the experiment of rearing identical twins in different cultures and comparing the results would be conclusive, for although the hereditary factor would remain constant and the cultural factor would vary, the structure of the family in which the twins were reared could not be exactly duplicated. Even if the experiment were undertaken in a uniform artificial environment, it would be impossible to reproduce identically the emotional influences upon the child of persons in contact with him. Some academic psychologists or sociologists might consider such an experiment conclusive, but no psychoanalyst would, since he knows too well the influence upon the child's development of adults in early contact with him.

The experimental method must therefore be replaced by less exact methods. Obviously the statistical method offers a second choice. The frequency of certain types of neurotic criminal and normal personalities in different cultural groups might indicate the varying influence of culture upon personality. If compulsion neuroses should prove more frequent among merchants, industrialists, and intellectuals than among peasants, more frequent in England and Germany than in Italy and France, or more frequent in the nineteenth century than in the fifteenth century in Europe, or if hysteria is more frequent among Catholic peasants and more common during the Middle Ages than in the twentieth century, important conclusions could be drawn as to the influence of different civilizations on mental development. Such comparative studies could be carried on in a cross section of our present civilization by studying the frequency of certain neuroses and personality types among different cultural groups, as well as by comparing the frequency of certain attitudes and neuroses in different historical periods. The most promising method is the comparison of psychoanalytic case histories of individuals belonging to different civilizations. The advantage of this method over all others is that only such clinical studies can give us a sufficiently detailed and reliable view of the actual structure of a human personality as it develops under certain cultural and specific family influences.

Although such comparative analytic studies of persons belonging to different cultures are not yet available, instructive observations have been made by analytically trained anthropologists concerning the relationships of culturally determined family influences upon personality formation (Benedict, Kardiner, Linton, Mead). Kardiner speaks of a basic personality characteristic for each culture and tries to demonstrate its cultural determinants, which consist in certain institutions which are again derived from the structure of the whole society.

In a classical study, Ruth Benedict [2] attempts to explain the typical personality structure of the Japanese from the typical childhood experiences in the family. She was most impressed by the sense of duty, obligation, and filial reverence characteristic of the Japanese. While American parents live for their children, Japanese children live for their parents. Their life is devoted to paying back a debt incurred toward their parents and predecessors. Filial duty consists in rigid obedience and in a consistent, unrelenting effort to preserve the purity of the family's name. This goes hand in hand with the unquestioned acceptance of hierarchy, both within the family and in society at large.

Another central feature of the Japanese personality is the extreme lack of spontaneity of action and feeling. The whole life of the Japanese is carefully mapped out for him. His behavior on every occasion is rigidly prescribed. To an outside observer, the life of a Japanese appears as a sequence of ritualistic performances which he executes with automatic precision. This he achieves by practicing the right kind of behavior just as he practices specific skills such as fencing or wrestling or gardening until their performance becomes perfect and automatic.

A third trait most difficult to understand is that in spite of

[2] Ruth Benedict: *The Chrysanthemum and the Sword; Patterns of Japanese Culture*. Boston, Houghton Mifflin Company, 1946.

rigid discipline, filial reverence and obedience, and acceptance of a hierarchical organization in which everybody's place is accurately defined, there is a paradoxical trend in the Japanese personality toward spontaneity which gives the Japanese personality a mysterious, contradictory, and unpredictable aspect. While self-discipline and submission to the hierarchical system and an extreme dependence on public opinion are the outstanding features, there is an occasional manifestation of indomitable rage and rebellion, and also a consistent indulgence in culinary and sexual enjoyment and a high degree of interest in artistic activities.

Ruth Benedict explains these contradictions by the Japanese principles of child rearing. The family is hierarchically organized and usually comprises three generations living together in the same home. The most eminent figures are the male members of the first generation; in the second place comes the father. From his early years, the child sees the complete obedience of his father to his grandfather and learns to feel the same way about his own father. The authority of the father is so undisputed that it does not require any extreme form of enforcement; it is instilled in the child so consistently that a facial expression, a wink of the eye, is sufficient to achieve extreme restrictions in the child's behavior. This rigid discipline, however, is not imposed upon the child from the beginning of his life. In his first five or six years, the child is indulged by his mother to an extreme degree. This is expressed in the early feeding habits, which are just the opposite of the American system of routine clock feeding. The mother's breast is constantly at the disposal of the Japanese child, who often continues nursing even after the next child is born, up to the second or third year. This oral indulgence is reciprocal, for to the Japanese mother, nursing the child is not felt as an obligation but is experienced as a keen physical pleasure. Toilet training is learned rather early but without drastic regimentation, and there is no intimidation of the child's early manifestations of sexual interest. Mutual sexual play among children is not in the least discouraged, nor is infantile masturbation.

These two successive periods in the life of the Japanese child explain convincingly the contradictory nature of the Japanese personality. An early period of almost complete freedom in which the satisfaction of the senses is uninhibited is followed by an extreme disciplinary regulation of life. Discipline which follows excessive freedom must be doubly strong to be effective. The Japanese acquires this extreme self-discipline, but he can save his mental equilibrium only by having vents in certain areas of his life.

How and why these family attitudes have developed, what their social meaning and origin are, is only vaguely indicated by Benedict. There can be no doubt, however, that this type of family organization is the reflection of a hierarchical feudal system which existed in Japan in an unchanged form for many centuries until the revolution of 1868. Even after the Meiji revolution, it has been pointed out by historians, the feudal system was not destroyed but was fitted with slight modifications into the modern, industrialized Japan.

Industrialization there, as in Germany, was not followed by democratization. Japan's history can be viewed as a gradual coalescence of smaller feudal units into larger ones. Finally, all particularistic loyalties of the subjects to their local lords fused into one central loyalty to the emperor. The ethos of the Japanese family clearly reflects the loyal attitude of the retainer toward his feudal lord. Naturally, blind obedience and emphasis on personal honor, combined with martial virtues, are at the core of every warring feudal society in which internecine warfare is the content of national life. Other feudal cultures show similar traits. The Japanese code of honor closely resembles the chivalry and loyalty of the Spanish knights and of the German *Ehre*. The emotional atmosphere of the Japanese family could not consciously have been planned to be more effective in producing loyal subjects for feudal lords. The indulgence in the Japanese child's early education is a great asset in making him more capable later of tolerating all kinds of extreme social restrictions by providing emotional outlet for him and allowing him freedom to gratify the most intense instinctive needs. Through these free areas, a balance is achieved which permits the Japanese to live his social life by iron discipline.

From all this, it becomes obvious that Japanese personality formation could be changed on a large scale only if the whole social structure itself were altered.

Similarly instructive is Margaret Mead's [3] analysis of the American character, which she explains as a result of family influences. In many respects the American character offers a direct contrast to the Japanese. Nothing is more characteristic of the American than his extreme informality, his lack of consistent patterns of behavior, his resultant adaptability, and his complete denial of social hierarchy. While virtue for the Japanese consists in the meticulous observance of rules prescribed for every situation, the supreme virtue for the American consists in individual accomplishment. While the Japanese has a lifelong sense of indebtedness and obligation which he must spend his life in repaying, the American puts emphasis on the fact that he does not owe anything to anybody except himself. The filial reverence and obedience of the Japanese is in sharp contrast to the American's slight respect for the older generation and for traditional ways of thought and action. The Japanese finds security by learning and following a traditional code; the American's security is based on what he himself achieves in competing successfully with others. While the self-

[3] Margaret Mead, *And Keep Your Powder Dry*, New York, William Morrow and Co., 1942.

respect of the Japanese is dependent on how successfully he can live up to the code of revering his predecessors, the self-respect of the American is based on how successfully he can outstrip the accomplishment of his predecessors. And to make the contrast even sharper, with all his self-reliance and lack of restrictions through customs and rules, the American in his sexual behavior is much more circumscribed than the Japanese. In Japan extra-marital relationships are openly indulged in; in the United States they are forbidden by law, disapproved of by public opinion, and indulged only through subterfuge.

Though the Japanese has a free outlet for his biological instincts, his social conduct is devoid of spontaneity and is rigidly prescribed. The American offers just the opposite psychodynamic picture; his basic instincts are highly regulated in expression and all inventiveness and spontaneity must seek outlet in business and social activities, which are free of rules and permit adventure and individual accomplishment.

Let us examine now how these characteristics can be explained from the structure and customs of the American family. As Benedict points out, the most striking difference between American and Japanese child rearing is the strict regulation of the vegetative functions in the American child at a very early age. Feeding rules and toilet habits begin early, and the child's protestations are completely ignored. Gradually, however, more and more freedom is given to the child, in contrast to the custom of the Japanese family, in which the child's freedom is more and more curtailed as he grows older. The American child becomes the center of family life, and he is allowed expression of his aggressive impulses. Continental dinner guests in the American home are often amazed at the way the child can run around the dinner table, pestering his parents and the guests. Very soon, however, a premium is placed on successful competition and accomplishment. As Mead puts it, the love of the American mother is conditional:

it depends on how well the child can measure up to other children. In school, good grades and athletic accomplishment become the conditions of his acceptance by others and—what is particularly important—by his mother. To measure up and to excel are the basic motive forces of the American personality; both love and security depend upon being successful in the race.

Particularly significant in American culture is the lack of rigid social stratification. The American lives in a fluid society which changes from generation to generation. This is most conspicuous in the immigrant family. The father is in a vulnerable position, since he does not master the language and customs of the new culture. The children and their children have to learn ways different from his and his wife's. These children cannot develop reverence for tradition; their trend is away from tradition. The child of this "second generation" has to find out everything for himself, with little or no aid from the parents. He learns from his teachers and from other children. Since immigration until recently has been a constant feature in the American scene, its influence upon American character cannot easily be exaggerated. The country was founded upon a protest against the old world, and this protest remained a characteristic feature of the new world. Many other traits of the American personality can be explained from sociological facts.

The American character shows interesting contradictions. With all the emphasis upon individual accomplishment, there is a conspicuous tendency to conformity. Certain external features of life, such as clothing and house furnishings, are standardized and thus become a source of security in a land where traditionally sanctioned, rigid regulations are lacking. Continuous competition in a fluid society in which one's status is never fixed creates a great amount of insecurity. This supplies a powerful and consistent impetus for further achievement and success. At the same time, competition separates individuals from each other and thus creates the opposite desire, to "belong." This need manifests itself in what might be called the American fraternalism, in the numerous social groups, clubs, fraternities, and sororities which mushroom as a reaction against the estranging effect of the extremely competitive social life. The American habit of holding frequent conventions of occupational groups has the same basis. Business and professional rivals in those conventions meet in the bar as friends, offering each other drinks and cigars, and inviting each other to dine. In this way the lonesome individual, who became separated from everyone else by his desire to measure up to others or to outdo them, finds his way back into a community.

These examples may suffice to demonstrate that personality traits characteristic of a nation are molded through the medium of the family and that ultimately the family attitudes themselves are determined by the total social configuration existing in a given culture.

2. GENERAL CULTURAL INFLUENCES

These cultural variations should not, however, obscure the influence of social institutions which operate in every form of culture, such as certain marital laws. Although these were described long ago by various anthropologists, their meaning was first recognized by Freud. In his pioneer work, *Totem and Taboo,* he explained the ubiquity of marital laws forbidding incest and showed the relation of these to totemistic rituals which, with considerable variations, appear in all primitive cultures. He claimed that the totem, usually a sacred animal but sometimes an inanimate object, is always a symbol of the father and that the rituals are designed to protect the totem from the aggression of the male members

of the social group. The two basic taboos in primitive societies are: (1) not to use a woman belonging to the same
totem group for sexual purposes and (2) not to kill the totem
animal. These together agree with and express the content of
the Oedipus complex. From this Freud concluded that the
nucleus of every social organization represents a defense
against the oedipal tendencies. The unity of the family can
be preserved only if the sexual interest of the sons becomes
diverted from the female members of the family, because only
thus can the rivalry between father and sons be circumvented.
This measure preserves the integrity of the family, and at
the same time exogamous marriage binds different families
together. According to his view, the family is the cell of the
society. Families become united through exogamy into clans,
which then become extended to tribes and finally into nations.

Freud dramatized this view with his theory of the primal
horde. This is the most primitive association of men. There
is a "violent jealous father who keeps all the females for himself and drives away the growing sons. . . . One day the ex-
pelled brothers joined forces, slew and ate the father, and
thus put an end to the father horde." The totem feast is
the commemoration of this criminal victory over the father.
The reaction to this primal crime is the beginning of civilization. "The sons hated the father who stood so powerfully
in the way of their sexual demands and desire for power,
but they also loved and admired him." After they had removed him their guilt and longing for a powerful leader
were aroused. "The dead now became stronger than the living had been." The two basic taboos originated from this
conflict. The sons "undid their deed by declaring that the
killing of the father substitute, the totem, was not allowed,
and renounced the fruits of their deed by denying themselves
the liberated women." Freud's explanation of the fact that
in totemism the father is represented by a symbol protected

by law, while the incest taboo is openly expressed, is that patricidal wishes are more deeply repressed. These must disappear from consciousness and no open trace of them can be tolerated. The father himself is therefore not mentioned in totemistic rites, but only his symbolic representative, the totem.

This ingenious theory of the origins of civilization, especially the hypothetical primal horde of brothers, has been repeatedly challenged, but the fundamental validity of the Freudian view has never been successfully contradicted. The gist of it is that social organization is possible only if its nucleus, the family, can be guarded by institutions regulating the relation of its members to each other. The most disruptive force within the family is the sexual jealousy of the male members. The infant's prolonged dependence upon the mother requires some form of family, and the family can survive only if it is protected from the natural jealousies and aggressions of the members against each other. The Oedipus complex therefore reflects the basic social institutions by which the integrity of the family is kept and must be considered as the nucleus of man's domestication.

BIBLIOGRAPHY

ALEXANDER, F.: "A Tentative Analysis of the Variables in Personality Development. Culture and Personality" (1938 Section Meetings), *Am. J. Orthopsychiat.*, 8:587, 1938.
———: *Mental Hygiene and Criminology.* The American Foundation for Mental Hygiene, Inc., 1930.
———: *Our Age of Unreason.* Philadelphia, J. B. Lippincott Company, 1942.
———: "Psychoanalytic Aspect of Mental Hygiene and the Environment," *Ment. Hyg.*, 21:187, 1937.
ALEXANDER, F., BURGESS, E. W., WARNER, W. L., and MEAD, M.: *Environment and Education.* Supplementary Educational Mon-

ographs No. 54. March 1942. Chicago, The University of Chicago Press.

BATESON, G., and MEAD, M.: *Balinese Character. A Photographic Analysis.* New York Academy of Sciences, Volume II, 1942.

BENEDICT, R.: *The Chrysanthemum and the Sword. Patterns of Japanese Culture.* Boston, Houghton Mifflin Company, 1946.

————: *Patterns of Culture.* Boston, Houghton Mifflin Company, 1934.

FREUD, S.: *Civilization and Its Discontents.* London, Hogarth Press, 1930.

————: "Contributions to the Psychology of Love. The Taboo of Virginity," in *Collected Papers,* IV. London, Hogarth Press, 1925, p. 217.

————: *Group Psychology and the Analysis of the Ego.* London, The International Psycho-Analytical Press, 1922.

————: *Totem and Taboo.* London, George Routledge & Sons, Ltd., 1919.

KARDINER, A.: *The Individual and His Society.* New York, Columbia University Press, 1939.

————: *The Psychological Frontiers of Society.* New York, Columbia University Press, 1945.

LINTON, R.: *The Study of Man. An Introduction.* New York, D. Appleton–Century Company, Inc., 1936.

MEAD, M.: *And Keep Your Powder Dry.* New York, William Morrow and Co., 1942.

————: *From the South Seas. Studies of Adolescence and Sex in Primitive Societies.* New York, William Morrow & Company, 1928.

ROHEIM, G.: *Australian Totemism.* London, George Allen & Unwin, Ltd., 1925.

Chapter VII

The Psychology of Dreaming

contradicts grey

1. THE SLEEP-PROTECTING FUNCTION OF DREAMS

FREUD ALWAYS considered his theory of dreams as the best-founded portion of psychoanalysis. This has been confirmed by the fact that this theory has been little changed either by himself or by his followers. It stands as valid in all its details and fundamentals and has been tested by long observations.

Although dreams have always attracted popular imagination and the interest of literary men, they have been neglected by science. There have been three main theories of dreams:

1. The prescientific view current in the ancient world attributed to dreams a prophetic supernatural significance. Wise men could predict the future from dreams.

The other two types of dream theories are scientific in their attempt to explain dreams from other known phenomena.

2. Physiological dream theories maintain that dreams have no psychological meaning but are the result of rudimentary activity in the brain cortex which reflects incoherently impressions of the previous day.

3. Psychological theories consider dreams as products of fantasy and attempt to explain them psychologically.

Freud's psychoanalytic theory of dreams belongs to this third group. In his book, *The Interpretation of Dreams,* he gave full credit to earlier literature but drew his own conclusions from the observation of patients before consulting the views of others. In fact, he learned practically nothing from these others, although he found later that Ives Delage, Scherner, and some others had vaguely anticipated some of his views. No one before him had advanced a comprehensive theory capable of explaining dreams.

Freud's interest was attracted to dreams by his patients' accounts, and he soon recognized their value for the study of repressed tendencies. His clinical work had begun with hypnosis, and he recognized the similarity of somnambulistic states to dreaming.

His book on dreams cannot be summarized effectively in a brief abstract; it must be studied in the original. This brief chapter is written to prepare the student for this task. The order of Freud's presentation will not be followed here, but the essentials of the theory are presented. The therapeutic use of dreams will be discussed in the later chapter on therapy.

The basic fact about dreams is that their function is to aid rather than to disturb sleep, and to prevent the dreamer from being awakened by internal stimuli. The physiological function of sleep is rest. We close our eyes to exclude optical stimuli; we cannot close our ears, and therefore we seek quiet, we withdraw interest from the outside world, and our mental activities are reduced to a minimum. We cannot, however, protect ourselves from such internal stimuli as a full bladder, an empty stomach, thirst, the pressure of unfulfilled wishes, frustrations, guilt, and worry. All these in spite of our need to rest continue to affect our mind, but dreams attempt to reduce them so that sleep may be prolonged. Dreams are not always successful, however, in preserving sleep.

DREAMS AS SATISFACTIONS OF PHYSICAL NEEDS

 The sleep-protecting function of dreams can be illustrated by the simplest type of dreams, which satisfy elementary demands like hunger or thirst. The hungry or thirsty subject dreams that he is drinking or eating, and by this hallucination achieves temporary gratification. He can continue sleeping instead of being awakened to satisfy these physiological needs. An overfatigued schoolboy sets his alarm clock for 7:00 A.M. in order to be at school at 8:00. He awakes, shuts off the alarm clock and decides to rest another ten minutes, falls asleep again, and dreams he is busily occupied in school. Here an unpleasant duty is visualized as fulfilled, and this permits the dreamer to deceive himself and continue to sleep.

SIMPLE WISH-FULFILLMENT DREAMS

The same dynamic principle operates in the dreams of small children. These are simple wish-fulfillments in which the child satisfies in fancy what it has been refused on the previous day. A five-year-old girl asked her parents for a birthday present of a toy automobile driven by foot which she had seen another girl playing with. On her birthday she was disappointed because she received a tricycle instead. The next morning she came into her parents' room saying triumphantly, "I dreamed that I had a big automobile and drove it alone all around the city." All dreams of simple wish-fulfillment have the same structure. Such expressions as "Not even in my dreams would I have expected this to happen" betray the intuitive knowledge of this function of dreams. It is directly expressed in the Hungarian proverb, "The hungry goose dreams of corn and the hungry pig of acorns." If all dreams were simple wish-fulfillments there would be no need for a special theory, and many scientific minds who pride themselves on their exactness would not have so long insisted that dreams have no meaning and are unworthy of psychological study.

DREAMS OF ADULTS

The dreams of most adults do not reveal their meaning as easily as the examples cited above. Dreams of simple wish-fulfillment are common only in children; adults express their wishes directly only rarely and under unusual circumstances, and mostly in great distress. When lost in the desert, or imprisoned, the victim may dream of drinking water or escaping from his cell. Most adult dreams, however, appear senseless, disconnected, and fragmentary and not only do not give direct satisfaction but sometimes even cause anxiety. The principle of wish-fulfillment which is obvious in children's dreams of satisfaction cannot be applied simply to the majority of adult dreams. Once Freud had arrived at his general view that dreams protect sleep he was faced with choosing between two conclusions: (1) either some dreams fulfill wishes, provide satisfaction, and protect sleep, while others are meaningless reverberations in the brain of the previous day's impressions, or (2) all dreams are meaningful and the apparently senseless and disconnected ones also can be explained psychologically. Freud's pursuit of the second alternative was the most significant of all his scientific achievements and resulted in his theory of dream interpretation.

The reason why adults' dreams are not the direct transparent expression of unfulfilled wishes is that most wishes of adults, unlike those of children, are thwarted not by external but by internal obstacles. The small child is almost completely dependent upon adults for the gratification of his desires and needs; they help him to satisfy or they prevent him from satisfying his desires. When the child is frustrated he imagines his wish to be fulfilled in the way denied him by reality. The desires latent in adults' dreams, however, are contrary to their own standards. The obstacle to their fulfillment is internal. The desire, for example, to hurt someone to whom we are obligated cannot be expressed simply by dreaming of beating or killing him. A direct expression of such alien desires would cause severe conflict, arouse fear and guilt, and waken the dreamer. The desire must therefore be disguised in the dream by replacing the object of the hostile impulse with someone whom the dreamer can justifiably hate or by casting someone else in the role of murderer. The unconscious tendency is thus expressed, and at the same time the conflict with conscience is avoided. The dream permits sleep by diverting the pressure of an unfulfilled wish to an expression permissible to the dreamer's own standards.

This theory required confirmation by facts, and a method had to be devised by which the hidden meaning of the dream could be reconstructed.

2. PRINCIPLES OF RECONSTRUCTING THE HIDDEN MEANING OF A DREAM

Freud differentiated between the manifest dream content, which is the plot of the dream, and the latent dream content, which is disguised because of its unacceptable nature. He called the process by which the latent dream content is transformed into the manifest dream content, the dream work. Dream work is the result of the censorship of the superego, which does not permit the alien desires to be expressed directly. Interpretation must penetrate the censorship and reverse the process of the dream work. Dream work transforms the latent content into relatively unobjectionable manifest content; interpretation reconstructs from the manifest content the latent conflict. The resistance to the analytic interpretation of dreams is offered by the same force which effected the disguise. Since the wish expressed in the dream has been rejected by the conscious personality, the penetration of its disguise provokes violent protest.

This resistance explains why most dreams appear meaningless and disconnected. Freud overcame it by free association and invented a way both to reconstruct the latent dream content and to account for its distortion. The dreamer associates freely to the different elements of his dream. The fragmentation of the manifest dream content into its elements is needed because only the whole dream in its context has an objectionable meaning; the elements in themselves are naturally harmless. In the course of associating to the manifest dream elements the dreamer arrives at the latent elements of the dream. The pressure of the repressed wish breaks through the lessened resistance, since this unconscious censorship during free association is not exerting conscious control over the trains of thought, and the repressed mental content emerges into consciousness. When all the elements of the dream have been thus illuminated, the associations themselves are assembled into a meaningful whole. As in calculus, no general rules can be given for integration, or, as no general rules can be given for solving a crossword puzzle, so the reassembling of associations to dreams is creative, the outcome of experience and ingenuity. Once, however, a solution has been found by a good guess, it can be accurately tested if enough is known, especially of the dreamer's emotional state at the time of the dream. Amateur dream analysis on social occasions has little to do with the scientific interpretation of dreams. This can be made effectively only during psychoanalytic treatment because the analyst is intimately acquainted with the dreamer's emotional life at the time of his dream and also knows his past.

All this can be explained more concretely by examples.

Before discussing these, however, certain other facts must be considered. Freud early observed that certain dream elements yielded no associations. These were common symbols of universal human experience. Some authors, particularly Jung, believed these symbols to have been inherited in a "racial unconscious." Freud's mind was divided on this question. I do not see the necessity for such an improbable assumption as phylogenetically predetermined symbols. Their universality can be explained from common experiences.

The knowledge of universal symbols has been derived from the dreams of a large number of individuals as well as from the study of language and folklore. Many of the same symbols which appear in dreams occur also in figurative speech. A king is a universal symbol for the father in both dreams and folklore and is often referred to as the father of the nation. The most common symbols involve members of the family, basic facts of life like birth, the sexual act, sexual organs, and death.

The father is symbolized not only as a king but as an animal, as, for example, in totemism, which represents the ancestor of the tribe as an animal. The mother is symbolized by nature, the earth, and water, from which all life stems. This symbol is also common in folklore and dreams. Birth is symbolized with surprising regularity by water and in scenes of rescue from drowning. In folklore, the birth of the hero is often related in this way, as Otto Rank has shown. The best-known example is the legend of Moses who was found by Pharaoh's daughter in a basket floating in the water, a symbolic intimation that he was her illegitimate son.

Procreation is variously symbolized by sowing, tilling, or manufacture. It is impossible to give here a complete list of these symbols, but wood as a symbol for the mother should be mentioned. In Latin *materia* means "matter" and *mater* means "mother"; in Spanish *madera* means "wood." There is here an unconscious equation between the mother and substances from which things can be created.

The sexual act, because surrounded by secrecy and repression, is usually referred to symbolically in dreams. The incestuous nature of infantile impulses, which are taboo in all civilizations, is a universal cause of sexual repression. The variety of their symbolic expression is great, but it is based on a few simple analogies like the penetration of hollow objects, traveling in the same conveyance with someone. The German *Verkehr* means both "traffic" and "sexual intercourse."

Children are commonly symbolized by little animals, as in the expression, "kids." Because of unconscious hostility in sibling rivalry these symbolic animals are often voracious and disgusting, like bugs and worms. Death is often referred to by means of departure.

The knowledge of common symbols and disguises is like familiarity with a language, and we often refer to it as the language of dreams. In the interpretation of dreams the technique of free association, therefore, is greatly aided by the interpreter's knowledge of this language. The characteristic mentality of dreams will be discussed later. Here a few examples will be presented to illustrate more completely the generalizations just stated.

DREAM NO. 1. A middle-aged German businessman sought treatment for a severe depression accompanied by suicidal impulses. The depression developed a year and a half after his return from military service as an officer in the first World War, when he was confronted with the task of assuming civilian responsibilities. Early in his treatment he reported the following dream:

"I am taking a walk with one of the ranking officers of the Russian army and become aware that it is the Tsar. Suddenly a stranger appears with a sword and wants to kill the Tsar. I wish to intervene to save the Tsar, but it is too late. The Tsar is killed." [1]

Following the technique of dream interpretation just described, I separated the dream into its component parts and asked what associations to each part could be produced.

The patient associated the Tsar with the fact that in Russian the *Tsar* is called "little father." He connected the officer in the dream with one of his war experiences. During a lull in operations the opposing forces agreed for a period not to shoot at each other from the closely adjoining trenches. The soldiers could see each other, talk, even knew each other by name and sight. On one occasion the patient violated the agreement, which appeared to him "strange" because in normal life "he wouldn't kill a fly." He vindicated his cruelty by the thought that the Russians were prepared to kill the wives and children of their enemies.

When asked to associate with the word "stranger," he hesitated. Nothing came to his mind, and he stated with annoyance that he did not know who the stranger was. He was then told that the stranger probably meant the strange part of his own personality which had committed murder. It was pointed out to him that he used the word "strange" when he described how unlike his naturally kind character it was to shoot at the Russians. The patient protested energetically and said, "How could it be myself when in the dream I try to save the Tsar?" It was then explained to him that he was the author of the dream and if he had wanted to, he could have saved the Tsar. Intellectually the point became clear, and he later produced memories in which hostile feelings toward his father were recalled.

In this dream several mechanisms are illustrated. (1) In

[1] This dream was described in *The Criminal, the Judge and the Public*, by Franz Alexander and Hugo Staub, New York, The Macmillan Company, 1931.

representing a part of his personality by a stranger he utilized the mechanism of *projection*. This was possible because the hostile actions were actually foreign to his ego and were repressed. His actual personality was kind and considerate. (2) He *substituted* for the father the Tsar, a king being a common *symbol* for father. The dream was mobilized by the hostile feelings provoked by the analytic situation. He transferred to the analyst the same ambivalent feelings which he had felt toward his father. This revived his childhood hostility. The dream was a concealed expression of hostility against persons in authority, a pattern formed in childhood. If the reaction pattern had not already been formed, he would not have reacted to the analyst with so much hostility. (3) In the dream he tried to save his victim, but this is obviously a hypocritical gesture. It is an example of *overcompensation*. Instead of killing he tried to save the Tsar.

This dream expresses hostility to authority precipitated by the therapeutic situation. The latter was a repetition of the early son-father relationship which the patient had never entirely outgrown. Returning from military service, in which his dependent needs had been satisfied, he must again resume the responsibility for caring for himself and his family. He was not ready to do this and so regressed to early dependent desires. In his childhood his father had stood between him and his mother, who had spoiled him. In his regressive mood he reacted to all authority as he had previously to his father's, and at the beginning of his treatment he reacted emotionally to the analyst as if the latter were his stern father.

DREAM NO. 2. A young married businessman reported the following dream in the early phase of his analysis:

He was standing on a balcony with the wife of his older brother. Another balcony belonging to the next apartment adjoined, and both apartments were on an upper floor. His sister-in-law jumped suddenly from the balcony to the adjoining one and motioned him to follow, but he was afraid to jump.

Associating to the dream, he mentioned immediately that he had spent the previous evening with his sister-in-law. They had dined in her home and were alone because her husband had some important meeting. This older brother had played a semi-paternal role in the patient's life. Their father had died when the patient was three years old and the brother was fourteen years his senior. The brother was now a very successful businessman who had helped the younger brother financially and morally.

At the time of the dream the patient owned a fashionable haberdashery which his brother had financed. His sister-in-law was associated in the business. On the preceding evening he had talked with her about the store. In reporting the dream the patient said that he had long felt a vague attraction toward his sister-in-law, and that on this evening he felt that his sister-in-law would be willing to accept his advances. In fact she had remarked provocatively that she would have no compunctions about extramarital relationship if she found the right man. The patient in reporting this event made the remark that he was too much devoted to his brother to give in to this temptation.

In the light of this situation the dream becomes intelligible if one remembers that in German—the analysis took place in Germany—*Seitensprung* means a "jump to one side" but is also a colloquial expression for extramarital relationship, equivalent to the slang expression "doing something offside." In the dream the same symbol is used to express the idea of extramarital relations. In the dream, however, as in reality, he did not have the courage to follow his sister-in-law's invitation. Since his own desire was not unconscious, the repressed emotion is not the sexual attraction itself but the fact that he did not dare to give in to it. He emphasized that his hesitation was moral but he was actually afraid. This was confirmed by material which emerged when the dream had been interpreted. The patient admitted that when he considered an affair with his brother's wife his first reaction had been fear lest his brother would take away his business and leave him without support. His main conflict was actually the struggle against his dependence upon his brother and his own insecurity. His attitude was inevitably ambivalent. To offset his shame at his dependence he felt a need to compete with his brother which he did not dare to express openly. In the dream the fact that the two balconies were on an upper floor expressed symbolically the danger of jumping into sexual relations with the sister-in-law.

In this dream other typical mechanisms could be pointed out. The act of jumping from one balcony to another enacts a figure of speech, a common device in dreams. Freud aptly compared the relationship of thought processes in dreams and waking to that of picture writing with the use of an alphabet. In dreams abstract ideas are enacted concretely following the figure of speech. For example, we call a parvenu an upstart. In dreams the wish to rise in the social scale may be symbolized by climbing stairs or a mountain. We speak of social climbers but do not think of the physical act of climbing. In dreams, however, references to abstract ideas are usually expressed in a primitive concrete form. The patient expressed his fear of losing his security by the danger of falling from a height. The idea that an affair with his sister-in-law might mean his "downfall" appears in the dream as the act of jumping at a height from one balcony to another, thus exposing himself to the danger of physical downfall.

3. DREAM MECHANISMS

CONDENSATION

The manifest dream content is a compression of its latent repressed elements. This brevity is in itself an effective disguise and is achieved by different techniques. Portions of the latent dream content are omitted or only unimportant fragments appear in the dream. Through a "displacement of emphasis," however, the parts convey the effect of the whole. The most important feature of condensation consists in fusing many latent elements possessing a common denominator in one idea or picture. A good example of condensation is contained in the following dream of a thirty-six-year-old businessman, the youngest of five brothers:

"In my parent's home there is in the living room a peculiar object. I can't quite make out what it is. It looks like a stove, a combination of a tile structure and radiators. It represents a collective gift which I and my brothers have given to my mother."

From his associations I learned that his mother's birthday had occurred a few days before. The patient lived away from his parents and had sent money to one of his brothers to buy a gift in his name. He connected "tiles" immediately with the fact that some of his friends had recently made a large sum in a transaction in which they had sold tiles. He connected radiators with the fact that his father had recently built a home for his mother and equipped it not with radiators but with inefficient and cheap heating equipment of another type. His mother had commented critically on his father's miserliness.

From previous material I knew the following salient facts: The patient was the youngest of five brothers. He was considered a poor businessman by his family, and he was the only brother who was not a member of his father's company. He worked in his own concern with only moderate success. He had married a divorcee who had been previously married to a very wealthy man, and his main ambition consisted in surrounding his wife with the same luxury which she had enjoyed earlier. The patient was greatly mortified by his family, their depreciation of his abilities, and his exclusion from his father's firm. His feelings of envious competition with his brothers, however, had been successfully repressed and could only be reconstructed from his symptoms and dreams.

The latent dream content can be reconstructed from his association and life history and is briefly this: "I want to outrival my father with my mother so I shall give her a radiator, which he did not. I want to be as successful in business as my friends who recently made so much money in tiles." This idea is only hinted at by the tiles in the dream. His rivalry with his father for his mother and his envy of successful friends in business are condensed in the gift to his mother, which combines radiator and tiles. In making the gift jointly with his brothers he denies his wish to outdo his brothers. Actually the gift to his mother caused him embarrassment, since he both wanted and did not want to compete with his brothers. He therefore sent the money and asked his brothers to buy a gift in his name. The competition with his brothers was desperate enough to be repressed. In his dream he expressed competition with his father openly by giving his mother a radiator, but he denied his wish to rival his brothers by joining in a common gift.

All these competitive desires to rival his father and brothers, his wife's first husband, and his successful friends are condensed in the combination of tiles and radiator in the dream.

ALLUSION

In dreams a seemingly unimportant detail often expresses a hidden personal allusion. "Parapluie politics" means appeasement, because of the allusion to Chamberlain's umbrella. Freud called one form of allusion *pars pro toto*. Instead of a whole person or a whole act the manifest dream contains only fragments. Allusion, however, may be more comprehensive and may contain any hidden reference, as is the case in ordinary speech.

TEMPORAL SEQUENCE REPLACING CAUSALITY

Temporal sequence in dreams often stands for causality. Two events occurring successively in a dream may indicate causal connection between them. Here again dreams reveal their primitive way of thinking.

A twenty-three-year-old university student under analysis was working through his competitive attitude toward his father and the guilt feelings connected with it. He dreamed that he took General Eisenhower's place and wore his uniform. He then had to go somewhere by airplane and must change his clothes. He searched but could not find them, could not attach his medals nor fasten his buttons, and missed the plane. The meaning was that he felt guilty at wishing to usurp General Eisenhower's, i.e., the father's, place and so he could not find his clothes, attach the medals, fasten the buttons, or catch the plane. This becomes clear if we interpolate between the first and second parts of the dream the word "because." "I cannot succeed because I want to replace my father."

On the other hand, in some dreams later occurrences explain earlier ones. A twenty-six-year-old woman with strong masculine aspirations was struggling under analysis with her hostility against her parents. She disliked her father for his coldness and her mother because she was domineering. In the dream she entered a department store to buy a hat. She had her own hat in her hand and opened it to inspect the stiffening in it. A small pocketbook dropped out of the hat. She decided not to buy a new hat but to keep the old one. The scene then changed and she was driving home from the store with her father. A man in her home town known as F.X. owned a building with a huge smokestack that threw off sparks which had kindled numerous fires.[2]

The patient associated with her old hat her satisfaction with her "own kind of femininity." The smokestack appeared to her as a sexual symbol. F.X. is a real person who mistreated his daughter, never helped her, and always sided with her cruel stepmother. This paralleled the patient's impression of the atmosphere in her own home. Further association showed that the patient tended to get money from her father, who paid for her analysis. Other details of this dream are here irrelevant, but these two fragments are clear if we interpolate between the second and first scenes the word "because." "Because my father has always mistreated me as F.X. mistreated his daughter, and because masculinity—the huge smokestack —arouses dangerous flames of passion, I prefer my own femininity—the old hat—which includes a strong element of masculinity—the stiffening. By holding on to it I profit—the pocketbook—since my father will have to support me and continue paying for my analysis."

REPRESENTATION BY OPPOSITES

Often in dreams a person or act is disguised by its opposite. Parental figures, for example, in sexual dreams are often represented by strangers or persons of a quite different race, like a Chinaman. Nothing can be more unlike one's parents than a stranger of another race. Representation by opposites is analogous with overcompensation. In the dream of the Tsar's murder the dreamer tried to rescue the Tsar. Rescuing instead of killing is representation by the opposite. A conspic-

[2] This dream was of a patient treated under my supervision in the Institute for Psychoanalysis in Chicago.

uously tall person may appear in a dream as very small, a fat one as thin, a dark one as blond.

PICTORIAL REPRESENTATION, PERSONIFICATION, AND OTHER REGRESSIVE THOUGHT PROCESSES

The thought processes of dreams are in general primitive. We have already seen that abstractions are expressed by concrete pictures. The logic of the mind is often replaced by what might be called a primitive logic of the emotions. Because of their primitive nature dreams afford an excellent opportunity to study infantile mentality. Freud insisted that even elementary logical postulates, such as that a thing cannot be in two places at the same time, are disregarded in dreams. The dreamer may appear as himself, yet certain of his attitudes may be personified as other persons or even as animals. Pursuing beasts often represent the dreamer's projected and personified hostile tendencies which create anxiety and from which he tries to escape. The personification of wishes and tendencies as living beings is analogous to the role of animals in primitive thought.

4. THE DYNAMICS OF DREAMS

Dreams can best be understood as the results of two opposing forces: the wish to express a desire or relieve tension and the opposite tendency to reject this desire. Close examination of the whole of a dream often reveals how the repressed wish begins to rise and tries to assert itself, but meets opposition and anxiety and tries to circumvent this opposition by disguises and modifications, but soon finds new obstacles which it tries to evade, just as water running down a hillside turns in one direction to get around a rock and soon is forced to turn into a new channel to avoid a new obstacle. There are numerous methods of evasion in dreams, from simple disguises to complex compromises with the repressing forces. When the disguise due to a concession to the repressing forces becomes too great, it sacrifices too much from its value for gratifying the repressed wish, and the demand for gratification requires more frank expression. If then the expression becomes too frank a more effective disguise becomes necessary. This is well shown in the dream of the Tsar's murder. It begins by cautiously representing the victim as a high-ranking officer. This is not a frank enough reference to the father, so the officer changes to the Tsar himself. The representation of the father is then clear enough, but the dreamer must not commit the murder himself and so personifies his murderous wish in the stranger.

The compromise between the gratification of an objectionable wish and guilt over it is illustrated by another dream of the same businessman who produced the radiator dream. To understand this dream two relevant facts in his history must be added. The youngest of five brothers, he was small in stature, but the tallest of the five males in the family. His most conspicuous neurotic symptom was extreme shyness, which became quite unbearable in the presence of tall men. He reported the following dream during an analytic session:

"We are together in the family circle, and a small man wearing very high boots, probably a clown, is performing a very comical dance." With the clown he associated his own imitation of a clown's dance which he had seen with some friends at a cabaret the previous evening. He did it very well and had met with great success. He could not at first associate anything with the high boots except that he had worn similar boots in the war. They had been very uncomfortable, and he had given them away. Suddenly, without any apparent connection, a memory of his childhood appeared. He was six years old and was playing with his father in the forest. They arranged a race. His father was a small and fat man but at the same time ran faster than his six-year-old son. The patient remembered that he was terribly angry that his father won the race. The unconscious link between this forgotten memory and the high boots is the well-known tale of the seven-league boots which enabled their owner to take seven-league steps. In his dream he wore such boots and realized somewhat tardily after thirty years his infantile wish to run faster than his father. Since this was almost a family of dwarfs and the patient was the tallest, he had actually succeeded in surpassing his brothers and his father in height. It was a tragicomic trick of destiny that his superior height, the point at which he won the oedipal battle, became in later life his weakest point, for his shyness and timidity were especially pronounced in the presence of tall men. He remembered in connection with his dream that on the previous evening he had been with his wife in a restaurant and had seen at an adjoining table several good-looking, tall men and had felt more envious of them than ever. In the associations which followed he became quite conscious that one foundation of his sense of inferiority was his small size. He had always been vaguely aware that this was connected with his timidity, but now he became quite conscious of it. In the dream he satisfied his infantile wish to run faster than his father and be taller than he, but the high boots, the symbol both of his ambition and of his desire for a larger penis, were the cause of the comic impression which the clown, personifying himself, had made in the dream. The high boots symbolized speed, height, and a big penis but also punishment for these wishes laden with oedipal guilt. The significance of the boots as punishment was expressed in the comical impression the small man made in them.

His first association with the boots was with a pair he had had in the war and which had been merely a hindrance. This dream is similar to the fairy story in which the envious boy is punished for his envy by growing a long and awkward nose.

The symbolic meaning of this fairy story is transparent. The long nose means the big penis which the boy envies and which he gets as punishment. The patient's wish to rival his father had also been fulfilled: he was taller than all his competitors in the family, and in the dream he wore the seven-league boots. His physical height, however, had become the nucleus of his neurotic timidity. His conscience punished him just at the point at which he was successful. Although he was the tallest in his family, he felt his smallness in comparison with other men. The compromise consists in the fact that he satisfied in the dream his most cherished desire—to impress his family, who considered him the inferior member of the family —but could do it only by a comical dance, like a clown, which satisfied his need for punishment and exhibitionism.

The swing between wish and repression can be best observed in dream pairs and series which occur during the same night.[3] The connection between such dream pairs is very close. For example, one expresses a forbidden act by disguising the person but pictures the act openly; the second disguises the act but reveals the person. Together they express completely the repressed wish. A typical example is the pair: (1) "I am driving with Mother in the car." (2) "I am having sexual intercourse with a strange woman." The incestuous desire is expressed in the combination of the two, while each remains unobjectionable in itself.

The first dream of a pair often makes the second possible by eliminating guilt: (1) "I ask someone to give me a newspaper. He curses me and refuses." (2) "A person changes a large bill for me. He gives me the change, but I do not give him the bill I want converted into small denominations." The day before this dream the patient had asked me to allow him to peruse the newspaper on my desk. I refused. The second

[3] F. Alexander, "Über Traumpaare und Traumreihen," *Internationale Zeitschrift für Psychoanalyse*, Band 11, 1925.

dream referred to another episode. He failed to pay the whole of his last bill and owed me a part of my fee. The dream expresses his desire not to pay his bill. He justifies this by pointing out my refusal of the newspaper. He made use of this insignificant episode to justify in the dream his desire not to pay my fee.

The second dream sometimes relieves guilt aroused by the first dream, in which too clear a gratification of a forbidden wish has been permitted. A gifted person became fascinated by psychoanalysis and soon mastered the fundamentals of psychoanalytic theory. He played with the idea of becoming an analyst after he had finished his cure, which, as is well known, is not exceptional. His identification with the analyst repeated his infantile identification with his father. Before the dream we had discussed the emotional basis of his plan to become an analyst later. In this connection he reported the following pair of dreams:

"My brother has stolen some patents and made much money from them." This was only a fragment of a long and complicated dream, most of which he had forgotten. The second dream on the same night was: "I have a denture, a kind of artificial jaw, which has fallen out of my mouth."

He associated with patents the fact that his brother had recently been much occupied with exploiting different patents. A few days earlier a young Hungarian physician had called on his brother and offered him some new inventions. The patient then went on to describe the Hungarian physician. His brother had been much impressed by this young man, who had formerly been a dentist but had also a real genius for technical inventions. He already had a number of registered patents, some very successful, and had even invented a new metal amalgam for fillings.

These associations suffice for an understanding of the first dream. He attributed to his brother his own tendency to steal something from the Hungarian physician, myself, for he knew that I was of Hungarian origin. What he wanted to steal from me was not a patent but the knowledge of psychoanalysis and my professional position. His wish to become an analyst expressed his wish to occupy my place. It was easy for him to replace psychoanalysis with a patent for a denture because the Hungarian physician with whom his brother had negotiated was a dentist. The two dreams have meaning only when taken together: "I want to steal a patent, i.e., psychoanalytic knowledge, from my analyst, but my punishment would be to lose my denture, i.e., the benefit of my treatment." He frequently compared psychoanalysis with a kind of prosthesis which only neurotic people need.

The full and exact meaning of these dreams can be understood only in connection with the preceding analytic sessions. The dream is an answer to my previous interpretation concerning his desire to become an analyst which he had felt to be an accusation. What I told him amounted to saying, "You want to become an analyst because you envy me and you would like to have my position." In the dream he answers: "That is not true. I don't want to steal anything from you; it is my brother who wants to steal something from a Hungarian physician. Moreover, why should I envy your knowledge and scientific ability, since the denture which you put into my mouth, i.e., psychoanalytic treatment, is no good and has no value for anyone? See, it has fallen out again." This pair of dreams can be considered as a dialogue between the patient's unconscious and his analyst. The first dream expresses his wish to usurp the analyst's position; the second appeases his conscience, aroused by the first dream.

It is noteworthy that the patient's projection onto his brother of his wish to steal did not suffice to calm his guilt. The need to punish himself remained along with the wish to depreciate any help given to him.

Every dream can be considered as an attempt to gratify wishes consistently with internal standards and external conditions. This might be called the problem-solving function of the dream (French).

Freud's contention that unconscious processes may be highly complex is confirmed by the fact that dreams may present the solution for difficult intellectual problems. Puzzles in chess or mathematics have been repeatedly solved in sleep. The dreamer goes to sleep after working hard on a problem and awakes with the solution in his mind. The fact that in dreams complex intellectual problems may be solved seems to contradict the view that the dream represents a less precise, more primitive type of psychological process than reasoning in the waking state. The process by which problems are solved in dreams is identical, however, with that phenomenon which also occurs in the waking state and is called intuition.

Intuition solves problems without taking cognizance of the intervening steps. It has challenged the interest of many psychologists, including Bernard Alexander, whose view agrees with psychoanalytic theory. He believed that intuition is a nonverbal form of thinking. Freud also defined conscious thinking as the connection between "notions of things" and words. Verbal thinking, expressed in words, is based on generalizations which become fixed as categories. The same name is given to similar objects. Once a word is given to an object it is difficult to include new ones in the same category or, rather, to discover similarities between seemingly disconnected objects. Intuition reverts to the stage when objects can be freshly and naïvely related to each other. Words give precision to our thought but may hinder the discovery of new connections. Intuitive or preverbal thinking, therefore, is useful in discovering new connections, while verbal thinking is more fixed and precise. Dreams occur on the preverbal level, and it is not astonishing that in dreams new intuitive correlations may be established. One of the best examples is Kekule's discovery of the carbon ring during his sleep. He was dozing off while working on a study of organic compounds, and in his dream atoms at first chaotically tumbled before his eyes, then took shape and moved like a snake. Finally the snake, consisting of groups of atoms, bit its own tail. Kekule awoke with the discovery of the carbon ring.

Ordinarily, however, the dreamer's problem is not a matter of an intellectual nature but the wish to gratify desires without arousing internal conflict. All the defense mechanisms previously described may be used for this purpose: projection of the repressed wish onto someone else (the patent-stealing dream), justification of a repressed wish by suffering (the newspaper dream), displacement (killing the Tsar instead of the father), and many other methods of self-vindication. This problem-solving activity of the dream can best be observed during treatment. The analyst's interpretation exposes or destroys defenses, and the dreamer is forced to find new methods of resolving the conflict between his standards and his alien tendencies. In his study of dream sequences occurring during treatment French has described this function precisely.

5. DREAMS WITH UNPLEASANT CONTENT

Dreams which are painful and from which the dreamer may awake with terror apparently do not fit into the theory of wish-fulfillment. It must, however, be remembered that a dream is an attempt to relieve tension caused by repression with as little conflict as possible and that the dream work is not always successful in disguising the objectionable content sufficiently. An act may be performed in a dream without sufficient disguise, and this causes the dreamer to awake in terror. In such cases the dream does not fulfill its purpose successfully. The pressure of the repressed desire may have been so strong that the inhibiting forces were not able to resist and organize it.

Most dreams with an unpleasant content, however, are not of this kind. They are dreams in which the motivating force is not a repressed wish but a guilty conscience. It is common knowledge that a guilty person cannot sleep in peace and we refer to one who usually sleeps soundly as "sleeping like a child." A person whose conscience has been aroused by the day's events goes to sleep with worry and the expectation of some impending evil which is the common sign of a guilty state of mind. As we have seen, the general method of relieving guilty feelings is to suffer. In dreams with an unpleasant content the patient satisfies the claims of his guilty conscience by imagining some kind of suffering. The purpose of the dream is to protect sleep from intensive stimuli; self-punishment is therefore reduced to a minimum. The expected punishment, which, in the unconscious, is usually castration fear and its derivatives, is disguised and replaced by some less terrifying experience. In this way the dream, although it is still unpleasant, satisfies the claims of conscience and allows the dreamer to sleep. If the punishment is insufficiently disguised the dreamer awakes in panic. Examples of a successful and an unsuccessful dream with self-punishment will be quoted.[4]

DREAM NO. 1.   A puritanical young married man became aware during analysis of the appeal of extramarital relationships. Since marriage he had believed that no woman other than his wife existed for him. He denied every extramarital desire and insisted that he was completely satisfied with his wife. One night he dreamed that he was a small boy,

4 F. Alexander, "About Dreams with Unpleasant Content," *The Psychiatric Quarterly*, 4:447, 1930.

and he and a little girl of the same age were about to get into bed. He believed that the bed was the same one in which he used to sleep when about that age. A man was already lying in the bed. "As I put my right foot on the bed the man pointed to my toes, which were dirty, and I felt ashamed that I had not washed them. My foot was its present size rather than that of a small boy."

He associated at first to an advertisement for cornplasters showing a foot with electric lights in the toes to represent the corns. A hand pointed to one of them. He had seen this cornplaster advertisement on the street the day preceding the dream. The little girl reminded him of a cousin with whom he had had his first puppy-love affair in childhood. They had kissed and hugged and on one occasion practiced mutual exhibition. Another girl stood on guard to warn them if anyone should approach. This dream occurred when the patient had begun to recognize extramarital wishes which he had previously repressed. These wishes brought fear nearer to consciousness. He also recalled that he had been accosted by prostitutes the evening before as he was going home late. He had passed the same corner almost every night, but this was the first time that he had been accosted. It is easy to see that he had been accosted because for the first time he had looked at the women and thus given them courage to address him. In the dream he replaced his present sexual desires with an earlier one. He was in a similar mood when he went to bed as he had been in childhood after his first sexual experience with his cousin, about which he felt guilty. He substituted the past conflict for the present. The second purpose of the dream was to replace the threat of an unknown but severe punishment by a trifle. The man on the bed pointed to his dirty toes, and he was ashamed that he had not washed them. In the dream he was about to commit a forbidden sexual act with the girl and was rebuked, not for this, but for a much smaller offense. Toes here are the symbols of genitals, and the menacing finger threatens castration. Although this dream was very unpleasant and accompanied by fear and shame, it saved the dreamer from a much worse fear. The dirt refers to sexual ideas, dealings with prostitutes, etc. The punishment is directed against the toes, much less vital organs than the penis, and the crime is reduced to dirty toes. A good bargain is made: he gets punishment for having dirty toes, which is a lesser evil than promiscuity.

It is clear that dreams with an unpleasant content follow the same dynamic principles as dreams of wish-fulfillment. In the latter a desire which disturbs sleep is reduced by imaginary satisfaction. If the dream-producing wish is forbidden by conscience, the relief is obtained by dreaming of its satisfaction in a disguised form. If the wish is thwarted externally, it is expressed in the dream directly. If the sleep-disturbing tension is caused by a guilty conscience, relief requires punishment. A dream of punishment is an attempt to relieve the tension caused by a guilty conscience because conscience can be satisfied only by suffering. Primitive people chastise themselves or sacrifice valuable possessions to their gods whenever they feel guilty. It is only human to satisfy conscience with as little sacrifice as possible. The young man who dreamed of his dirty toes offered his conscience self-humiliation in admitting he was dirty, but this was a lesser crime and deserved a lesser punishment than extramarital intercourse.

DREAM NO. 2. This dream was reported during the analytic treatment of a young businessman, a hypochondriac, who had lost his money during the inflation in Germany and at the time of his dream was beginning to re-establish himself.[5] After his financial breakdown his older brother had helped him, and in the weeks preceding the dream he was

[5] Another dream of the same patient was discussed on pages 163–164.

in a difficult conflict with his conscience. He played with the idea of buying a new motor car, since he had been forced to sell his own beautiful car when he had lost his money. His conflict was due to the fact that his brother had lent him money for business investments and not for the purpose of buying a new car. Finally he bought a small car and was planning to take his first trip with his wife. On the night preceding the trip he had the following dream:

"I am driving in the big white car which I owned before my financial breakdown. My wife is with me, and we are passing through the market place of a small provincial town and have to drive slowly. I hear the people in the market place talking about me. They point at me saying, 'There is the profiteer, Mr. B.' It was a terrible experience."

He woke in anxiety, bathed in cold perspiration. His first feeling was intense relief that it was only a dream. He next thought of the trip he was about to take and expressed his pleasure in the following way: "How silly this dream was, since tomorrow I am going for a drive anyway but in my new small car."

In further associations the patient described his feelings toward his older brother, and we succeeded in tracing the deeper sources of his sense of guilt connected with the motor car. It became evident that this was a reaction to the repressed envy he felt toward his successful brother, who owned a beautiful and powerful car. The car was a symbol of everything for which he envied his brother—his abilities, money, success with women, etc.

This dream is a clear case of a punishment dream and was produced merely by the claims of his conscience. He went to sleep with an intense sense of guilt over the excursion which he had planned to make in his new car, which was the symbol of his competitive feelings toward his brother. The dream served to relieve this sense of guilt by putting him in a painful situation. While the tension of repressed wishes can be relieved through imaginary satisfactions, the demands of the conscience can only be fulfilled by punishment, suffering, or sacrifice. The dream gained its subject a quiet conscience. In it he revived the past and fancied himself in a painful situation as a profiteer, which he no longer was. He also succeeded in exchanging his guilt toward his brother for the more remote conflict of having once been a profiteer in the period of inflation and of making much money easily but somewhat disreputably.

The dream was an attempt to get rid of guilt in the easiest possible way. He had to suffer, for his conscience was roused by the purchase of the motor car, but the point of the dream was to reduce the necessary self-punishment as much as possible. The influence of the pleasure principle in such a mental situation must lie in diminishing unavoidable psychic pain. This dream succeeded in restoring his disturbed mental balance so that he could make his excursion the next day with an easy conscience, having paid the price for it by the painful experiences of the preceding night. It failed, however, to save his sleep.

All this amounts to the fact that a person cannot even in his dreams disregard those social standards which he has incorporated as a part of his personality. These social attitudes represent dynamic forces which, if aroused in the form of guilt, may become sleep-disturbing stimuli just as unfulfilled desires do.

French has shown that reality cannot be completely ignored by the dreamer. Fantasy is only partially free, and its limitations, as in all other forms of thoughts, are the facts of reality and the internally accepted standards which the ego had to learn to respect during its development. The dream is a regressive process but cannot completely extricate itself from the ego's adjustments, which have become an organic part of its nature. These consist of the recognition of external and internal obstacles which oppose subjective needs and desires.

6. SUMMARY

A dream is an attempt of the organism to protect sleep from disturbing stimuli. These stimuli are physiological needs like thirst and hunger, or more complex desires which life does not grant, or wishes which we deny ourselves, or unpleasant duties which press upon the mind, or a guilty conscience. In all these instances dreams attempt to eliminate tension by imaginary gratification of the physiological need or of the externally thwarted or internally denied wish, or by visualizing an unpleasant duty as fulfilled, or by suffering and punishment. In wishes denied by ourselves and in self-punishment dreams distortion is operating. In wish-fulfillment dreams of children imaginary gratification is undistorted.

BIBLIOGRAPHY

ALEXANDER, F.: "About Dreams with Unpleasant Content," *Psychiatric Quart.*, 4:447, 1930.

————: "Dreams in Pairs and Series," *Internat. J. Psycho-Analysis*, 6:446, 1925.

ALEXANDER, F., and STAUB, H.: *The Criminal, the Judge and the Public.* New York, The Macmillan Company, 1931.

EDER, M. D.: "Dreams—as Resistance," *Internat. J. Psycho-Analysis*, 11:40, 1930.

FRENCH, T. M.: "Insight and Distortion in Dreams," *Internat. J. Psycho-Analysis*, 20:287, 1939.

————: "Reality Testing in Dreams," *Psychoanalyt. Quart.*, 6:62, 1937.

FREUD, S.: *The Interpretation of Dreams.* London, George Allen & Unwin, Ltd., 1932.

————: "Some Additional Notes upon Dream-Interpretation as a Whole," *Internat. J. Psycho-Analysis,* 24:71, 1943.

JUNG, C. G.: *Psychology of the Unconscious.* New York, Moffat, Yard & Company, 1916.

STEKEL, W.: *Die Sprache des Traumes.* Wiesbaden, Bergmann, 1911.

Chapter VIII

Unconscious Factors in Wit and Aesthetic Appeal

IT IS UNNECESSARY to argue at length that the appeal of art is based on unconscious psychological processes. If anyone is asked why he was touched in reading a novel, why he laughed at seeing a comedy, or why he found a picture beautiful, he cannot give an adequate answer. It is usually quite easy to show that his attempted explanations are rationalizations invented to explain spontaneous and immediate responses. Literary criticism, which attempts to explain and describe the appeal and significance of literature, is the best proof of the unconscious nature of aesthetic appeal. What scholars try to explain is understood instinctively by even the least educated spectator, even though he could not put it into words.

The first conclusion is that the appeal of art is unconscious. The question is what unconscious psychological processes the aesthetic response consists of. Many emotions in various combinations produce aesthetic enjoyment. In view of the great variety of tragic, humorous, comic, or purely beautiful effects, the hope of finding a single common denominator appears remote.

Obviously it is not the emotion itself, expressed through art or literature, but rather the form of its expression which produces an aesthetic experience. It seems probable that the artistic effect depends upon certain dynamic relationships, on the analogy of Freud's explanation of wit and the comic on such a basis. Our reaction with laughter to a joke or anecdote is, though somewhat different, related to what we call artistic effect. The effect of a caricature or comedy is similar to the effect of a joke so far as the nature of the psychological processes involved is concerned.

Freud's monograph on wit and humor is one of his most thorough studies, paralleled only by his book on the errors of everyday life and surpassed only by his interpretation of dreams. The psychological riddle of laughter at wit and the comic has challenged the minds of men like Bergson, Lipps, Jean Paul, and others but was finally solved by Freud. The value of Freud's theory of wit is that it applies *mutatis mutandis* to beauty, a field hitherto equally obscure.

The essence of Freud's theory of wit is that its pleasure derives from the free expression of repressed feelings otherwise unacceptable to the conscious personality. A psychic charge used to repress an alien tendency is suddenly liberated and discharged in laughter. In jokes the repressed tendency is usually an aggressive impulse against authority or against a sexual object, at whose expense we laugh. This is the content of jokes. The elimination of repression by what Freud calls the technique of wit lies in its form. The latter achieves the joke's point and releases the repressed tendency.

The proof that the form and not the content makes a remark witty is that the same content often does not provoke laughter if otherwise expressed. A parvenu who was famous for exaggerating his business success turned to his friend and exclaimed boastfully: "How much do you think I made last year?" "About half," replied his friend. The humor would be completely ruined if his friend's answer had been: "I know you are always exaggerating, so I shall believe only half the sum which you mention."

A famous example used by Freud originates from Heine. A simple citizen was bragging about his relationship to Baron Rothschild. He said, "Believe it or not, I was sitting beside Baron Rothschild and he treated me as his equal, quite *famillionaire.*"

Freud translates the same content in another form to show how the witty effect is completely lost if the story is told thus: "Rothschild treated me quite as a member of the family, of course as much as a stuffed shirt can do." In both jokes the content is aggressive and deprecatory, but the effect is achieved by the form in which the wit attacks his victim.

Freud examined a great variety of humorous techniques, such as the condensation of several words into one, double meaning of words, and pseudo-logic masquerading as real logic, and succeeded in finding a common denominator. In wit the form element consists in the gratification of the universal psychological tendency to regress from complex acquired ways of thinking to simpler infantile ones. The pleasure derived from the similarity in sound of words with different meanings, from the double meaning, or even from lapses in logic is essentially childish. Comparison of two things only roughly similar also causes infantile delight. In the first joke quoted above the reply disregards precision and logic. To earn "half" makes no sense without knowing half of what. Moreover, one word suffices to replace a long sentence. In the second joke the form element evokes a childish pleasure in playing with the sound of words but disregarding their meaning. Here also two words serve for a long sentence and there is, furthermore, childish pleasure in creating a neologism. In reverting to these primitive forms of thought and usage the finer distinctions are disregarded and the training on which they are based ignored. All wit makes use of regression to diverge from the reality principle to more comfortable if less adequate ways of thinking governed by the pleasure principle. The form of wit involves irresponsible play with words or meanings to relieve for the moment the strictness and strenuousness of rational thinking.

The success of a joke depends upon a combination of content and form. The content releases repressed hostility in laughter, but its expression is made possible by diverting attention from the hostile content to the harmless pleasure and relief afforded by the form element. The mild infantile pleasure derived from the form serves as an excuse to give way to the hostility.

The same economic and dynamic principles can be applied to explain the related phenomena of artistic appeal. Sachs and Rank have pointed out that in literature rhyme provides an infantile pleasure and rhythm an elementary organic pleasure. The content of a poem or story can be presented in a manner devoid of any artistic appeal. Most people have emotions and fantasies which might be literary material, but only a few are capable of endowing them with artistic form.

The content of literature, as of wit, expresses repressed or thwarted desires. The artistic effect is created by the form, which permits covert indulgence of emotions which would be conflictful if brought into the open. Everyone has the feeling that another's complaint at desertion by a lover is ordinarily an imposition and rouses contempt rather than compassion. Complaint about unreturned love in verse obviates this and the listener can vicariously relieve his own sorrow. The pleasure in the form is solely responsible for this. Without it the content of most love poetry would appear weak and sentimental.

The relation of content and form varies in different artistic media. This is not the place to apply the Freudian formula of wit to all varieties of artistic expression. In literature the content seems to outweigh the form and offers the best opportunity to examine its nature. If reduced to their skeletons, literary themes can be condensed into a comparatively few basic plots. Their paucity in comparison with the variety of forms in which they are expressed is most striking. The most common motif is some variety of oedipal situation. The hero is the son, who after many adventures overcomes all difficulties and obtains the maiden of his choice. These difficulties represent the father as the first obstacle to the child's erotic desires. From Homer's Odysseus to Horace Greeley, stories of success are constructed on this simple formula. In a variant of this theme the emphasis shifts from winning the mother to elimination of the father, as in *Hamlet* or *The Brothers Karamazov.*

Male authors as a rule do less justice to the female oedipus situation, which is complicated by the peculiarities of the female castration complex. Variations of this are found in Wilde's Salome, Hebbel's Judith, and the Biblical story of Samson and Delilah. The man is eventually decapitated, or at least deprived of his masculine power, by a jilted woman.

Rivalry between sisters appears in all variations of the Cinderella pattern, but it is basically always the same story. The same conflict among brothers appears in the story of Cain and Abel and has been incomparably represented in De Maupassant's "Pierre et Jean."

The mechanism described by Freud in his article on the common degradation of sexuality is one of the preferred themes of the Victorian era. The son who is inhibited by his fear of incest can gratify his sexual desires only with degraded objects. Manon Lescaut and Camille are well-known examples of this.

The tragedy of parents with their children is another, though less common, basic plot. Père Goriot and King Lear are the most noble representatives of the tragedy of the deserted father. The heroine of De Maupassant's *Une Vie* is a classic example of the tragic outcome of the transposition of a mother's frustration to her son which eventually destroys them both.

The effect of all these masterpieces of literature lies in their release of deeply repressed attitudes through their form, style, economy of narration, and virtuosity in reproducing reality and making it more real than life by distilling and condensing the essentials.

In music it is more difficult to distinguish between form and content. In graphic art, painting, and sculpture, the element of form outweighs the content element.

The relationship between the two is illustrated in a study of caricature by E. Kris. The content is obvious, and it consists in an aggressively comic distortion of a face or body. The artistic appeal, however, derives from the subtlety of form and the economy and primitiveness of design.

The essence of artistic appeal, according to this view, is based on saving mental energy. This gain is achieved by the fusion of the effect of form with that of content. The form permits regression to an infantile mentality, the content expresses repressed wishes.

The fusion of form and content is the essence of art. Form makes possible the gratification of a repressed wish because the emotional discharge is attributed to something acceptable —namely, to pleasure afforded by the form. This pleasure veils the release of repressed tendencies. When form is weak, art loses its appeal. When its content appears in all its nakedness, drama becomes melodrama and comedy an unsavory burlesque, painting becomes mere photography or pornography, the dance an imitation of sexual license, and wit a brutal derision or an undisguised sexual attack.

BIBLIOGRAPHY

ALEXANDER, F.: "A Note on Falstaff," *Psychoanalyt. Quart.*, 2:592, 1933.

———: "Unconscious Factors in Aesthetic Appeal," *Deuxième Congrès International d'Esthetique et de Science de l'Art*, Tome I. Paris, Librairie Felix Alcan, 1937, p. 217.

BERGSON, H. L.: *Laughter. An Essay on the Meaning of the Comic.* New York, The Macmillan Company, 1912.

FREUD, S.: "Dostoevsky and Parricide," *Internat. J. Psycho-Analysis*, 26:1, 1945.

———: *Wit and Its Relation to the Unconscious.* New York, Moffat, Yard & Co., 1917.

JONES, E.: "A Psychoanalytic Study of Hamlet," in *Essays in Applied Psychoanalysis.* London, The International Psycho-Analytical Press, 1923, p. 1.

KRIS, E.: "The Psychology of Caricature," *Internat. J. Psycho-Analysis*, 17:285, 1936.

LIPPS, T.: "Komik und Humor," in *Beitraege zur Aesthetic*, 6:1, 1922. Herausgegeben von T. Lipps und R. M. Werner. Leipzig, Verlag von Leopold Voss.

RANK, O., and SACHS, H.: *The Significance of Psychoanalysis for the Mental Sciences.* Nervous and Mental Disease Monograph Series No. 23. New York, Nervous and Mental Disease Publishing Company, 1915.

REIK, T.: *Nachdenkliche Heiterkeit.* Wien, Internationaler Psychoanalytischer Verlag, 1933.

———: "The Psychogenesis of Analytical Interpretation and of Wit," in *Surprise and the Psychoanalyst.* New York, E. P. Dutton & Co., Inc., 1937, p. 62.

SACHS, H.: *The Creative Unconscious.* Cambridge, Sci-Art Publishers, 1942.

———: *Gemeinsame Tagtraeume.* Leipzig, Internationaler Psychoanalytischer Verlag, 1924.

———: "Kuenstler Psychologie und Aesthetik," in *Bericht ueber die Fortschritte der Psychoanalyse,* 1914–1919. Wien, Internationaler Psychoanalytischer Verlag, p. 234.

————: "Schillers 'Geisterseher,' " *Imago,* 4:69, 145, 1915–1916.

————: "The Tempest," *Internat. J. Psycho-Analysis,* 4:43, 1923.

Chapter IX

Psychopathology

THE PRIMARY purpose of this book is to make clear the psychodynamics underlying psychopathological phenomena in general, and no attempt is made to describe in all detail the different forms of psychoneuroses and psychoses. Full case histories will not be offered in illustration, but only extracts.

The preceding discussion of the ego's defenses will help the understanding of the psychopathological phenomena. Whenever healthy, integrated behavior breaks down, the original impulses emancipate themselves from the adjusted patterns and the ego uses against them various defense mechanisms. The nature of a neurosis or psychosis is to a large extent determined by the nature of the defenses the ego chooses for its protection. In order to present a comprehensive picture of the problem of neurosis, certain repetitions will be unavoidable.

1. DEFINITION OF NEUROSIS

Neurosis is a disease. Although in many respects it differs radically from other diseases, it has one characteristic common to most diseases: it causes suffering and discomfort. Like every disease it is also rooted in disturbances in the functioning of the organism. In most physical diseases one or more organs are involved; in neurosis the central co-ordinating core of the organism, the ego, is disturbed.

The ego is that part of the organism which assumes the task of harmoniously gratifying our needs and desires. These are often in conflict both with each other and with external conditions. The ego must reckon with different desires and interests and accepted standards and must compromise and muddle through by giving as much satisfaction as possible to each, even when they are in conflict among themselves or with the environment. Whenever the ego proves incapable of performing this task we speak of the failure of its governing and co-ordinating function. This is the essence of a neurosis.

A healthy ego can best be compared to a democratic state which recognizes private needs of all kinds, gives them a hearing, and meets the conflicting interests by mediation and compromise. This insures a stable but fluid state of affairs. The neurotic personality is comparable to an autocratic government which suppresses all opinions and aspirations that do not conform to its ruling principles. As long as rebellious opinions and demands can be controlled by an iron rule, unity prevails. It is built, however, on a volcanic foundation. Whenever the autocracy is weakened the outlawed rebels break through and destroy the whole system. The energy spent in keeping unruly desires in check is diverted from constructive use. Fear and coercion are the only motives operative, as the cultural sterility and lack of creativeness in totalitarian systems prove.

A neurotic personality is comparable to such an autocratic country impoverished in initiative, governed by anxiety and coercion. The analogy should not, however, be carried too far, and we now turn to the specific facts of the human personality. The central dynamic factor in neurosis is repression and those defense measures by which the ego attempts to keep all the unacceptable impulses out of its territory.

As we have seen, repression is normal in a child but undesirable in an adult. Of course, even a healthy person takes recourse to repression to some degree. Only an ideally efficient ego would function without it. The ego develops gradually with growth. It does not belong to our hereditary equipment but is a product of learning. Needs and impulses such as hunger, sex, and raw aggression, however, are present from the beginning. To co-ordinate these impulses and their derivatives and to satisfy them consistently with conditions in nature and society is the ego's task. It must learn how to exercise this complex executive function. In young children only the dynamic building stones, the primitive impulses, exist, from which the socially adjusted person must be constructed.

The impulses which the child represses because his ego cannot manage them become a problem in his later life. Their pressure is felt from time to time, and he will have to take defensive measures to keep them out of consciousness. These repressed, unconscious impulses are preserved in their original form as in an icebox and emerge in dreams in strange and unintelligible images, the language of the infantile mind, in waking life in neurotic symptoms, irrational anxieties, obsessions, and impulsive behavior.

Our first question, then, is, why does not everyone develop a neurosis? Everyone has similar infantile experiences, everyone has to repress some of his early impulses because his infantile ego was weak and could not assimilate, control, and modify them.

First of all, we must remember that neurosis and normality are not wholly different. The psychology of neurosis and of normality is the same in quality; the differences are merely quantitative. We have seen that repression is not an efficient method of adjusting needs to life's requirements. It does not permit the modification of unadjusted impulses. What is repressed is no longer amenable to education, since this is the function of the conscious mind. It is true that the unity of the ego is preserved by excluding everything disturbing to its unity, but this is accomplished at a great price. The repressed energy is lost for outward-directed activity, and the ego is impoverished. Moreover, since repressed impulses continue to exist, the need for constant defense against them consumes the available energies. This not only means further impoverishment but also constitutes a threat. It is obvious, then, that the less the child has to repress and the more his adjustment is based upon efficient control, the sounder will be his development.

We have compared the healthy ego to democratic government which permits expression of private particularistic needs. Naturally, all aspirations cannot be fulfilled in their original form. The parliamentary system, however, allows free expression and negotiation leading to compromises inclusive of all interests as far as possible.

The conscious ego performs this function in the personality. It is therefore important that the conflicting desires should become conscious. Some must be radically modified, others renounced in their original form so that more important interests can be safeguarded. The final solution is a compromise reconciling different needs in the light of their relative importance and practicality under the given circumstances. The ego must therefore get a full report from within concerning subjective needs and must know the conditions upon which their gratification depends. It must confront the facts about itself and those about the surrounding world. Repressed wishes and desires are excluded from this process of mediation and compromise. Since they are lodged in the unconscious, they are inaccessible for adjustment either to other needs or to the environment.

The ego in infancy and early childhood is too weak to judge, to endure frustration and renounce, and therefore must exclude many desires from consciousness. How, then, does the ego learn its co-ordinating function?

Repression operates according to automatic patterns almost like a reflex. Once the child has become fearful of expressing his hostile impulses and has learned to repress them, a pattern becomes established and the ego tends to repress all hostile impulses. The result is a timid, inhibited person who can never assert himself in later life. A child who has been taught to repress all sexual impulses will later find that all sexual impulses provoke anxiety and guilt. (The frequent claim that over fifty per cent of women are sexually frigid is explained by radical repression of sexual impulses in early years.)

It may seem a miracle that any ego ever becomes strong enough to make an adequate adjustment. If, however, a child is not checked too ruthlessly in the expression of his sexual or aggressive impulses, he will be in a better position to modify them gradually and adjust them to social standards. Healthy development of the ego is not by any means based on a licentious gratification of all impulses. In order to work, however, with impulses as raw materials—and there is no other material to work with—these must become conscious. It is not so difficult to define theoretically the parental attitudes which will permit the expression and gradual modification of the natural impulses of the child. The practical application of these principles, however, is quite another question.

We have seen that every child's ego is too weak to handle judiciously the difficult adjustment of diverse needs. In order to save himself from frustration and pain he tends, therefore, to repress impulses which cause him trouble. The less this drastic procedure is used, the less chance there is for a neurosis to form in later life. Democracy must be acquired through education. The ego must also learn to mediate between desires and given conditions and can learn this only if given an opportunity to come to grips with the impulses. It cannot master its executive function if it represses those forces which should be harmonized. As the ego gains co-ordinating and integrating power through experience, it becomes increasingly able to endure temporary frustrations and to control, modify, and harmonize needs with accepted standards.

Every experience which has an overwhelming, intimidating effect is called traumatic and favors repression, thus counteracting the ego's chances to learn how to handle its original impulses which need adjustment.

The severity of early traumatic experiences differs from person to person. The most important factor is the parental attitudes. Pre-Freudian psychiatry was much more acceptable to parents because most neurotic and psychotic difficulties were blamed on heredity. Heredity is a major force, is unalterable, and involves no responsibility. Moreover, the blame is shared by grandparents and great-grandparents, fortunately on both sides. Psychoanalytic theory traces the origin of neurosis to the early parental influence upon the child, although it does not deny completely the importance of heredity. The same parental influences may hurt a child with a susceptible hereditary equipment more than one of more robust stock. Heredity remains a factor, but psychoanalysis has demonstrated that in addition to heredity childhood experience also contributes to the formation of neuroses. Some experiences are accidental, but the majority and the most important, permanent, and insidious ones, consist in the uninterrupted pressure of parental attitudes. Whether the child's ego will be encouraged to learn how to deal with its needs and impulses or will withdraw from this task by repression depends largely upon the parents.

We must answer another important question: Why does a person with infantile repressions remain free of neurotic disease for a considerable length of time and break down at some later phase in his life? Some of us are never bothered again with these old problems. Why do others succumb to them? The early phases of ego development exposed to family influences neither fully explain the origins of neurosis nor its onset at a particular time. There must be other factors which account for the development of an actual neurosis. Early experience is responsible for vulnerable spots which in many cases, however, never lead to neurotic disease unless other later influences come into play. Neurosis results from the failure of the ego to co-ordinate needs harmoniously with each other and with external conditions. Allowing for considerable individual differences, this capacity is always limited. Nothing has shown this more clearly than the gruesome psychiatric experiment which the war has supplied. At Guadalcanal a large number of Marines, carefully selected, well-adjusted and steady individuals, developed strikingly similar neurotic symptoms under prolonged strain. Anyone can be subjected to experiences so overwhelming that they surpass his ego's functional efficiency. Of course, a vulnerable ego will yield to less pressure than a strong one. An exceptionally well-adjusted person fails only under exceptional and prolonged strain.

Early discoveries in psychoanalysis influenced many of us to minimize the importance of actual difficulties in causing neurosis. We referred to them as "only the precipitating cause," looking for the real cause in childhood. The relative significance of childhood experiences and more recent events, however, is not the same in all cases. A simple analogy may illustrate this. A man buys a truck, and after a while one of its springs breaks. He takes it back to the company saying that the truck broke down because the spring was weak. The company says that the truck was all right but that he overloaded it and under such a load it had to break down. Without knowing the quantitative facts precisely this argument cannot be decided. It is obvious that the contention that the spring was too weak is a relative statement—it was too weak for the load. Trucks may break down because of a flaw in construction, but a perfectly good truck may also break down under an excessive load. The same reasoning is applicable to the causation of neurosis. Some persons become neurotic primarily because of a defect in construction, in hereditary equipment. Some may develop during an early vulnerable period weak spots which yield to the impact of even the average vicissitudes of life. Others may break down because they are exposed in later life to excessive strain or to confusing and novel conditions for which they have had no preparation. All personality traits are rooted in the experiences of childhood, and it depends to a large degree upon later circumstances whether some will cause neurotic difficulties or not. Early traumatic experiences may prove overwhelming and reduce the ego's functional capacity, but the struggle with early traumatic experiences may also strengthen the adaptive faculties and the ego may emerge better equipped from the struggle.

It is a natural propensity of the human mind to seek a simple solution for everything. It seeks to operate with two-dimensional correlations and is disinclined to complexity, but nature has no regard for our mental laziness. Events in nature have not one but many causes. Psychiatry at first blamed most diseases on infection or heredity. As soon as a parent, brother, or uncle was found to have been insane, committed suicide, or suffered from chronic headaches, the etiological requirements were satisfied. At the beginning of the Freudian era the importance of childhood experiences was discovered and claimed as *the* cause of neurosis. Gradually we have come to recognize at least three sets of factors which together in varying degrees contribute to neurotic disease. These factors are heredity, early experiences of life, and actual difficulties. A patient with poor hereditary equipment may be destined to develop neurosis no matter what happens to him. In another case the early experiences may have been so unfavorable and have created so many vulnerable spots that the individual cannot later withstand ordinary difficulties. There are, however, many neurotics whose hereditary equipment and childhood experience were not particularly unfavorable but who in later life were exposed to situations beyond their control. The relationship between these three sets of factors is complicated by the fact that the later events are largely determined by infantile experiences. Our fate is, partially at least, determined by ourselves.

This view might be called the relativistic interpretation of neurosis. A patient is not neurotic per se but becomes so because he is involved in a certain situation with which he is unable to cope. Our complex civilization confronts one with a great variety of situations. Even a person with an unhappy childhood may adjust to a certain kind of life, and if he can stay in it may never develop a neurosis. A sensitive, introspective young man, interested in music and literature, might have been a complete misfit in a frontier town of the last century in America. He would have been the object of ridicule and could not gratify his special interests. The same person in the *fin de siècle* literary society of Paris might have been highly esteemed and encouraged. Anyone who has read Margaret Mead's description of the Balinese personality would agree that the average Balinese, with his introverted, dreamy disposition, would be considered in American society either a schizoid personality, a case of ambulatory schizophrenia, or a prepsychotic personality. On the other hand, an American traveling salesman who fell in the hands of a Balinese psychiatrist would run the danger of being incarcerated as a potentially dangerous hypomanic.

In our diversified society there is place and need for a great variety of different personalities. What is weakness in one social situation may be an advantage in another.

In defining neurosis one must be well aware of this principle of relativity. Neurosis is due to the inability to gratify needs harmoniously in a given situation. It registers a discrepancy between the individual and his environment. If the environment were constant in all cases, only the personality need be considered. In our civilization, however, environmental settings vary greatly and neurosis can be defined only by considering both the individual and his surroundings.

This relativistic concept of neurosis has been confirmed by experience during the last war. In spite of all efforts to eliminate obvious neurotics, many psychopathic personalities eluded diagnosis and entered the services, where they often functioned with surprising success. On their return to civilian life, however, their neurotic problems reappeared. These were persons who needed more guidance than is compatible with our free society, and their dependent needs were satisfied in a large organization which took care of them and told them what to do. In civilian life they were again thrown on their own resources and felt frustrated. Their need to depend upon others created deep conflict and hurt their pride. In order to remedy this injury to their self-esteem they were driven into spasmodic acts of bravado and disregard of convention. They needed to prove to themselves and others that they were not frightened and dependent and still in need of maternal or paternal protection. They proved this by a rebellious and aggressive display of pseudo-masculinity. This often brought them into conflict with the law. But when such individuals could satisfy their need for dependence and obedience in a large organization like the army, which puts a premium on obedience, their conflict was resolved and they became excellent soldiers. Their need for dependence was satisfied in an acceptable manner, and also their need to be tough and brave found a legitimate expression in the army. The old problem returned only when they were again thrown on their own and had to resume the responsibilities of civilian existence.

This shows that a neurosis must always be defined as a relationship between a personality and its social setting. Most people are neither born neurotic nor become inevitably so through early experience. Neurosis sets in when heredity and infantile experience combine in conflict with the environment.

One further aspect of this subject requires more consideration. The ego has been defined as an apparatus which coordinates conflicting desires and adjusts them to the environment. This we call adaptation. The measure of the functional efficiency of the ego is determined by the extent of its adaptability. Obviously that adaptation is simpler if conditions remain unchanged. By experiment and the guidance of parents the ego adopts suitable behavior patterns, which, once learned, need not be changed. Just as muscles deteriorate if they are not used, the ego loses its flexibility in an unchanging environment. For example, set provincials are uncomfortable away from home. The typical Parisian or Viennese is a fish out of water elsewhere. These fine representatives of their native culture do not even attempt to change their way of life when they emigrate but create little Parises and Viennas abroad. A similar example is the tragedy of the older generation in a rapidly changing world. Superb representatives of their own age who were well adjusted and happy become disgruntled and neurotic when a rapid social change forces them to live in a new era. This problem did not arise during relatively static periods like the feudal period in Europe. At such times conditions and customs remained the same from generation to generation and the place of each individual in society was rigidly determined. The same patterns of behavior descended from parents to children for centuries. Sociologists correctly emphasize rapid social change as the most conspicuous feature of our present industrial era. Not only do two subsequent generations live under different conditions, but an individual during his own lifetime has to readjust himself repeatedly to rapidly changing material and ideological conditions. As a youngster he lived in a world of rugged individualism, in his twenties he was taught the blessings of political paternalism, only perhaps to face in his mature years a renaissance of individual initiative. From this it is obvious that the first requirement of industrial civilization is a highly flexible and adaptable personality. As we have seen, the instrument of flexible adaptation is the conscious ego. The comfort of living according to well-tested traditions is not enjoyed by man in the modern era. Habitual behavior patterns do not require conscious deliberation but become routine. Men living in a period of rapid change, however, must develop the faculty of rapid adjustment. They must therefore be more aware of themselves and of their needs than was necessary for their predecessors.

In its struggle for self-preservation humanity develops in each period of history the knowledge and skills it needs for survival. One of the crucial problems of our industrial era has been to create sanitary living conditions for people in large cities. An understanding of contagious diseases became a question of life or death, and bacteriology and physical hygiene arose to meet the problem of congested areas. Dynamic psychiatry plays a similar role with the psychological difficulties arising from rapid cultural change. The aim of psychoanalysis is to increase the effectiveness of the conscious ego by replacing automatic adaptations and repressions with conscious control and flexible adjustments to the changing conditions of modern life. This requires facing facts not only outside but within ourselves. The Greek maxim, "Know yourself," may once have been a luxury; today it is a necessity. Man can adjust himself to his changing environment only by knowing himself, his desires, impulses, motives, and needs. He must become wiser, more judicious, and more self-reliant. Otherwise he will become confused and frightened and regress to his dependent childhood and become the prey of power-seeking minorities who will induce him to believe that his security lies in doing what he is told.

2. GENERAL CHARACTERISTICS OF PSYCHONEUROTIC AND PSYCHOTIC SYMPTOMS

a. PSYCHONEUROTIC SYMPTOMS

(1) *Irrationality*

Neurotic symptoms appear both to the patients themselves and to observers as less rationally motivated than normal psychological processes. Fear in a dangerous situation is rational, but anxiety at walking in the street or sitting in a crowded restaurant or theater appears irrational. Sadness upon losing a person one loves is rational; a depression over a minor frustration is unreasonable. More paradoxical is a depressive reaction to promotion in business or professional life. The irrationality of obsessional ideas of hurting another with sharp instruments, which may cause anxiety at the sight of a knife or needle, is obvious because there is no conscious motivation for such hostile acts.

(2) *Disconnectedness of Symptoms*

The second characteristic of neurotic symptoms is their dissociation from conscious psychic life. The mother who is obsessed with the idea of strangling her children while they are asleep is actually deeply devoted to her children and there is nothing in her conscious mind which she can remotely connect with her symptom. The compulsion to wash one's hands continually appears inexplicable. In the course of the disease it may become rationalized as fear of germs or of soiling others.

(3) *Regressive Nature of Symptoms*

This can be best recognized by realizing that the psychological content of neurotic symptoms would appear "normal" if the patient were a child. Fear of the dark or of being alone in crowded places or the streets of a big city are common reactions of the small child. The fear of great open spaces is also universal when the child is learning how to walk. Rapid changes of mood provoked by trifling rebukes or momentary frustrations also belong to the normal psychology of the small child. The wish to use sharp instruments for destructive purposes is part of the child's natural retaliation for being pushed around by adults. The rituals of washing and orderliness are also manifestations of childish obedience designed to appease adults. They are the marks of a "good child."

It is not so easy to prove the regressive nature of the conversion symptoms. They are, however, the revival of early traumatic experiences which have been repressed.

As soon as the unconscious links in symptom formation are reconstructed, the symptom loses its irrational and disconnected appearance. The knowledge of the repressed motivation makes it intelligible and shows its connection with the rest of the personality.

In reconstructing the repressed motives, the mother's obsession to strangle her children in their sleep becomes intelligible as a reaction to her self-sacrificing maternal attitude and her regression to early sibling rivalry when she took care of her younger siblings and received less attention from her parents than she felt she deserved. A phobic's fear of people is intelligible as a reaction to his early hostility against anyone who distracted his mother's attention from him.

b. PSYCHOTIC SYMPTOMS

Psychotic symptoms, in common with neurotic symptoms, are irrational and regressive but are not always disconnected. This is particularly true of paranoid delusions. In paranoid psychoses alien tendencies break through the barriers of repression, becoming part of the conscious personality, which often loses its own cohesiveness. The paranoid patient is aware of his hostile impulses and rationalizes them with delusions. He attacks others because he feels persecuted. The symptom is not isolated like an aggressive obsession, for the patient assumes full responsibility for it. Delusions are attempts to create imaginary situations in which the symptoms appear rational and acceptable. Because the ego's critical sense is impaired the irrationality of the symptoms is apparent to everyone except the patient. This is often called "lack of insight," but the paranoid's capacity for rationalization is often remarkable and he often succeeds in convincing others of the rationality of his behavior.

The regressive nature of psychotic symptoms is self-evident. According to Freud, the hallucinatory gratification of needs is characteristic of the infant who has not yet differentiated between the inner and outer worlds. Delusions about one's own person, self-aggrandizement, and self-depreciation are regressions to infantile attitudes toward the self. The little child who plays at being a big-game hunter or a bus conductor gratifies in fantasy his wish to be as big and powerful as his father. The psychodynamics of delusions of grandeur are based on similar overcompensation for feelings of inferiority. Delusions of self-depreciation are regressions to infantile feelings of inferiority in the adult world.

3. THE GENERAL DYNAMIC STRUCTURE OF A
PSYCHONEUROSIS

We have seen that a neurosis develops whenever a person cannot satisfy his emotional needs in a given situation without internal conflict. This conflict may arise in human relations, in occupational activities, or in his sexual life. Usually there is a struggle before recourse is taken to regressive neurotic gratifications. Neurosis consists, according to one of Freud's formulas, in replacing suitable behavior with regressive symbolic substitutes. Real objects of mature emotion are replaced by family figures of early childhood, and the desires directed toward them are necessarily infantile compared with behavior expected from adults. This is why neurotic conflict arises. The anxieties and frustrations which forced the child to give up his older attachments are revived now, and their content is repressed. Neurotic symptoms and behavior are manifestations of the ego's defenses against these early emotions. The axis of the neurotic structure is anxiety which keeps the regressive tendencies repressed. Their continued pressure would keep anxiety constantly active if the ego did not defend itself against them. The different forms of neurosis correspond to the different methods of defense employed by the ego. Neurosis is therefore an attempt to relieve anxiety created by conflicts which repeat earlier conflicts and are reactivated by regressive desires. The development of neurosis can be divided into two phases: (1) the attempt to relieve the pressure of actual frustration by regressive substitutive satisfactions; (2) the attempt to eliminate by various defense measures the conflict and anxiety resulting from regression.

Substitutive gratifications themselves can be divided into different types: (1) Conversion symptoms. These are unconsciously motivated innervations in the voluntary muscles and sensory organs that have an unconscious symbolic meaning which they substitute for realistic gratifications. This is most commonly observed in hysterical personalities. (2) Phobias. Everyday acts such as walking, writing, talking, washing become charged by unconscious alien tendencies and assume a symbolic meaning. (3) Gratification of unconscious alien desires in isolated fantasies which have lost their connection with the rest of the conscious personality and appear as obsessive states. Compulsive symptoms which are designed to reduce guilt aroused by these fantasies by moralistic rituals. (4) Depressions and delusions of grandeur, in which repressed unacceptable tendencies are turned against the self. (5) Paranoid projections, in which alien tendencies are projected upon others. (6) Hallucinatory and delusional gratification of alien tendencies in schizophrenias. (7) Impulsive behavior directed by unconscious strivings in character neuroses (psychopathic personalities) and the manic phase of manic-depressive psychoses.

The defenses against neurotic anxiety are also various. All the defense mechanisms described before are current, but it is not always possible to distinguish clearly between neurotic gratifications and defenses, because symbolic gratification in symptoms is in itself a defense. This alone, however, does not suffice to allay anxiety resulting from unconscious guilt, and in all neuroses specific defenses are aimed at relieving the sense of guilt.

4. THE DEVELOPMENT OF A NEUROSIS

The most common development of a neurosis in an adult may be schematized in the following diagram:

(1) *Precipitating factors*
↓   The actual situation with which the patient cannot cope.
(2) *Failure in the solution of actual problems*
| Unsuccessful attempts at adaptation of shorter or longer
↓   duration.
(3) *Regression*
| The replacement of realistic effort to gratify needs by
↓   regressive fantasies or behavior.
(4) *Primary conflict revived by regression*
| The revival of old conflicts by regression to old adaptive
↓   patterns abandoned in the course of growing up.
(5) *Self-punitive measures*
| A futile struggle to resolve neurotic conflict by a combina-
| tion of substitutive gratifications and self-punishment ex-
| pressed in symptoms. The futility of the attempt to re-
| solve the conflict is due to the fact that the regressive de-
| sires, the guilt, and the resulting need for self-punishment
| are all unconscious. Only their disguised representations
↓   are conscious.
(6) *Secondary conflict and the impoverishment of the ego*
    The longer a neurosis continues, the more fully a vicious
    circle develops. Symptoms absorb a patient's energies and
    make him less effective in dealing realistically with life.
    This is called secondary conflict and necessitates further
    regression and symptomatic outlets, which in turn in-
    crease conflict and absorb more energy.

This formula may be illustrated by the history of the young
businessman presented before, who developed a severe depression while advancing rapidly in his career.

THE PRECIPITATING FACTOR

The precipitating factor was evidently his promotion. His
employer, who took such a fatherly interest in him, became

his sole competitor, the only remaining obstacle to his becoming the head of the business. This aroused guilt and turned the hostile impulses defensively toward himself. He could not solve the problem of competing with his benefactor.

REGRESSION

The intensity of the conflict can be understood only from his previous experience with his parents. The earlier Oedipus guilt was revived by the actual situation. This regression is confirmed by the revival of dependency on his mother. In the four years after his father's death he had been his mother's sole support, but now he became emotionally dependent upon her. He returned to the oedipal situation by identifying his employer with his father, but regressed to an even earlier pregenital dependent relationship with his mother, renounced the guilt-laden desire to replace his father, symbolized by his employer, and refused to accept the increased responsibility in his work required by his promotion.

PRIMARY CONFLICT REVIVED BY REGRESSION

The regression from the actual conflict with his employer to oedipal fantasies precipitated the earlier guilt toward his father.

SELF-PUNITIVE MEASURES

His self-accusation, servility, and refusal to accept more salary were self-punitive measures designed to relieve guilt.

SECONDARY CONFLICT

The regressive evasion of the actual conflict provoked by his promotion caused a new conflict. The fact that he was the sole support of his mother forced him to continue in his position and struggle against his neurotic desire to escape into complete dependence upon his mother or, alternatively, to commit suicide. This secondary conflict caused him to seek help from an analyst.

IMPOVERISHMENT OF THE EGO AND THE NEUROTIC VICIOUS CIRCLE

The continuous struggle against the regressive desires which interfered with his activities consumed a great part of his energy and increased his need for dependence. If this vicious circle had not been treated it would have led to a progressive aggravation of his condition. A severe depression with possible suicide could have been expected.

The question arises why he did not develop a depression after his father's death, when his childhood desire to replace his father with his mother had been suddenly realized. Why did not this event precipitate oedipal guilt and necessitate self-punitive measures? The answer is that after his father's death both he and his mother faced a grave emergency. The uncle to whom they had appealed for help turned them down. This relieved any possible sense of guilt and saved him from a depression. The image of the "bad father" was supplied by fate so that he could turn his hostility against his uncle. This solution appeared in the dream in which he replaced his kindly employer by his ungenerous uncle. An emotional situation arose only when his fatherly employer, who had overwhelmed him with kindness, became the target of his hostility. Then his competitive feelings had to be turned against himself. The wish to destroy his benefactor was more than he, a spoiled only child, could reconcile with gratitude and love for a father.

5. SECONDARY GAIN

Being incapacitated by illness may have certain advantages. Among the most transparent is financial compensation for accidents. Illness may serve also as a legitimate excuse to avoid unpleasant duties and discard pressing responsibilities. It provokes sympathy and attention and assures the sufferer a privileged position. These advantages retard recovery and make therapy particularly difficult.

They are secondary consequences of neurotic illness and do not belong to its dynamic structure or to the motivation which produces neurosis. This is particularly true of financial compensation for accidents. It is, however, extremely difficult to draw a sharp line between earlier dependent longings of patients and their secondary exploitation of illness to satisfy passive dependent needs. Many authors—Fenichel, for example—attempt to isolate the secondary gain artificially. In many instances what Fenichel designates as "gains from the superego" belong to the basic structure of the neurosis. The use of suffering for obtaining gratifications alien to the ego is one of the most fundamental mechanisms in every neurosis. Every neurosis involves suffering because the social standards incorporated in the superego require punishment for transgressions of the accepted code. The gain in relief from neurotic guilt through suffering cannot be considered as secondary since it is the very essence of neurosis. Although Fenichel is right in maintaining that "nobody becomes neurotic just for the purpose of suffering," suffering is a constituent part of neurosis and makes gratifications alien to the ego possible.

The concept of secondary gain must be applied with great precaution. Any adult person who prefers support from others to the productive use of his own powers is unduly dependent. This infantile trait is always a significant, and frequently the most significant, factor in his neurosis. The important consideration is that the emotional and financial gains derived from illness contribute to the prolongation of illness. It is sound therapeutic tactics to reduce these gains whenever possible.

6. A BRIEF REVIEW OF PSYCHOPATHOLOGICAL PHENOMENA

a. ANXIETY NEUROSIS

The outstanding symptom is anxiety which is not consciously motivated but "free-floating," so that patients have difficulty in describing it precisely. Occasionally they describe it as a fear of death, of some vague impending catastrophe, of fainting or of behaving in an irrational, uncontrolled, and insane fashion, but these descriptions are vague and changing. In some cases patients feel anxiety only in the presence of certain persons, in others only when they are alone. The anxiety is a reaction to repressed impulses which threaten to emerge into consciousness. These are usually impulses aroused by frustrations in personal relations. Sexual desires are frequently involved but seldom cause anxiety directly, although they may arouse competitive hostility and resulting anxiety. Neurosis develops when failure is experienced in important social or sexual situations and the response to failure is regression to early hostile and destructive tendencies. Suitable ways to achieve ends are abandoned, and frustration is met with un-co-ordinated rage which is repressed. Only the resulting anxiety, the fear of conscience, appears in consciousness. The unconscious content of this anxiety is in men the fear of castration; in women certain typical masochistic fantasies are its equivalent.

An anxiety state is often the initial phase of a neurosis. It is rarely chronic in its purest form, in which periodic attacks of free-floating anxiety recur. The ego gradually develops defenses by which the anxiety can be curbed. The later course of the disease assumes different forms, depending on the type of defense employed. If the causative hostile impulses are turned against the self, depression develops. If they emerge into consciousness as disconnected ideas, an obsessional neurosis may develop. If the hostile impulses are overcompensated by trivial behavior like repeated washing or meticulousness, compulsions result. If they are projected upon others, delusional symptoms of persecution develop. Sometimes hostile impulses are diffused in general impulsive behavior, and in this way a neurotic character disturbance arises. They may periodically overpower the ego, as in the manic phase of manic-depressive psychoses. Conversion symptoms may also drain unconscious hostile impulses. In most neurotic symptoms guilt resulting from the expression of destructive impulses necessitates self-punishment.

Free-floating anxiety may introduce almost any form of neurosis or psychosis. It is seldom a stationary condition, although in many cases recurrent anxiety may persist for a long time as the only manifest symptom. Every neurosis has a complicated psychological structure aimed at eliminating anxiety. Anxiety neurosis is a state in which the ego has not yet succeeded in defending itself against anxiety. A very common outcome of an initial anxiety state is the gradual development of specific fears which appear only in specific situations. These are the phobias.

b. PHOBIAS

The most common types of anxiety to which phobic patients are subject are fear of crowds, fear of darkness, fear of large spaces (agoraphobia), fear of high places (acrophobia), of writing, of driving in a car, of walking—usually downtown in crowded sections—and of enclosed places (claustrophobia). These situations are usually connected with childhood fears. Phobic patients regress to an early anxiety-laden situation with which they replace an actual one. This is obvious in the fear of darkness, or of people. The fear of going downtown corresponds to the child's first experience with the noise and bustle of a large city. This is evident in patients who feel no anxiety on the street as long as they can see their home. This is really a fear of being lost. Height phobias correspond to an early fear of falling when learning to walk, and agoraphobia probably has a similar origin. It reflects the stage when the child is learning to walk and goes from one piece of furniture to the next and the space between them appears to him enormous.

While these common childhood situations are the earliest roots of anxiety, the real etiological factors consist of tendencies alien to the ego. These are more individual and are covered by the more common infantile patterns, which are merely regressive substitutes for them. The activities avoided have an unconscious symbolic meaning, which is often sexual. Walking on the street may represent in women an unconscious fantasy of prostitution. The soiling of a white sheet of paper by writing on it may represent a reaction to early anal sadistic fantasies. Heights often evoke unconscious competitive, narcissistic ambitions to be in a superior position. The fusion of childhood fears with similar later ones is complicated. Walking was once a daring accomplishment, an adventure, undertaken in competition with adults. A similar combination of feelings reappears in adolescence. When a young girl begins to "go with boys," a rebellious emancipation from her mother is often woven into this emotional pattern. Walking on the street may be connected with adventurous fantasies of making casual acquaintances, and this leads to fantasies of "streetwalking" and prostitution. In a street phobia all these unconsciously associated anxieties form one "gestalt," a unit which is activated regressively when there is a failure in meeting the demands of life. It is not unusual for a street phobia to develop in a young woman after her second or third romantic failure, when she feels defeated in her competition with other girls. Regression to early competitive situations in her family appears in unconscious fantasies of rebellion against the mother. This precipitates anxiety and further regression to a helpless state so that she cannot even walk alone on the street or leave home. In the final stage of a severe phobia every self-assertive action is avoided with anxiety, and the patient may become confined to her home like a helpless dependent infant.

A woman married to a businessman but always frustrated in her sexual desires and completely devoted to her children developed a street phobia at the approach of her climacteric. Before it was too late she wanted to experience an adventure, which in her unconscious took the form of illicit love and prostitution. Her phobia was restricted to walking on those streets in which the night life of the city was centered. At the same time she developed the obsessional idea of strangling her children during the night. This obsession sprang from the same emotional source and indicated her rebellion against her married life, which stood in the way of her freedom.

Three phases in the formation of a phobia can be distinguished: (1) failure in life and loss of initiative; (2) regression in fantasy to earlier competitive situations—oedipal or sibling rivalry—with corresponding anxiety and guilt; (3) the substitution of dependence for self-assertion. The phobia is an attempt to localize the anxiety within a single situation while saving the ego from recognizing the real unresolved problem and tackling it. Localized anxiety often gives place to a gradually spreading anxiety, multiple phobias develop, and in malignant cases there may be a regression to complete helplessness. Such patients may spend years locked up alone in their rooms, and their condition can easily be mistaken for schizophrenia.

C. OBSESSIVE-COMPULSIVE STATES

The fully developed symptoms combine obsessive ideas and compulsive rituals. The obsessive ideas are asocial, like hitting people, having incestuous intercourse, killing near relatives or children, and putting disgusting objects into the mouth. They are disconnected and appear to have no relation to the rest of the personality. They are usually undisguised and express openly otherwise repressed infantile impulses.

A man of forty-two suffered from the obsession of wanting to hit people on the head with an ax. At first this idea bothered him only occasionally and he would avoid hardware shops. Later any object even slightly resembling an ax precipitated the same obsession and its accompanying anxiety. Every rectangular object, e.g., a doorway, renewed his fear, and later he dreaded reading because capital "L" reminded him of an ax. His whole professional life was affected by his compulsion, and he continued work only with the greatest effort. He suffered constantly and for twenty-five years had had few quiet moments. His whole life was occupied with his obsession and different ways to overcome it.

Analysis revealed a common emotional situation. He had an elder brother and a younger sister and in his youth was envious of both. The younger sister had all the advantages of the youngest member of the family. When she was born she deprived him of the parents' attention and care. His elder brother, on the other hand, enjoyed all the privileges of being older. Thus the patient had neither advantage. The result was a competitive and hostile attitude toward his brother which roused guilt.

A forgotten memory which appeared in analysis gave a clue to the understanding of his obsession. When he was six years old he was digging potatoes with the son of a neighboring farmer. Each boy had a hoe, and the patient accidentally hit his friend on the head so that the boy fell bleeding to the ground. Fearing that he had killed his friend, he developed severe feelings of guilt.

The analysis showed that the intensity of these guilt feelings originated in his attitude toward his elder brother, which he transferred to the farmer's son. Hitting the farmer boy on the head with the hoe meant for him his unconscious hostility toward his brother. He had forgotten this incident entirely, but it nevertheless contributed to his obsessional symptoms. These represented the crime and at the same time the self-inflicted punishment for it. In fantasy he hit people on the head with an ax as he had actually done to the farmer boy, but his obsession was also the source of painful neurotic suffering.

In most cases it is impossible to trace the origin of obsessional ideas to such an isolated repressed event. They usually represent asocial impulses common in early childhood. The form of the asocial impulses is probably always determined by specific experiences, which are usually not so dramatic as the one described in this case.

Compulsive rituals, in contrast to obsessions, are frequently exaggerations or caricatures of social behavior. The most common are repeated handwashings or prolonged ceremonial baths or showers, and exaggerated meticulousness. Shoes must stand exactly parallel and symmetrically in front of the bed. Doors and drawers are closed carefully, objects in the bathroom or pocket are scrupulously counted, all stations between Chicago and New York rehearsed, the names of the presidents recited in order. Sometimes more individuality is shown. One patient kissed his dead father's picture fifty times, touching the glass with both lips at the same time, before going to bed. Symmetrical repetition, as, for example, doing with the left hand what is done with the right, is quite common ("undoing"). Touching plays a particularly important role. The urge to isolate things from each other is often an outstanding factor. Two different activities must be separated. A patient may not touch his face after touching his suspenders or engage in sexual acts on Thursdays, because his son had died on that day. As a rule the one act represents something good or clean, the other something bad or dirty. The face is clean, while suspenders, connected with the trousers and eventually with the penis, are dirty. The son's death is sacred, but sexuality is bad. They must therefore be separated.

Equally typical are certain character trends. These patients are usually inhibited in all activities, are considerate, punctilious, and rigorous in observing the small courtesies and conventions of society. They suffer from a paralyzing doubt which pervades their whole personality and behavior. They look at everything from all sides and finally cannot decide to do anything. In their personal relations they are very dependent on others, their parents, wives or husbands, and their professional superiors, although superficially they may appear to be independent.

These symptoms and character trends constitute a dynamic structure which is a precarious balance between repressed tendencies and repressing forces of the ego. The obsessional symptoms represent a breach in the repressive defenses through which alien wishes emerge. By isolating them from the rest of his personality the patient does not feel them to be his own and assumes no responsibility for them. Thus assertion of the most frankly asocial tendencies in conscious fantasies is made possible by a mechanism described as bribing the superego. The compulsive patient is hypermoralistic, exceptionally clean, punctilious or truthful, industrious, meticulous, and conventional. He overdoes all this and can therefore allow himself to indulge in prohibited fantasies. These two sides of his personality, the "good" and the "bad," social and asocial, clean and dirty, hostile and considerate, are in a constant struggle with each other, and the whole neurosis consists in preserving their equilibrium. Only when the superego's social demands are satisfied can indulgence be enjoyed without anxiety. The whole ritualistic symptomatology is a complex structure of defenses which serve to allay anxiety caused by asocial impulses. The compulsion is a derivative of this dual orientation. The paralyzing doubt, too, which may completely incapacitate the patient and prevent him from doing anything effectively, is the result of this emotional schism. Since he is always the servant of two masters, he feels that everything he wants to do has a double motivation. He cannot commit himself to either side with conviction because his impulses are at odds and his main concern is to maintain their equilibrium. No energy is left for constructive activity, since the psychic forces—social and asocial—are engaged in the never-ending and futile task of balancing each other.

One basic feature underlying obsessive-compulsive states is that fantasy and thought processes in general regressively assume the same exaggerated significance as they have in early childhood; i.e., imagining doing something becomes equivalent to doing it. Fantasy is able to gratify the need, but it also evokes guilt and anxiety if the imagined act is a forbidden one. This phenomenon has been called the "magic of ideas" or the "omnipotence of thought," which is characteristic of the child, who, on account of his limited powers, often has to content himself with fantasy for the gratification of his wishes.

I have described in an earlier publication [1] an extreme example of how thought may completely substitute for action. During the analytic hour this patient asked what time it was. I replied that it was half-past nine. After several seconds, he asked the same question and begged me to repeat my answer. When I then requested him to tell me why he had asked the question twice, he explained it by telling me of his

[1] F. Alexander, *The Psychoanalysis of the Total Personality*, Nervous and Mental Disease Publishing Co., New York and Washington, 1930.

obsessive doubt: He had suddenly become uncertain whether I did not say that it was half-past ten, and if it actually was half-past ten now, then a whole hour had elapsed without his knowing what he had done during this period of time. He was therefore afraid that perhaps without knowing it he had been to a prostitute and become infected with syphilis. His anxiety was quite sincere; he asked me two or three times whether I had really said half-past nine. When I answered "Yes," he asked after several seconds, "Did you say yes or no?"

The idea of going to a prostitute provoked the same anxiety as if he really had gone. This example also shows the role of doubt in compulsive states. The same patient often had a compulsion during analytic sessions to turn around to see whether I was still sitting there, because his fantasy that I was dead was so realistic that he had to convince himself of its unreality.

The repressed tendencies at play in obsessions and compulsions have been thought by most psychoanalytic authors to be anal-sadistic. The emphasis on cleanliness and punctuality accompanied by hostile and coprophilic ideas is the basis of this thesis, and there is no doubt in the majority of cases about the anal-sadistic character of the fantasies. It appears, however, that the obsessions and compulsions are sometimes oral and phallic. The characteristic of the disease is the type of defenses employed by the ego against pregenital impulses, among which the anal-sadistic are unquestionably outstanding.

d. DEPRESSIONS

The main symptoms of depression are melancholy and hopelessness, embitterment, and, in fully developed cases, self-critical and sometimes suicidal impulses, and a retardation of psychic processes with a general lack of initiative. Hostile impulses are inhibited and turned inward. A sense of guilt is predominant. It is aroused by hostile impulses which become self-destructive. A characteristic of depressed patients is their dependence in love relationships. Whenever this is frustrated they react with hostility which is turned against the self. This both discharges the hostility and relieves the sense of guilt. A further feature of depression is the appeal for sympathy and love by the patient's self-critical and self-punitive behavior (Rado).

A common precipitating cause is the loss through death or some other cause of someone whom the patient has loved. Freud has shown that the psychology of melancholia is an exaggerated and morbid form of mourning. In both mourning and melancholia the main factor is the unwillingness to renounce the loved person in whom so much love was invested. The withdrawal of interest from the world in both cases is the result of the incapacity of reinvesting love into other objects. In melancholia, however, withdrawal of interest from the world is combined with self-accusation as the predominant feature. Freud explained this from the melancholic's basically ambivalent relationship to love objects. In the melancholic patient the latent hostility toward the person lost is turned against the self. The narcissistic nucleus of the ego feels itself abandoned. All the love invested in the object was withdrawn from the narcissistic reservoir. Desertion often turns love into hate. Murders of passion are based on this mechanism. Death, however, is an insuperable obstacle to hate and its sole remaining object is the lover himself. This is the basis of suicide after a murder of passion, and the situation in the mind of the melancholic is analogous. A surge of hostility against the world in general is a common initial phase in a severe depression; this occurs before the hostility mobilized by the loss is turned back against the self. The introversion of hostile impulses is facilitated by introjection of or identification with the object. The re-creation of a love object within the personality through identification as a defense against its loss is a conspicuous feature of severe depressions. All these features, in a less pronounced form, are also present in mourning. The ambivalence toward the lost object is less pronounced, hence the self-destructive manifestations are not so blatant. However, the mourner also indulges in all kinds of self-imposed restrictions, indulges in guilty meditations about not having been kind enough toward the deceased, and does not allow himself any pleasurable pursuits. Mourning ceremonies, too, such as throwing ashes on one's head or fasting, are definite manifestations of guilt which originates in ambivalent feelings. All this shows that for the narcissistic nucleus of the personality all love objects constitute a threat and that all human relations have a trace of ambivalence.

The relation of the depressed patients to their love objects, however, is more markedly ambivalent, oral, and dependent. The inversion of hostility is aided by unconscious fantasies of oral incorporation of the ambivalently loved object. The self-destructive tendencies are attacks upon the introjected object. It is questionable, however, whether such fantasies are the most essential factor, no matter how frequently they may occur. The deflection of thwarted hostility inward is probably more elementary. When a small child attacks a stronger person in rage and is repeatedly pushed away he realizes his attacks are futile and begins to stamp on the ground and hit his head and chest with his fists.

A depression may develop as a reaction to sudden mobilization of hostile impulses in persons habitually inhibited in this regard. Guilt further contributes to the inversion of hostility. Since oral incorporation is the most primitive manifestation of hostility, it is not surprising that oral fantasies often accompany depressions. Feasts during wakes originate in this emotional need. Anal fantasies, however, are also quite common and underlie mourning ceremonies like putting ashes on the head or throwing earth and stones on a grave. The primary characteristic of the depressed is not the quality of his hostile impulses but their sudden release against otherwise beloved persons, which creates unbearable guilt. The combination of hate, love, and guilt is the essence of ambivalent relations. Ambivalence is, then, one of the basic dynamic factors in depressions as well as in compulsion neurosis. The compulsive patient relieves his guilt by rituals of expiation; the melancholic by inverting his hostility. A depressive patient develops much stronger attachments than do compulsives. The latter often make a cold, intellectual impression, whereas depressives are warm and emotional.

It must be remembered that all human relations contain some degree of ambivalence because for the narcissistic nucleus of the ego every object loved is an enemy. Dreams of the death of dearest relatives are common among healthy people because deeply repressed death wishes against dear relatives belong to the psychology of normal love. Love given to another reduces self-love. Circumstances which arouse this elementary narcissism may provoke death wishes toward loved persons. The predisposition to depression, therefore, is as universal as mourning. Only quantitative differences can account for the fact that one person works through his ambivalence conflict during a normal process of mourning of weeks or months while another person develops a chronic depression.

e. THE MANIC-DEPRESSIVE REACTION

The depressive states described above are reactions to common experiences, often to bereavement or frustrations and, though exaggerated and prolonged, are analogous to mourning. One group of patients develops alternatively depressive and elated states of varying intensity and duration. The older clinical descriptions give the impression that an endogenous condition prevails in which both the depressive phase and the elation occur without external provocation. When the precipitating factors are found, they usually appear insignificant. They are therefore thought to set in motion an organic, constitutionally determined process. The adjective "reactive" has been applied to depressions in descriptive psychiatry to emphasize a distinction between "psychogenic" depressions and manic-depressive conditions which were considered to be "endogenous."

The transition from moderately healthy people with a cyclothymic rhythm in their moods to disturbed manic-depressive psychotics is gradual. This gradual transition makes improbable the assumption that the ultimate cause is a primary metabolic or endocrine disturbance. Moreover, many severe cases have been helped by psychoanalysis. This would not be decisive were it not for the fact that these patients, when not treated, as a rule continue their extreme swings of mood indefinitely. The success of psychotherapy, which affects the underlying emotional configurations, shows that psychological factors operate in at least a number of cases.

The psychoanalytic studies of Freud and Abraham afforded the first psychological insight into these seemingly unmotivated mood swings.

The depressive phase of these patients is similar to a reactive depression. The psychological processes are retarded, the mood depressed, interest in the environment reduced, and the tendency toward self-criticism, self-depreciation, and self-destructiveness more pronounced than in a simple depression. A patient sitting in a hospital room brooding, scarcely noticing the physician, and answering after a long silence in monosyllables in a barely audible mumble may the next day greet the doctor with an exuberant flow of words, noticing all the details of the doctor's attire and remarking on them. The sequence of ideas appears often disconnected, the former retardation gives place to a veritable "flight of ideas." Elated and self-confident, the patient is full of plans and sees no possible obstacles. As the elation gains momentum and the hypomanic phase becomes fully manic, inhibitions disappear and the patient becomes aggressive, irritable, and sexually unrestrained. Psychologically, the manic phase is the exact opposite of the depressive, but the two are related as a convex arch to a concave.

DEPRESSIVE PHASE	MANIC PHASE
Retardation	Acceleration (flight of ideas)
Inhibition	Lack of inhibition
Introverted interest in self	Extroverted interest in environment
Lack of initiative	Extreme un-co-ordinated initiative
Lack of self-confidence	Unlimited confidence
Self-accusation	Aggressive fault-finding
Self-destruction	Uninhibited aggressive behavior
Melancholy	Elation
No sexual interest	Sexual licentiousness

The psychodynamic basis of this shift in attitudes is a change in the ego's handling of rejected impulses, especially hostile and aggressive ones. In the depressive phase the hostile impulses are inverted by guilt. The patient feels like a sinner who deserves punishment. In the manic phase the same impulses are turned outward. The restraint of conscience which was responsible for the introversion has been removed. The clue to a psychological understanding of the manic-depressive reaction lies in the reasons which remove the inhibitory influence of the conscience. Freud found the answer in the psychology of guilt feelings.

The depressive phase can be considered as a reaction to the manic period. In the latter the patient expresses freely alien impulses which are otherwise repressed. He is inconsiderate, boastfully aggressive, and sexually uninhibited. The conscience is temporarily ignored, but it soon reasserts itself. For a time the patient appears released from the superego's inhibitions and, like an overdisciplined child in the absence of parents and teachers, indulges in an orgy of uncontrolled behavior. In the depressive phase the conscience imposes the punishment which appears appropriate to the crimes of fantasy committed during the manic period. This is the period of atonement. Punishment, however, also has its limitations. The depressed patient makes punishment an orgy of self-abasement. Once the balance is restored, he has paid—or rather overpaid—for his guilt. He can now defy his superego and make the undeserved punishment an excuse for licentiousness. This is another example of bribing the superego, which we have already observed in the compulsive and obsessive states. In the latter the obsessions express openly the patient's repressed wishes, and his compulsive rituals serve as expiation. In the manic-depressive condition transgressions and punishment are separated into a licentious manic and a self-punitive depressive phase. We may call the obsessional-compulsive neurosis a one-phasic and the manic-depressive condition a two-phasic process.

We are dealing here with a disease of the conscience. Its severity provokes manic rebellion, which reactivates the superego. The two phases are both the causes and the effects of each other, and a vicious circle is established. When the superego has been made tyrannical by early experience, every event which increases the severity of repressions provokes a revolution in the form of a hypomanic or manic attack which necessitates in turn a period of atonement. It is therefore as correct to call the manic phase a reaction to the depressive phase as to consider the depressive phase a reaction to the manic.

If one knows these psychodynamic connections, it is not difficult to discover anamnestically the precipitating circumstances. Manic-depressive attacks do not come out of the blue. The first phase, which may be either depression or elation, is always precipitated by an event which disturbs the equilibrium between the repressed and repressing forces in the personality.

A nineteen-year-old girl entered college, became depressed and self-critical, lost initiative, and could not continue. She was the oldest of four sisters and two brothers, strongly attached to her father, a professional man of high standing, and involved in a competitive ambivalent attitude toward her mother and younger sisters. This was the source of her guilt. She was her father's favorite, the two other girls the mother's, although this was only vaguely apparent. A cousin with whom she had compared herself unfavorably had recently married. This, plus the competitive atmosphere of the college, activated the repressed family rivalry, and she reacted with a prolonged depression. She left school and returned home, but her behavior became unbearable to her mother. She stayed in her room, neglected her appearance, and burst into tears at the slightest provocation. In the first months of her treatment, which started in this depressive phase, she made the transition to uninhibited behavior. She began one morning to talk animatedly to a strange young man on the bus. A few days later she took a trip and picked up a stranger whom she met in a hotel lobby.

The competition in school, the marriage of her cousin, the scholastic and social successes of her sister, combined to mobilize her repressed hostility toward her mother and sister. The depression was a repressive measure like police action against revolution in an autocratic state. The manic phase, again, was a counterrevolution against the exaggerated punitive measures and released what she had previously repressed. Her unconventional behavior was a spiteful challenge to her mother and to her conscience, which represented her mother's discipline.

The events which upset the internal equilibrium were innocuous in themselves. A superficial anamnestic study might easily have passed them over, and the attack could have been then attributed to some unknown organic, possibly endocrinological, cause. As it was, the patient's guilt was the precipitating cause. It had developed in the rivalry between the four female members of the family and was stimulated by her father's preference for her and her mother's rejection. All this prepared the first depressive attack. The equilibrium between female rivalry and repressed guilt was so precarious that anything might upset the balance and provoke an attack. It is not unusual for normal endocrinological developments and the increase of sexual drives to upset this equilibrium. The cause, however, is not a particular endocrinological disturbance but the reaction of the ego to the sexual impulses of maturity. In this case this was one of the etiological factors.

The psychodynamic formula for this case is: increased sexual rivalry—increased guilt feelings—self-punitive depression—a manic counterreaction in which the repressed sexual urge broke through. Why the ego in some cases selects the one-phase compulsive-obsessional type of defense and in others the two-phase manic-depressive one cannot be answered with certainty at present. The constitution of the total personality is most probably the decisive factor. The outstanding character traits of the preneurotic personality in patients who develop compulsive or obsessional symptoms are quite different from those in patients who become manic-depressive. Strict repression demanded by the superego is common to both, as well as the fact that the requirements of conscience are not thoroughly assimilated by the ego and remain dissociated. The distinction between the superego and the ego was derived mainly from the study of compulsive-obsessional and manic-depressive patients. In a normal person a clear distinction between the ego and superego cannot be made, for the social attitudes are harmonized and cannot be regarded as a separate compartment of the personality. The difference between the typical compulsive and the typical manic-depressive patients' preneurotic personalities is illustrated by their personal attachments. The former is usually a highly intellectual person who has learned to detach his emotions from his reason. He is inclined toward abstract thinking, believes often fanatically in abstract causes and principles, and is apt to neglect the practical aspects of life. He is loyal to causes rather than to persons, is a theoretical lover of mankind but somewhat detached from immediate associates. The manic-depressive is a warm, often practical person, with a preference for the concrete over the abstract. He develops strong emotional attachments, and his emotions rule his reason.

The structure of the compulsive-obsessional neurosis exhibits an almost mathematical precision, which rests, however, on the precarious dissociation of emotion from emotional content. The letter of the law dominates its sense. The manic-depressive patient's lapses are more emotional and the punishment more realistic and emotionally transparent.

In manic-depressions as well as in reactive depressions the orally dependent attitudes and identification as a defense against frustration are conspicuous in contrast to the anal-sadistic patterns prevalent in compulsive and obsessive states.

It is claimed by psychiatric statisticians (Kretschmer, Sheldon) that obsessional compulsives have an asthenic longitudinal (ectomorphic), the manic-depressives a pyknic (endomorphic) physical build, but there are too many exceptions to this rule to attribute to physical constitution a primary importance. The basic psychological structure of the personality, however, is unquestionably an important factor in the choice of the neurotic defenses which ultimately determine the symptoms.

f. THE HYPOCHONDRIAC SYNDROME

Hypochondriasis was a common diagnosis when psychiatry was mainly descriptive and lacked the dynamic understanding of symptoms. Actually it is not a disease entity, but a syndrome which appears in different neurotic and psychotic symptoms, particularly in depressions and schizophrenias. As a fear of disease it may represent a phobia such as syphilophobia or cancer phobia. Descriptively the syndrome consists in an anxious preoccupation with the whole or one part of the body which the patient believes to be diseased. A depressive mood, anxiety, and various bodily sensations are the outstanding emotional features. The ideational content varies from pronounced somatic delusions to a fearful expectation of disease and death.

Preoccupation with the body is a normal reaction to pain. Bodily pain as a rule prompts the withdrawal of interest from outside objects to the self. A painful disease often serves as the beginning of hypochondriasis, of the obsessive preoccupation with an organ which may persist long after the organic condition is healed. Such increased interest in the body, however, persists only in response to certain emotional needs.

Psychodynamically, three major components can be differentiated: (1) a narcissistic withdrawal of interest from objects to the self; (2) a need for punishment caused by guilt feelings; (3) a displacement of anxiety. The withdrawal is most clearly observed in the preoccupation with their bodies of once beautiful, highly narcissistic women who cannot reconcile themselves to growing old. Severe hypochondriasis is a common symptom in such women. When frustrated in their demands for admiration by others they themselves give their bodies all the attention they previously received from their admirers. Frustration also mobilizes competitive hostile impulses which had been dormant as long as they received love and attention and competed successfully with other women. These hostile impulses revive earlier competitive conflicts of family life, oedipal guilt, and sibling rivalry. This guilt creates a need for suffering. The hypochondriac symptom satisfies both needs: the patient gives love and attention to her own body and at the same time she relieves her guilt by suffering. Suffering becomes a condition of and excuse for the exaggerated self-interest.

This basic pattern is observable in most cases. Increased narcissistic need caused by frustration of the wish to be loved is the primary factor. Frustration creates hostility, then guilt and the need for suffering. The combination of the wish to be loved and to suffer at the same time gives rise to the hypochondriacal symptoms.

The displacement of anxiety is a defense against castration fear. Neurotic guilt arouses the infantile fear of retaliation, the fear of castration. The hypochondriac displaces this fear to another organ as if he would offer his guilty conscience a less highly cherished organ as a substitute for his genitals. Essentially this is a mechanism similar to that seen in phobias.

In psychotic cases in which hypochondriacal ideas become delusional, introjection of ambivalently loved and hated objects which are identified with the supposedly diseased organ is the foundation of the syndrome.

The selection of the specific organ depends partially upon the nature of the guilt conflict and partially upon more accidental factors. A formerly diseased organ or a questionable diagnosis may be the first occasion for hypochondriasis in persons in whom the psychodynamic situation is ripe for the development of such symptoms. In some cases the selection of the organ is determined entirely by psychological factors.

A middle-aged businessman developed a morbid fear of cancer of the stomach, a disease which had actually caused his father's death. He was a determined, ambitious man who had achieved success largely by his own efforts. His whole personality was geared to making and saving money. His relation to women was immature; he demanded love and attention, returning almost nothing except material values. On one occasion he exacted monetary compensation from a woman who caused him some small material damage in a traffic accident. For this he felt guilty for many months and lived in dread of retaliation. Soon after this the patient developed his hypochondriacal ideas. His cancer phobia was based on a deep-seated guilt about his oral aggression which characterized his relation to his mother and later to all women. His guilt toward his father was also involved because in his possessive dependence he had claimed his mother entirely for himself and considered his father as a competitor. The choice of the stomach as the seat of his hypochondriac fears was doubly determined: the stomach is the organ of incorporation, the needs of which were first satisfied by his mother, and it was also the location of his father's cancer.

g. NEUROTIC CHARACTER

(Synonymous expressions for this category are: Fate Neurosis, Moral Insanity, Psychopathic Personality, Behavior Disorders, Impulse-Ridden Personality.[2])

First of all, these patients distinguish themselves from other neurotic sufferers in that they derive their neurotic gratifica-

---

[2] This group comprises a variety of types which externally, from the descriptive point of view, show marked differences. This may account for these various expressions.

tions and need for punishment not from symptoms but from their co-ordinated behavior and the important vicissitudes of their life. In this respect they are more like normal people. They are not satisfied with the substitutive gratifications which neurotic symptoms offer. They "act out" their neurotic impulses, in contrast to psychoneurotics, whose most important activity is in their fantasy. The tragedies of a compulsive-obsessional take place in the bathroom or in bed and no one knows about them except those closely associated with the patient. The neurotic character is an actor on the stage of life, and his disturbed behavior affects everybody in his environment. The unconscious meaning of his behavior is intelligible only in terms of the whole rhythm of his life. His unconscious needs are not expressed in fantasy, but his destiny is shaped by the relentless pressure of unconscious neurotic patterns.

The contrast between ordinary neurotic symptoms and the acting out of unconscious alien tendencies can be illustrated by Ferenczi's concept of autoplastic versus alloplastic adaptations. The organism has two fundamental mechanisms at its disposal to satisfy its needs: (1) changes within the organism; (2) changes in the environment. The need for heat can be satisfied by increasing the muscle tone, reducing the body surface by huddling, by exercise, or by making fire. The first three are autoplastic, the last an alloplastic adaptation. Phylogenetic development can be considered a series of autoplastic changes within the organism which adapt the body to a given environment; for example, in the arctic region animals develop heavy furs. Culture is alloplastic adjustment which changes the environment to fit needs. Protection against cold is secured by building houses with fireplaces in them. Neurotic symptoms are all autoplastic measures by which emotional tensions are relieved internally by conversion symptoms, fantasy activities, etc. Neurotic symptoms have little effect upon the environment; they belong to the patient's private life. Actual gratification through effort is alloplastic and affects the environment. The longing for someone may be temporarily relieved by fantasy, but it does not actually satisfy the desire. Expressing love and marriage change the actual situation. This corresponds to Freud's view of neurotic symptoms as substitutes in fantasy for successful action. This group of neurotic personalities aims at gratification of unconscious alien tendencies, not by mere fantasy, but by their conduct in life toward other people. In contrast to the ordinary neurotic symptoms, this type of expression of neurotic tendencies can be considered alloplastic.

The contrast between autoplastic symptoms and alloplastic behavior applies strictly only to the difference between conversion hysteria, anxiety neurosis, compulsion, obsessive neurosis, and neurotic personality. In the manic phase the cyclothymic patient acts out his unconscious tendencies, and the depressive patient may satisfy his need for punishment by suicide. Paranoid schizophrenics may also act out their impulses. But in all these conditions fantasy is the important outlet and irrational action is occasional. For neurotic characters action is the primary outlet, although they may also develop neurotic symptoms which replace action. Classification always narrows types, while most actual cases exhibit mixed symptoms. Only the prevalence of one type of neurotic pattern can serve as the basis for classification.

In spite of this a neurotic character is no more difficult to diagnose than other psychiatric conditions. The contention that a diagnosis of psychopathic personality or neurotic character merely covers ignorance is based on an insufficient understanding of the dynamics of these cases. There is no condition in psychiatry about which more confusion and error exist than this field.

Many patients with neurotic characters were long considered wicked, asocial, untreatable, lacking conscience, or constitutionally defective. It took a long time for a scientific attitude to replace a moralistic one in the psychiatric treatment of these patients. The old psychiatric expression, first used by Prichard, "moral insanity," expresses this antiquated attitude as clearly as the latest one, "constitutionally inferior, psychopathic personality." The truth is that in these cases environmental influences play a role at least as important as in most forms of mental disturbance. These patients are less inclined to introverted fantasy gratification and, like healthy persons, require realistic activity to satisfy their needs. Only their adjustment to the social environment is based on faulty principles. The disturbance of social patterns is the effect of the early parent-child relations, and it is most illuminating to observe how often parents bring children with this type of behavior problem to the psychiatrist and insist that the child was born a failure. In this way they defend themselves against their own unconscious feeling of responsibility for the child's difficulties.

These patients can be divided roughly into two groups: psychopathic criminals and eccentrics. This is, however, only a practical division. Social position is important, for the more privileged express their hostility more frequently in eccentricity than in delinquency.

It would be nonsense to classify neurotics by occupation, claiming, for example, that compulsive neurotics are usually artists, professors, or businessmen. They are found in all walks of life, for their occupation has little connection with their neurosis. Possibly statistics would show that the majority are engaged in intellectual pursuits. Occupation has quite a different significance for neurotic characters. They too may be found in all occupations, but usually in those which permit action. Adventurers, speculators, sportsmen, collectors, swindlers, confidence men, and all kinds of delinquents are found in this group, but seldom lawyers, physicians, executives, whose occupations involve co-ordination, control, and responsibility.

As has been stressed before, this group of neurotic characters includes a great variety of personalities. The unconscious motivations which are responsible for unadjusted behavior and lead to the repetition of certain interpersonal situations are manifold. Apart from criminals and eccentrics, some of these patients' neurotic behavior may be characterized by repeated marriages ending with the same type of failure, professional failures which repeat themselves in the same way, or other neurotic interpersonal relationships. A well-known group has been characterized by Freud as those who always fail after success because of their deep-seated guilt feelings which do not allow them to enjoy any success. In spite of this great variety there are common features typical for neurotic characters. Their neurotic acting out is characterized by three major features: (1) irrationality; (2) the stereotyped repetition of behavior patterns; and (3) self-destructiveness.

The irrationality is due to the dominance of unconscious factors, and the stereotyped repetition can be traced to the same cause. Unconscious motivations cannot be modified by conscious adaptations, and these stereotyped behavior patterns are equivalent to symptoms. They are often called "symptomatic behavior," because the underlying unconscious conflict is not amenable to the ego's control.

Self-destructiveness is prompted by the superego's rigid dictates, which sustain unconscious guilt. The neglect of this unconscious guilt is a common error in the psychiatric evaluation of this group. The phenomenon of bribing the superego can be even more clearly observed in these patients than in other groups. Freud first perceived the significance of guilt in neurotic criminals and spoke of "crimes committed from a sense of guilt." The central mechanism is the displacement of guilt stemming from repressed conflicts, usually from the oedipal situation, to some tangible conventional crime. By stealing or swindling they engage in a forbidden act much less objectionable than the forbidden desire they harbor in the unconscious. Their neurotic gain is punishment for a trivial offense and relief from greater guilt. Their behavior is therefore doubly motivated. It expresses, like a neurotic symptom, an alien impulse and its expiation. They are usually apprehended, because their mistakes are unconsciously deliberate. The popular belief that there is no perfect crime is due to an intuitive grasp of this fact. In *Crime and Punishment* Dostoievski described this unconscious need for expiation more realistically than any actual case history. After severe punishment for a relatively minor offense the conscience is relieved and the neurotic offender is emotionally ready for recidivism.

The psychiatric superstition that these patients are incurable stems from this psychodynamic phenomenon. They remain incurable as long as society conforms to their neurosis by punishing them. Their neurosis is an adaptation to punitive methods of education. Punishment atones for crime. By provoking punishment they relieve their own guilt and freely commit new offenses. This game of offense and punishment continues interminably. Therapy must break this pattern. Therapeutic success with this group, like Aichorn's, is based on embarrassing the neurotic delinquent by a novel, kind, and forgiving reaction to his provocative behavior. This upsets his equilibrium, which was an adjustment to the harsh and repressive treatment which he had previously received. Victor Hugo suggested this type of therapy in *Les Miserables* sixty years before Freud formulated his notion of the superego.

Among neurotic criminals the destructiveness and self-destructiveness can be easily recognized, but they are more successfully concealed by the eccentrics, who express both their aggression and their self-destructiveness less openly. They often engage in competitive and dangerous sports or hobbies. They climb mountain peaks which have never before been reached, set speed records, or try to make collections more complete than others' at excessive cost. Self-destructiveness is here satisfied by extreme danger and sacrifice. Narcissistic gratification derived from these competitive accomplishments is a further motivating factor.

Gamblers form a distinct group. Aggressive acquisitiveness and self-destructiveness are gratified simultaneously by the appeal to chance. The difference between eccentrics and criminals is often determined by social position, but the nature of the hostile impulses and previous experience may also be important.

h. ALCOHOLISM AND DRUG ADDICTION

The chronic consumption of alcohol and drugs is usually a habit acquired as a secondary complication of depressions and character neuroses. Morphine is taken first to relieve pain, but the motive changes when it becomes an addiction and its aim is to relieve mental distress. The third phase is the physiological adaptation of the organism to the drug. These are overcompensatory innervations directed against the inhibitory effects of the drug, and they are responsible for the great physical distress at the withdrawal of the drug.

Of all addictions, alcoholism is the most prevalent in both its chronic and its periodic variety. Oral dependence and self-destructiveness interplay, as shown by Knight. Earlier authors stressed latent homosexuality as a common factor.

In the majority of cases the underlying neurosis is a depression. Many patients employ alcohol as an escape from a depression or a substitute for it. The initial stimulus of alcohol produces a hypomanic state and permits the patient to overcome inhibitions due to guilt. The adverse consequences of drinking replace admirably other forms of self-punishment. Neurotic characters often resort to alcohol as an aid to acting out their unconscious tendencies.

The social sanction of alcohol and the actual pleasure obtained from the release of inhibitions only partially explain the difficulties in the psychotherapy of alcoholism. The assumption that victims of this habit suffer from a basic weakness of the ego cannot easily be rejected. It is at least partially confirmed by the fact that supportive measures such as are offered by Alcoholics Anonymous are often more effective than analytic therapy, which requires a greater amount of integrative capacity and control on the part of the patients than they possess.

i. ACUTE NEUROTIC REACTIONS TO TRAUMATIC EXPERIENCES (TRAUMATIC NEUROSIS)

From the psychodynamic point of view the conventional separation of neurotic reactions to physical trauma occurring commonly in industry and war as a specific disease entity cannot be justified. Every experience in which the ego is suddenly overwhelmed by stimuli which it cannot reduce to the level of its homeostatic equilibrium is traumatic. The objective nature of the traumatic event is of secondary importance. Of course, violent experiences in combat, which were generally referred to during World War I as "shell shock," would be traumatic for everyone. Emotional privations in war—dislocated conditions and separation from home and family—may produce effects similar to violent physical experiences beyond the ego's adaptive faculties. Under war conditions overwhelming emotional and physical experiences are interwoven, and it is difficult to separate their neurotic effects. Well-trained psychiatrists in the last war were impressed by the fact that the death of a "buddy" and the resulting guilt reactions were more common traumatic experiences than exposure to physical strains and injuries.

In this connection it is important to realize that every neurosis is a reaction to a situation which is beyond the ego's adaptive faculties. What characterizes the group called "traumatic neuroses" is not the trauma, which is present in every neurosis, but the acuteness of the condition. In chronic neuroses traumatic experiences are less dramatic and have a slow cumulative effect through the repetition of emotionally trying situations. In conditions called traumatic neuroses we are dealing with the acute sequelae to sudden emotionally and physically overwhelming stimuli. This group may deserve consideration from the descriptive point of view as a nosological entity only because of its massive clinical symptomatology and rapidly changing course.

The traumatic symptoms observed in the war following exposure to a combination of emotional and physical stress and those seen after industrial accidents show an extreme variety, such as loss of consciousness, severe disturbance of sleep with recurrent nightmares, tremors, loss of co-ordinated activities like walking or speaking, epileptiform convulsions, extreme irritability, diffuse aggression and sudden mood swings, functional disturbances of all vegetative systems, particularly the gastrointestinal, cardiovascular, and respiratory. Generally all these symptoms can be understood as prolonged effects of anxiety. The majority of the symptoms clearly manifest regressive responses to extreme stress and anxiety. The patients become frequently like helpless children who have lost all those faculties which they acquired gradually during growth. They must often relearn how to speak, walk, or use their hands. Loss of consciousness is the most radically regressive retreat from contact with a reality which has proved itself too inhospitable.

The vegetative disturbances are exaggerations of the normal vegetative responses to emotions. Normal vegetative responses such as an accelerated heart rate from fear are transitory reactions, but neurotic symptoms perpetuate normal responses chronically and persist long after the danger is over. The persistence of emergency psychology long after the danger has ceased is most clearly seen in the characteristic "startle reaction" to the slightest noise. This may continue after the other acute symptoms have disappeared.

All these reactions can be explained as signs of damage to the ego, which, under the intimidating influence of the trauma, abandons its mastery of co-ordination and regressively retreats to helplessness.

War neuroses have recently stimulated a considerable controversy about their position among neurotic disturbances. Kardiner laid special emphasis on the loss of "mastery" and tried to isolate "traumatic neurosis" from other forms of psychoneuroses as an essentially different type of condition.

On the basis of chronic cases studied after World War I he came to the conclusion that the nucleus of traumatic reactions is a "physioneurosis," which is different from the so-called "transference neurosis." After trauma the ego's mastery over the body, gradually achieved during growth, is suddenly disturbed. The traumatized ego relinquishes its faculties and regresses. It has at its disposal only disorganized fragments of previously co-ordinated activities. Its futile attempts at mastery of the dangerous external stimuli with its own impaired faculties results in irritability and aggressive, often explosive, behavior. Kardiner somewhat artificially separates these acute disturbances of the ego's capacity for mastery over the body from the pre-existing neurotic problems of the patient which appear as the condition progresses into its chronic phase.

Grinker and Spiegel, led by their extensive experiences in World War II, maintain that traumatic neuroses do not constitute a unique mental illness but consist of various neurotic reactions similar in cause and effect to all other neuroses and distinguished only by the sharpness and severity of the precipitating factors and the special color imparted by them. According to them, anyone may develop a traumatic neurosis if the stress is severe enough or attacks the individual where he is vulnerable or when he is overloaded with mastering other problems. They emphasize that all human beings have limited integrative capacities but that every reaction to trauma, mild or severe, depends upon the individual's previous psychological patterns and upon the experience to which he has been sensitized before the trauma. Furthermore, the trauma may be not an overwhelming fear of death but the reaction to incidents such as the death of a loved one or an envied comrade. Helplessness and immobilization when need for action is paramount and numerous other interpersonal situations are also relevant.

They maintain, on the basis of extensive therapeutic experience, that the complex fusion of acute traumatic reactions and old emotional conflicts cannot be entirely separated. They point out that the subjective meaning of the objective situation is of paramount importance in producing neurotic effects. For example, the death of a comrade may be sensed as the magical result of an unconscious hostility toward him, or the fear of death may be greatly enhanced by pre-existing guilt, which makes the soldier expect death as a deserved punishment. Moreover, the damaged and intimidated ego will become more vulnerable to old conflicts which were previously under control. This explains why, if untreated, many of these acute neurotic conditions of war tend to progress into a chronic phase, which consists of a fusion of residual symptoms of the acute phase with old neurotic conflicts which the ego no longer can handle because its integrative faculties have been impaired by the acute trauma. Accordingly, their therapeutic approach is comprehensive and attacks the total condition, both the intimidating results of the recent combat experiences and the reactivated pretraumatic problems. In treating the acute condition they stress the importance of restoring confidence by a protective physical environment and personal influence. By the use of sedatives in a procedure they call narcosynthesis they allow the soldier to re-experience the overwhelming situations in fantasy under more favorable conditions, when the anxiety is reduced by the influence of the drug and the reassuring presence of the physician. In this way the ego regains its mastery and is better prepared to deal with the chronic neurotic problems.

Traumatic neuroses offer simple and convincing evidence for the basic fact that the ego's functional failure in preserving homeostatic equilibrium has a prolonged effect in undermining its morale and inducing it to retreat regressively from its executive tasks. This is the essence of every neurotic disturbance.

j. CONVERSION SYMPTOMS

These are chronic innervations of the voluntary muscles and sense organs motivated by unconscious alien impulses. They express repressed wishes and at the same time reject them. The term "conversion" was invented by Freud to indicate that a physical symptom replaces an emotionally charged idea and can be considered a dynamic equivalent to it. The expression is unfortunate in suggesting a mysterious transformation of a psychological to a physical quantity.

Physiologically conversion is no different from any normal innervation by which we express emotions, such as weeping, laughing, or blushing, or from voluntary behavior. To satisfy our subjective needs we carry out under their motivational influence appropriate co-ordinated muscle innervations. No leap from the psychic into the physical occurs. Cerebral processes which are registered as feelings and ideas are the central stimuli which lead to voluntary muscle innervations. The same is true of expressive movements like laughter or weeping. Hysterical conversion is motivated by unconscious impulses which are repressed because they are alien to the ego. There is a short circuit in which an emotion is expressed without passing through the conscious ego. Hysterical conversion is an inadequate substitute for the repressed tendency, which could be relieved only by action. Repression inhibits action, and since the tension caused by the unconscious tendency cannot be relieved it becomes a chronic innervation. Since conversion symptoms occur in the voluntary system, which is ordinarily under the ego's control, they are often misinterpreted by uninformed observers as malingering. Before Freud many physicians were inclined to consider hysterical symptoms as simulations, and this belief was strengthened by the fact that no organic basis for the symptoms could be found. In a hysterical contracture the peripheral nerves and ganglia involved remain unimpaired, but the possibility that the difficulty might be of central origin, in the highest centers of the brain, where the intellectual and emotional processes are localized, was not considered.

The classical example of a conversion symptom is the great hysterical attack described by Charcot. During the attack the patient is unconscious and undergoes convulsive movements of the whole body, which indicate a great amount of passion. The movements are suggestive of the sexual act and express repressed desires for intercourse which are rejected by the conscious mind.

In distinction to these periodic acute conversion attacks, the most common hysterical symptoms are chronic, such as paralyses, contractures of the limbs, anesthesias, paresthesias, and hyperesthesias occurring in the different sense organs. The last occur most commonly on the skin and disturb the tactile sense. Hysterical blindness or deafness is much less frequent. Constriction of the visual field, called tubular vision, is, however, common in cases of hysteria. The most common hysterical conversion symptoms were called stigmata—such as the disappearance of the pharyngeal or corneal reflexes and strange sensations of a foreign body in the throat (globus hystericus). The relative uniformity of hysterical conversion symptoms can be explained from the fact that many are based on certain typical infantile experiences and conflictful situations. This is particularly true of the so-called stigmata. Because conversion symptoms often release the emotional charge of unconscious tendencies, the patients appear impassive and unemotional (*"la belle indifference"*).

Hysterical symptoms have a double symbolic meaning. They express both a wish and its rejection. In acute attacks of grand hysteria the fulfillment of the wish is more conspicuous, and its denial comes to expression only in the fact that the patient is unconscious. In more common forms, like hysterical contractures and paralyses, the rejection of an intention is in the foreground. In his clinical demonstrations Charcot produced experimentally, by hypnotic suggestion, hysterical paralysis of the arm expressing the denial of the desire to strike someone with the affected hand.

The hysterical conversion symptom often serves as a substitute for a co-ordinated act and expresses only a part of the total act. The wish to be embraced may be expressed, as in the case of Freud's Dora, by a pain in the chest, representing the pressure of embracing arms which she had experienced in the past.

The voluntary portion of such vegetative functions as eating may be the content of hysterical conversion, as in hysterical vomiting. This often expresses the denial of some sexual desire—usually impregnation. It is a common symptom in young hysterical girls and is based on the widespread infantile fantasy of oral impregnation.

The unconscious meaning of hysterical vomiting, however, is not always as specific as this. The infantile expression of the wish for something is to put it in the mouth. Hysterical vomiting may be the rejection of any alien desire and an expression of disgust.

The hysterical contracture of a leg may express unconscious castration wishes, the contracted limb symbolizing the breaking off of an erect penis. This motivation has been illustrated by the analysis of a young hysterical girl described by Bosselman. The contracture of the leg in this case was also a defense against sexual attack.

In a case of torticollis I analyzed, the turning of the head to one side had a complex overdetermination. First, it represented an unconscious wish for fellatio. The symptom first developed when the patient, a salesman, was sitting in a barber chair. Second, at a deeper level, it probably represented turning toward the mother and corresponded to the nursing position. The symptom developed in this patient when the defenses against his passive oral dependence collapsed because of an accumulation of circumstances. He lost one of his legs in an accident when he was eight years old, and as a defense against weakness and dependence he developed an extremely independent and proud personality. He eventually became the support of his older brothers and was always helpful to others. In his early adult life he developed neurotic stomach symptoms based on his repressed dependent oral tendencies, but he paid little attention to them.

He adopted the son of a deceased sister and gave this young man all the care and attention he would have liked to receive from others but which he had never permitted himself because of his extreme sensitiveness at appearing weak and in need of help. The only person upon whom he could lean to some extent was one of his sisters, and his symptom developed shortly after her death and at the time when his adopted son was entering military service. Thus two important vents for his dependent needs were eliminated. The sister had satisfied his dependent needs directly; his adopted son provided him a vicarious gratification of the same need. When deprived of both outlets he developed the torticollis. This represented a repressed infantile dependence on men in fellatio fantasies and on women in sucking their breasts. This patient was successfully treated by psychoanalysis.

Many authors claim that the emotional conflicts underlying conversion symptoms are on the genital and phallic level, and in many cases this is undoubtedly true. Oral dependence constitutes, however, another common basis. Repressed aggressive impulses, e.g., toward castration, are also frequent. The genital theory of hysteria may be argued by maintaining that the original conflict is on a mature sexual level from which the patient often regresses to pregenital substitutes. The symptoms represent defenses partly against sexual wishes and partly against their regressive substitutes. This pattern applies, however, to many other neuroses in which the precipitating conflict is on the mature sexual level, from which the patient regresses first to oedipal fantasies and thence to pregenital attitudes. The question is, what unconscious wishes do the symptoms express? In my experience conversion symptoms may express repressed tendencies of any kind and belong to any level of emotional development.

It is another question whether one type of personality is more prone to conversion symptoms than others. This leads us to a group of patients to which one usually refers as hysterical, who reach more completely than other neurotics the genital or at least the phallic level of psychosexual development. Before discussing this group in detail it must be admitted that the extremely immature oral dependence of many hysterical patients seems to contradict the generalization that they are further advanced in their psychosexual development than other psychoneurotics. In fact, many patients who later develop melancholia seem to be capable of more mature human relationships before their illness than typical hysterics. In any case the attempt to explain the inclination for certain types of symptom formation from fixations to definite phases of development needs further investigation. This theory seems most applicable to schizophrenias and compulsion neuroses. In the former the tenuousness of the ego's relationship to external reality and its inclination to substitute fantasy for reality indicates the disturbance of the early phases of ego development in which the differentiation between the ego and external reality takes place. The prominence in compulsion neuroses of anal-sadism and of such character traits as exaggerated punctuality, cleanliness, and orderliness, which develop as a result of early severe toilet training, is generally recognized. The prevalence of oral fantasies and dependent affective relationships is equally conspicuous in depressions, hysterical conversions, and hysterical personalities. Hysterical conversion is not restricted to certain types of personality, and this is not surprising, as the voluntary and sensory systems are the organs of emotional expression. The symbolic expression of repressed tendencies by innervations within these organ systems is found occasionally in all types of neurosis.

The belief that conversion hysteria has a particular affinity to genital conflicts may be attributed to various causes. Hysterical conversion symptoms were first studied by Freud when he was realizing the significance of repressed sexual desires but had not yet developed his theory of pregenital sexuality. The convulsions in grand hysteria act out the fantasy of sexual intercourse, and a certain type of neurotic personality which has been called "hysterical" is actually characterized by severe repression of genital impulses. These patients are for the most part women who are exhibitionistic and are apt to dramatize emotions not actually felt. This spuriousness is confirmed by the fantastic lies with which these patients try to impress others and themselves. They struggle desperately to express inhibited sexual feelings. The convulsive attacks represent an extreme form of the same dynamic process which appears in the dramatic display of emotions by hysterical patients. The impression of lack of genuineness is created even though the hysterical person's external behavior is about what it would be if he actually felt those emotions which he displays. The exaggeration and theatrical display of emotions is so conspicuous that lack of actual emotions can easily be recognized even by unskilled observers.

Conversion symptoms often imitate organic illness, just as hysterical behavior makes a pretense of emotions not experienced. The truth is that the unconscious tendencies operative in hysterical personalities usually, though not always, are phallic or genital. This is the basis of the view that hysterical conversion symptoms always express phallic or genital impulses. This is largely true of *hysterical behavior,* but not of all *conversion symptoms.*

It should be emphasized in this connection that our knowledge of the etiology responsible for the various forms of neurosis is still limited.

The theory of conversion hysteria was erroneously extended to all physical disturbances in which emotions play a role, even to disturbances of the visceral organs which function under the control of the autonomic nervous system. Careful psychosomatic investigation of emotionally conditioned dysfunctions of the stomach, the bowels, and the endocrine, circulatory, and respiratory systems have shown that the underlying physiology and psychodynamics of these cases are essentially different from those of conversion mechanisms.

The study of the emotional component in diseases of the vegetative organs has proved to be of great significance. It introduced a new era of "psychosomatic medicine," which will be discussed in a separate volume.

k. THE SCHIZOPHRENIAS

The contribution of psychoanalysis to this group is more explanatory than therapeutic. There is great difference of opinion about the causes of schizophrenia, which includes a variety of conditions. Some emphasize the importance of psychogenesis, others consider schizophrenia a progressive organic disease process and regard its psychological manifestations as "epiphenomena." This divergence is due to ignorance of the facts. It seems highly probable that in the majority of cases of schizophrenia a constitutional element still undefined is of fundamental significance.

The psychodynamic difference between psychoses and neuroses has been formulated thus: The former are occasioned by a conflict between the different structural parts of the mental apparatus, and the latter by a disturbance in the personality in its relation to the outside world. It is true that during episodes or in progressive stages the psychotic loses touch with external reality because he falsifies the data of his sense perceptions. He is so vulnerable to the pressure of his own maladjusted demands that he cannot accept a reality which opposes them, and so falsifies it. The most extreme forms of this falsification are hallucinations, but illusions and delusions have a similar significance. This falsifying tendency is transparent in delusions in which the psychotic perceives in himself unacceptable hostile or sexual tendencies, refuses to accept them as his own, yet cannot repress them and so projects them on others. The resistance of paranoiacs to all explanations of their symptoms and the impossibility of convincing them of the error of their delusions is due to their perception of hostile and sexual emotions in themselves which they are unable to repress. Their error consists only in wrongly locating these emotions. They will not admit their possession and so project them in delusions, the vividness of which is derived from their actual inner experience. This may be expressed otherwise by saying that the psychotic has, in a sense, no respect for reality. It is easier for him to relinquish his contact with reality than to control his own emotions, and as a result he solves his inner conflicts by changing the picture of reality to suit his subjective demands.

It is important here to distinguish between two kinds of conflicts in psychotics. The first can be stated in the following way: "The world is not as I should like to have it. I do not want to live in such a world and therefore prefer to live in a world of fantasy. I am therefore ready to sacrifice real satisfactions for hallucinations of my own choosing."

The second type of conflict produces delusions and all paranoid phenomena and is identical with conflicts in the psychoneuroses. These conflicts arise, not because external reality is unsatisfactory, but because certain emotions are unacceptable. In the neuroses unacceptable hostile and sexual impulses are repressed but emerge in disguise as neurotic symptoms and find in this way a substitutive satisfaction. In the psychoses rejected tendencies are not repressed but projected. They are not recognized as one's own but are attributed to external reality. While paranoid mechanisms are falsifications of both internal and external reality, hallucinations and illusions are only falsifications of external reality. The hallucinating patient changes the picture of the external world, but the paranoid denies something in himself.

The combination of neurotic and psychotic mechanisms in paranoid conditions can be best illustrated by Freud's dynamic formulation of underlying persecutory delusions. He demonstrated that passive homosexual desires are repressed and overcompensated by hostile feelings. The unconscious "I love you" is transformed into the conscious "I hate you." This is a typical result of neurotic repression. In the second phase the hostile attitude is projected, and "I hate you" is transformed into "You hate me." According to this, a repressed passive homosexual desire is the ultimate dynamic basis of persecutory delusions. This is unquestionably a most frequent etiology. It appears, however, that any intensive hostile impulse, no matter what its origin, may be projected onto others when the ego's reality-testing function is impaired, if the impulse cannot be repressed or justified by acceptable motivations.

These two categories of symptoms, the falsification of reality and the paranoid symptoms, provide a basis for classification of various forms of schizophrenia. The paranoid mechanisms resemble the neuroses more closely, for the more highly organized portions of the mind still function unimpaired. They possess the dynamic efficiency of a socially adjusted ego, for paranoid patients cannot evade the influence of their superego standards. The fact that they project emotional tendencies proves that they cannot accept them. Repression, the neurotic's method, is impossible for them, for their ego cannot exclude from consciousness tendencies which the neurotic can conceal or distort. The paranoid psychotic can neither repress nor accept alien tendencies, and his only solution is projection. Hallucinations and illusions do not presuppose such an inner conflict, for they are merely solutions of a conflict between the ego and external reality. These mechanisms are therefore more infantile, because they correspond to an early stage of development, in which the conflict between subjective demands and reality is not yet inwardly reproduced as a conflict between subjective demands and the superego.

Paranoid hallucinations occupy an intermediary position, for in them the threats of the conscience are projected on external reality in an attempt to get rid of them. If we remember that the standards were internalized by assuming and embodying the moral and educational prescriptions of the parents, paranoid hallucinations may be considered as a regression to the period in which the ego was controlled merely by others and the child sacrificed his desires from fear of his parents' restrictions.

In schizophrenia, the ego also loses its synthetic function of harmonizing the different and often contradictory instinctual demands. Sudden unmotivated aggressive attacks and self-destructiveness are clear signs of disintegration in the structure of the ego. It seems to me unjustified to regard the impulsive self-mutilations of schizophrenics as reactions of a harsh superego. It is impossible to assume that the schizophrenic who can no longer feel pity and disgust and who indulges in coprophilia should be affected by the moral need for punishment. The self-mutilations are symbolic of self-castrations and are manifestations of isolated feminine wishes which are released after the synthetic function of the ego is destroyed. The polymorphous, manic behavior is the manifestation of disorganized instinctual demands which have lost their interconnections and seek independent outlets.

These considerations indicate a distinction between two main groups of schizophrenia, the one characterized by the predominance of paranoid hallucinations and delusions, the other by simple falsifications, hallucinations, and illusions. The theoretical and therapeutic evaluation of cases with pronounced paranoid symptoms must be different from others. Paranoid cases permit a greater participation of acquired standards and show a less deteriorated ego structure. A common factor in both cases, however, is the ease with which the psychotic gives up his connection with reality and falsifies it to suit his demands. The ability to dispense with reality is a characteristic of schizophrenia which differentiates it from neuroses, in which so radical a flight from reality is impossible. The neurotic is too loyal to reality to be able to deny its objective nature and consequently must work out the conflict within himself. The dynamic relation between the ego and the emotional demands is exactly reversed in psychoses and neuroses. In neuroses the ego overpowers the emotional demands and the neurotic symptom is a protest of the restricted impulses; in psychoses the ego yields to impulses, and hence the apparent lack of repression. In psychoses the impulses overpower the ego and it abandons its acquired function of recognizing reality. At the same time the ego loses its other function of harmonizing the different instinctual demands and turns out to be weak in the face of both external reality and the pressure of the primitive unadjusted instinctual impulses.

Our knowledge of the developmental phases of the mind permits a more precise evaluation of the difference between psychoses and neuroses. We have many reasons for assuming that the infant's psychic processes are similar to those which adults manifest only in their dream life and are also similar to the hallucinations of schizophrenics. Many years ago Bleuler referred to the similarity of dream processes to schizophrenic manifestations. The differentiation between the ego and the external world is one of the first accomplishments in the individual's development, and is based on the acceptance of the external world. We may say, therefore, that the hallucinating psychotic relinquishes his first adjustment to external reality, whereas in neuroses the later social adjustments are disturbed. We must assume that patients who develop schizophrenia have not secured this first step and the distinction between ego and nonego has never been firmly established.

The precipitating causes of psychoses emerge in adolescence or adult life and are in effect identical with those which operate in neuroses. In his flight from the conflicts of adult life the psychotic reverts to a very early period when he was unable to distinguish between fantasy and reality, and it is precisely this depth of regression which is characteristic of psychoses. The developmental difference between psychoses and neuroses is that adjustment to reality in the former has been disturbed at a very early period, while in neuroses the disturbance dates from the emotional conflicts with others in the period of the development of the superego.

Because the foundations of schizophrenia are laid in infancy or early childhood, it is reasonable to suppose that inherited constitution plays a more important role than in neuroses. It is difficult to imagine that external influences alone are responsible for this early weakness of the ego, which prevents the most elementary adjustment to physical reality, unless unusual and violent psychological influences can be discovered in the majority of cases to explain this early rejection of reality. Inherited constitution, however, operates in the development of all personalities, and its relation to environmental influences is complementary. Under extremely unfavorable circumstances even a strong constitution may suffer early damage which develops later into schizophrenia.

It must be admitted that the constitutional theory is too general to be satisfactory, but until we have more knowledge it may serve to avoid an overemphasis upon psychogenic factors. The influence of postnatal development is clearly of real importance in many cases. All influences which strengthen the connection with reality or tend to make reality more acceptable to a weak ego will decrease psychotic withdrawal. Similarly, all later influences which make it difficult for the ego to accept external reality will increase the likelihood of a schizophrenic disorder. An adequate theory of schizophrenia, however, must explain why the conflicts and influences of later life can drive these personalities back to such an early stage of development. The inability to distinguish reality from fantasy cannot be explained by influences subsequent to the growth of this ability. Traumatic influences even in late infancy cannot be responsible for the weakness of a faculty acquired at an earlier phase of development. Many people do not like the world as it is, but only psychotics reject it so forcibly.

Modern psychiatric hospitals display an intuitive grasp of these considerations. Their general tendency to make the environment as agreeable as possible to the patients is a therapeutic measure quite in harmony with the views developed here. The positive results of occupational therapy can be similarly explained. If the patient finds a place which he can fill successfully he will be more inclined to readjust to at least part of reality and abandon his flight from it. The principle of adjusting institutional environment to the personalities of schizophrenics is most consistent in the therapeutic methods of H. S. Sullivan, who advocates adjusting even the human environment to the emotional life of patients by employing as attendants schizoid personalities who have lost their "natural conviction as to right and wrong" and who consequently have an understanding of the peculiarities of the insane. He suggests special training for these "sensitive, shy, and ordinarily considered handicapped employees" in order to teach them to "cease to regard the schizophrenics in more or less traditional ideology as insane" and to see significant resemblances between the patient and attendant. Sullivan reports unusually good results from this method. Frieda Fromm-Reichmann, Knight, and recently Rosen have further pursued these sound therapeutic principles. Rosen reports surprising therapeutic results, which are apparently based primarily on strong positive transference and countertransference.

The principle of selecting attendants with personality traits similar to those of the patients agrees with the observations of H. Nunberg and K. Landauer, that the re-establishment of the patient's relation to the external world is based on an identification with a person or persons with whom he has had continuous contact. It is obvious that such identification is more easily effected with individuals of a similar emotional make-up. This also explains the frequency of pronounced homosexual tendencies in schizophrenics, for the homosexual object relation of schizophrenics is a pseudo-object relation, since it is essentially a narcissistic identification.

There are indications that the schizophrenic's withdrawal from reality, if it persists for a long time, may lead to physiological dysfunctions, probably metabolic, which may encourage further emotional withdrawal. All this has to be reserved, however, for future psychosomatic research.

1. PSYCHOLOGICAL FACTORS IN ORGANIC BRAIN DISEASES

The contribution of psychoanalysis to the organic psychoses consists mainly in the dynamic understanding of the psychological content of the symptoms. It has little to contribute to their etiology and therapy. This is quite natural, because many psychoses are due to major organic changes in brain tissue, as in the post-infectious, toxic, and degenerative psychoses of old age. In these cases, however, the symptoms can be understood as reactions of the personality to these organic changes. The best-known example is the explanation of the grandiose ideas of general paretics as compensatory defenses of the ego against the perception of waning mental faculties (Ferenczi-Hollos). The filling in of memory gaps with fictitious inventions in cases of Korsachow psychosis also follows psychodynamic principles, for the content of the fictions is determined by unconscious desires. In toxic delirium repressed impulses determine the content of fantasies.

The psychological content of senile psychoses also is determined by the personality structure and earlier conflicts. The outstanding factor is the ego's reaction to physiological decline. This may be overcompensatory, paranoid, or depressive, or it may tend simply to deny the fact of aging. The over-compensatory reaction may be of an adolescent type, with manic hyperactivity, sexual license, heightened competitiveness and aggressiveness, bragging, or euphoric denial of decline. The paranoid reactions are due to the projection of hostile impulses mobilized by the frustrating perception of decline. The depressive reactions are caused by introversion of the same hostile impulses against the self.

m. PERVERSIONS

Descriptively, one can differentiate two categories of sexual perversions: (a) perversions consisting in the distortion of the quality of the sexual strivings, and (b) perversions in which the object of the sexual striving is abnormal. Sadism, masochism, exhibitionism, voyeurism, and transvestitism belong to the first group; homosexuality, pedophilia, and zoophilia, to the second. In fetishism both the object of sexual striving and its quality are altered.

Perversions depend on fixations or regressions to early immature forms of sexuality, but the former is more significant. Even with regression, however, a large element of fixation must be assumed.

In general, the normal sexual development of such individuals has been interrupted on account of emotional involvements in the family arising from the Oedipus complex. On account of this the pregenital forms of sexual gratification are retained according to specific fixation points. All emotional tension which the ego cannot utilize and release in co-ordinated behavior may become the cause of sexual excitation. Sexuality in essence is based not on the quality but on the quantity of impulses and the mode of their release. Perversions confirm this thesis and exhibit an extraordinary variety of different emotional tensions which become the sole content of the sexual impulse.

If an aggressive impulse contributes and is subordinated to utilitarian goals like overcoming an obstacle, or attacking an enemy, it has in itself no sexual connotation. The discharge of aggression and hostility for its own sake and the infliction of pain as an end in itself is a sexual phenomenon, sadism. There is a constant accumulation of hostile aggressive impulses in the child because of its weakness and dependence upon adults which prohibits the free release of hostile impulses. Cruelty toward weaker objects, younger siblings, or small animals is the sadistic release of these pent-up feelings.

When an accumulated need for punishment and suffering is erotized it becomes masochism. The nonsexual counterpart of masochism is contained in the reality principle and involves voluntary subjection to strain, or even pain, if necessary to achieve a desired goal. A frugal life of self-denial in working for a cherished goal is not masochistic, although it means voluntary, self-imposed suffering. Only a person who takes pleasure in punishing himself and endures pain not as a necessary evil but as an aim in itself is properly called a masochist.

In exhibitionism the child's need to attract attention and his desire to impress adults with his body is erotized. Voyeurism is an erotized expression of curiosity.

During growth the child exercises its different faculties in a pleasurable erotic way for their own sake. Because of his dependent position he does not require the use of these faculties to survive. All surplus energy is released in this playful, erotic manner. In the child the desire for mastery, painful striving, curiosity, showing off, and getting attention are all sources of erotic pleasure. In perversion, these early erotic satisfactions continue to appeal because normal and mature sexual release is blocked. The same is true of perversions in which the choice of sexual object is abnormal because infantile.

Since the mature sexual impulse absorbs many early erotic elements, one might be inclined to consider perversions a result of the disintegration of the mature sexual instinct into its constituent parts. This is only partially correct. The most important factor in the mature sexual impulse is the emotional expression of the fact that the organism has achieved its growth and that its surplus energy seeks a constructive outlet in the form of love and procreation. This, as has been emphasized before, is a new factor which has not been present in the earlier phases of life. The mature sexual impulse is determined by emotional tensions which do not contribute to self-survival but transcend the limits of the individual. In maturity growth is no longer possible, but sexuality and love express a tendency to transcend this limitation. Another reason why perversions cannot be considered merely as the disintegration of mature sexuality is that in many perversions the integration of pregenital impulses into mature sexuality has never really taken place. Perversions are the result of a failure in the integration of the pregenital components of sexuality into a mature form.

The emotional factors responsible for this interrupted sexual development are numerous. The prevalence of the hostile, competitive components of the Oedipus complex is important. Fixation to this competitiveness along with sibling rivalry causes sadism. Anxiety and guilt aroused by competitiveness in the oedipal situation and sibling rivalry cause masochism and homosexuality. In the latter, competition is avoided by submission to the parental rival. Identification with the parent of the opposite sex achieves the same purpose. We often see an interesting fixation on intermediary goals connected with the early Oedipus situation. To separate the parents a boy may assume a feminine and seductive attitude toward the father which later contributes to his homosexual development. Originally the wooing of the father was subordinate to the normal Oedipus drive to separate the father from the mother. Gradually, however, this becomes an erotized end in itself (Silverberg). Another common factor in certain types of homosexuality is the boy's identification with his mother, which prompts him to give to a younger boy the kind of love he wished to receive from his mother and thus to enjoy vicarious satisfaction. Similarly in the development of masochism punishment at first relieved guilt engendered by hostility toward the father or mother. Gradually the punishment itself becomes erotized. This obtains also in sadism, in which originally aggressions toward a parent or sibling were aimed at obtaining the exclusive love of the other parent. Gradually the release of the aggression becomes an end in itself as sexual sadism.

In voyeurism curiosity originally played a subordinate role in the Oedipus situation and was encouraged by sexual interest in a member of the family. Gradually the curiosity itself became erotically charged. Similarly in exhibitionism the child's desire to draw admiring attention to himself becomes an erotic aim. In every perversion there is always a fixation to a specific mode of relieving overwhelming emotional tensions which have been aroused by the early family situation.

Transvestitism contains both exhibitionistic and homosexual components in a complex dynamic configuration.

The sources of fetishism are particularly intricate. The most important factor here is the attempt to control overwhelming castration fear aroused by the boy's discovery of the anatomical difference between the sexes. The fetish may be part of the female body or a piece of dress which substitutes for the dreaded female genital. It has always a phallic connotation and denies the absence of the penis in the woman. That fetishism is a perversion of men alone accords with this view.

Since we are restricting ourselves to fundamentals in this

PSYCHOPATHOLOGICAL PHENOMENA [1]

PSYCHONEUROSES						PERVERSIONS	PSYCHOSES
SOMATIC SYMPTOMS		PSYCHOLOGICAL SYMPTOMS					
Changes in voluntary neuromuscu- lar and sensory system	Responses to emotional states in the vegetative organs	Irrational anxiety	Irrational thoughts and rituals	Distortions of mood	Irrational behavior	Abnormal sex aim	Disturbed judgment (falsification) about one's own person and the environment in the form of hallucinations and delusions
Conversion hysteria	Vegetative neurosis (Organ neurosis)	1. Anxiety states (free-floating anxiety) 2. Phobias (Circum-scribed anxieties)	Obsessive-compulsive neurosis	1. Depres-sions 2. Manic-depressive reactions	No neurotic symptoms but irrational behavior in interpersonal relationships Neurotic character (Psychopathic personality) 1. Eccentrics 2. Neurotic criminals	Abnormal sex object Sadism-masochism Fetishism Exhibitionism and scoptophilia Homosexuality Zoophilia Pedophilia	1. Manic-depressive psychosis 2. Schizo-phrenias Simple Catatonic Hebephrenic Paranoid

[1] Drug addictions are secondary complications of other underlying psychoneurotic conditions, such as depression and person-ality disorders (neurotic character).

volume, we shall not go into a detailed description of the various psychodynamic mechanisms responsible for fixations to these early forms of erotic release. It appears that apart from the emotional vicissitudes described, conditioning plays an important role. Once the child has discovered certain modes of erotized release, he tends to repeat them. This is an example of the inertia principle. It is frequently possible to establish during psychoanalytic treatment the original conditioning experience which supplied the basis of a particular perversion. It is important to bear in mind, however, that such conditioning experiences in childhood become pathogenic only if normal sexual development is blocked by insoluble emotional conflicts aroused by experiences in early family situations.

BIBLIOGRAPHY

ABRAHAM, K.: "A Complicated Ceremonial found in Neurotic Women," in *Selected Papers*. London, Hogarth Press, 1927, p. 157.

———: "Notes on the Psycho-Analytical Investigation and Treatment of Manic-depressive Insanity and Allied Conditions," in *Selected Papers*. London, Hogarth Press, 1927, p. 137.

———: "The Psychological Relation between Sexuality and Alcoholism," in *Selected Papers*. London, Hogarth Press, 1927, p. 80.

———: "The Psychosexual Differences between Hysteria and Dementia Praecox," in *Selected Papers*. London, Hogarth Press, 1927, p. 64.

———: "Zur Psychogenese der Strassenangst im Kindesalter," in *Klinische Beitraege zur Psychoanalyse*. Wien, Internationaler Psychoanalytischer Verlag, 1921, p. 124.

ALEXANDER, F.: "The Neurotic Character," *Internat. J. Psycho-Analysis*, 11:292, 1930.

———: *The Psychoanalysis of the Total Personality*. Nervous and

Mental Disease Monograph Series No. 52. New York, Nervous and Mental Disease Publishing Company, 1929.

ALEXANDER, F.: "Zur Theorie der Zwangsneurosen und der Phobien," *Internat. Ztschr. f. Psychoanal.*, 13:20, 1927.

ALEXANDER, F., and HEALY, W.: *Roots of Crime*. New York, Alfred A. Knopf, Inc., 1935.

ALEXANDER, F., and STAUB, H.: *The Criminal, the Judge and the Public*. New York, The Macmillan Company, 1931.

BLEULER, E.: "Dementia Praecox oder die Gruppe der Schizophrenien," in *Handbuch der Psychiatrie*. Spezieller Teil, 4. Abteilung, 1. Haelfte. Herausgegeben von Prof. Dr. G. Aschaffenburg. Leipzig, Franz Deuticke, 1911.

————: *Textbook of Psychiatry*. London, George Allen & Unwin, Ltd., 1923.

BLUEHLER, H.: *Die Rolle der Erotik in der Maennlichen Gesellschaft*, Band I und II. Jena, Eugen Diederichs Verlag, 1921.

BOEHM, F.: "Beitraege zur Psychologie der Homosexualitaet," *Internat. Ztschr. f. Psychoanal.*, 6:297, 1920.

BREUER, J., and FREUD, S.: *Studies in Hysteria*. Nervous and Mental Disease Monograph Series No. 61. New York, Nervous and Mental Disease Publishing Company, 1936.

BRUNSWICK, R. M.: "A Supplement to Freud's 'History of an Infantile Neurosis,' " *Internat. J. Psycho-Analysis*, 9:439, 1928.

DEUTSCH, H.: "On Female Homosexuality," *Psychoanalyt. Quart.*, 1:484, 1932.

————: *Psychoanalysis of the Neuroses*. London, Hogarth Press, 1932.

ENGLISH, O. S., and PEARSON, G. H. J.: *Common Neuroses of Children and Adults*. New York, W. W. Norton & Company, Inc., 1937.

FEDERN, P.: "Psychoanalysis of Psychoses, I–III," *Psychiatric Quart.*, 17:3, 246, 470, 1943.

FEIGENBAUM, D.: "Analysis of a Case of Paranoia Persecutoria: Structure and Cure," *Psychoanalyt. Rev.*, 17:159, 1930.

————: "Paranoia and Magic," *J. Nerv. & Ment. Dis.*, 72:28, 1930.

FENICHEL, O.: *The Psychoanalytic Theory of Neurosis*. New York, W. W. Norton & Company, Inc., 1945.

————: "The Psychology of Transvestism," *Internat. J. Psycho-Analysis*, 11:211, 1930.

————: "Remarks on Common Phobias," *Psychoanalyt. Quart.*, 13:313, 1944.

FERENCZI, S.: "Materialization in Globus Hystericus," in *Further Contributions to the Theory and Technique of Psycho-Analysis*. London, Hogarth Press, 1926, p. 104.

————: "On the Part Played by Homosexuality in the Pathogenesis of Paranoia," in *Contributions to Psycho-Analysis*. Boston, Richard G. Badger, 1916, p. 131.

————: "The Phenomena of Hysterical Materialization," in *Further Contributions to the Theory and Technique of Psycho-Analysis*. London, Hogarth Press, 1926, p. 89.

————: "Washing Compulsion and Masturbation," in *Further Contributions to the Theory and Technique of Psycho-Analysis*. London, Hogarth Press, 1926, p. 311.

FERENCZI, S., and HOLLOS, S.: *Psychoanalysis and the Psychic Disorder of General Paresis*. Nervous and Mental Disease Monograph Series No. 42. New York, Nervous and Mental Disease Publishing Company, 1925.

FREUD, A.: *The Ego and the Mechanisms of Defence*. London, Hogarth Press, 1937.

FREUD, S.: "The Aetiology of Hysteria," in *Collected Papers*, I. London, Hogarth Press, 1924, p. 183.

————: "Analysis of a Phobia in a Five-year-old Boy," in *Collected Papers*, III. London, Hogarth Press, 1925, p. 149.

————: "Certain Neurotic Mechanisms in Jealousy, Paranoia and Homosexuality," in *Collected Papers*, II. London, Hogarth Press, 1924, p. 232.

————: "Fragment of an Analysis of a Case of Hysteria," in *Collected Papers*, III. London, Hogarth Press, 1925, p. 13.

————: "From the History of an Infantile Neurosis," in *Collected Papers*, III. London, Hogarth Press, 1925, p. 473.

————: "Further Observations on the Defense-Neuro-Psychoses," in *Collected Papers,* I. London, Hogarth Press, 1924, p. 155.

FREUD, S.: *A General Introduction to Psychoanalysis.* New York, Boni & Liveright, Inc., 1920.

————: "General Remarks on Hysterical Attacks," in *Collected Papers,* II. London, Hogarth Press, 1924, p. 100.

————: "Heredity and the Aetiology of the Neuroses," in *Collected Papers,* I. London, Hogarth Press, 1924, p. 138.

————: *Inhibitions, Symptoms and Anxiety.* London, Hogarth Press, 1936.

————: "Neurosis and Psychosis," in *Collected Papers,* II. London, Hogarth Press, 1924, p. 250.

————: *New Introductory Lectures on Psycho-Analysis.* New York, W. W. Norton & Company, Inc., 1933.

————: "Notes upon a Case of Obsessional Neurosis," in *Collected Papers,* III. London, Hogarth Press, 1925, p. 296.

————: "Obsessions and Phobias. Their Physical Mechanisms and Their Aetiology," in *Collected Papers,* I. London, Hogarth Press, 1924, p. 128.

————: "Psycho-analytic Notes upon an Autobiographical Account of a Case of Paranoia," in *Collected Papers,* III. London, Hogarth Press, 1925, p. 390.

————: "The Psychogenesis of a Case of Homosexuality in a Woman," in *Collected Papers,* II. London, Hogarth Press, 1924, p. 202.

————: "Sexuality in the Aetiology of the Neurosis," in *Collected Papers,* I. London, Hogarth Press, 1924, p. 220.

————: "Some Character Types Met with in Psycho-Analytic Work," in *Collected Papers,* IV. London, Hogarth Press, 1925, p. 318.

FROMM-REICHMANN, F.: "Psychoanalytic Psychotherapy with Psychotics," *Psychiatry,* 6:277, 1943.

GRINKER, R. R., and SPIEGEL, J. P.: *Men under Stress.* Philadelphia, The Blakiston Company, 1945.

HARNIK, J.: "Introjection and Projection in the Mechanism of Depression," *Internat. J. Psycho-Analysis,* 13:425, 1932.

HINSIE, L. E.: *The Treatment of Schizophrenia.* Baltimore, William & Wilkins Company, 1930.

HITSCHMANN, E.: "Bemerkungen ueber Platzangst und andere neurotische Angstzustaende," *Internat. Ztschr. f. Psychoanal.*, 23: 393, 1937.

———: "Paranoia, Homosexualitaet und Analerotik," *Internat. Ztschr. f. aerztl. Psychoanal.*, 1:251, 1913.

———: "Urethral Erotism and Obsessional Neurosis," *Internat. J. Psycho-Analysis*, 4:118, 1923.

HITSCHMANN, E., and BERGLER, E. *Frigidity in Women. Its Characteristics and Treatment.* Nervous and Mental Disease Monograph Series No. 60. New York, Nervous and Mental Disease Publishing Company, 1936.

HOLLOS, I.: "Psychoanalytische Beleuchtung eines Falles von Dementia Praecox," *Internat. Ztschr. f. aerztl. Psychoanal.*, 2:367, 1914.

HORNEY, K.: *The Neurotic Personality of Our Time.* New York, W. W. Norton & Company, Inc., 1936.

KARDINER, A.: "The Bio-Analysis of the Epileptic Reaction," *Psychoanalyt. Quart.*, 1:375, 1932.

———: *The Traumatic Neuroses of War.* Psychosomatic Medicine Monograph, II–III. Washington, National Research Council, 1941.

KNIGHT, R. P.: "Psychotherapy of an Adolescent Catatonic Schizophrenia with Mutism," *Psychiatry*, 9:323, 1946.

———: "The Psychodynamics of Chronic Alcoholism," *J. Nerv. & Ment. Dis.*, 86:538, 1937.

———: "The Relationship of Latent Homosexuality to the Mechanism of Paranoid Delusions," *Bull. Menninger Clin.*, 4:149, 1940.

LANDAUER, K.: "Spontanheilung einer Katatonie," *Internat. Ztschr. f. aerztl. Psychoanal.*, 2:441, 1914.

LEWIN, B. D.: "Analysis and Structure of a Transient Hypomania," *Psychoanalyt. Quart.*, 1:43, 1932.

———: "Claustrophobia," *Psychoanalyt. Quart.*, 4:227, 1935.

———: "Comments on Hypomanic and Related States," *Psychoanalyt. Rev.*, 28:86, 1941.

LORAND, A. S.: "Dynamics and Therapy of Depressive States," *Psychoanalyt. Rev.*, 24:337, 1937.

LORAND, A. S.: "Fetishism in Statu Nascendi," *Internat. J. Psycho-Analysis,* 11:419, 1930.

MASSERMAN, J. H.: "Psychodynamism in Manic-depressive Psychoses," *Psychoanalyt. Rev.,* 28:466, 1941.

MENNINGER, K. A.: *Man against Himself.* New York, Harcourt, Brace and Company, Inc., 1938.

————: "Polysurgery and Polysurgic Addiction," *Psychoanalyt. Quart.,* 3:173, 1934.

————: "Psychoanalytic Aspect of Suicide," *Internat. J. Psycho-Analysis,* 14:376, 1933.

NUNBERG, H.: *Allgemeine Neurosenlehre auf Psychoanalytischer Grundlage.* Bern, Hans Huber, 1932.

————: "Ueber den Katatonischen Anfall," *Internat. Ztschr. f. Psychoanal.,* 6:25, 1920.

————: "Der Verlauf des Libidokonfliktes in einem Fall von Schizophrenie," *Internat. Ztschr. f. Psychoanal.,* 7:301, 1921.

OPHUIJSEN, J. H. W. VAN: "On the Origin of the Feeling of Persecution," *Internat. J. Psycho-Analysis,* 1:235, 1920.

RADO, S.: "An Anxious Mother," *Internat. J. Psycho-Analysis,* 9:219, 1928.

————: "The Economic Principle in Psychoanalytic Technique," *Internat. J. Psycho-Analysis,* 6:351, 1925.

————: "Pathodynamics and Treatment of Traumatic War Neurosis," *Psychosom. Med.,* 4:362, 1942.

————: "The Problem of Melancholia," *Internat. J. Psycho-Analysis,* 9:420, 1928.

————: "The Psychic Effects of Intoxicants: An Attempt to Evolve a Psycho-analytical Theory of Morbid Cravings," *Internat. J. Psycho-Analysis,* 7:396, 1926.

————: "The Psychoanalysis of Pharmacothymia," *Psychoanalyt. Quart.,* 2:1, 1933.

REICH, W.: *Der triebhafte Character.* Wien, Internationaler Psychoanalytischer Verlag, 1925.

————: "Ueber Characteranalyse," *Internat. Ztschr. f. Psychoanal.,* 14:180, 1928.

ROSEN, J. N.: "The Treatment of Schizophrenic Psychosis by Direct Analytic Therapy," *Psychiatric Quart.,* 21:3, 117, 1947.

SACHS, H.: "Zur Genese der Perversionen," *Internat. Ztschr. f. Psychoanal.,* 9:172, 1923.

SADGER, J.: "A Contribution to the Understanding of Sado-Masochism," *Internat. J. Psycho-Analysis,* 7:484, 1926.

SCHILDER, P.: *Introduction to a Psychoanalytic Psychiatry.* Nervous and Mental Disease Monograph Series No. 50. New York, Nervous and Mental Disease Publishing Company, 1928.

SILVERBERG, W. V.: "The Personal Basis and Social Significance of Passive Male Homosexuality," *Psychiatry,* 1:41, 1938.

SIMMEL, E.: *Kriegsneurosen und psychisches Trauma, ihre gegenseitigen Beziehungen, dargestellt auf Grund psycho-analytischer und hypnotischer Studien.* Muenchen, Otto Nemnich, 1918.

STAERCKE, A.: "The Reversal of the Libido-Sign in Delusions of Persecution," *Internat. J. Psycho-Analysis,* 1:231, 1920.

SULLIVAN, H. S.: "Conceptions of Modern Psychiatry" (The First William Alanson White Memorial Lectures), *Psychiatry,* 3:1, 1940.

———: *Proceedings of the Second Colloquium on Personality Investigation.* Baltimore, Johns Hopkins Press, 1930, pp. 46, 47, 107.

TAUSK, V.: "On the Origin of the 'Influencing Machine' in Schizophrenia," *Psychoanalyt. Quart.,* 2:519, 1933.

WEIGERT-VOWINCKEL, E.: "A Contribution to the Theory of Schizophrenia," *Internat. J. Psycho-Analysis,* 17:190, 1936.

WITTELS, F.: *Die Welt ohne Zuchthaus.* Stuttgart, Hippokrates Verlag, 1928.

ZILBOORG, G.: "Affective Reintegration in the Schizophrenias," *Arch. Neurol. & Psychiat.,* 24:335, 1930.

———: "Ambulatory Schizophrenias," *Psychiatry,* 4:149, 1941.

Chapter X

The Principles of
Psychoanalytic Therapy

IN THIS CHAPTER no attempt is made to present the development of psychoanalytic therapy historically, since this has been done in other publications. Only the basic therapeutic principles are described here and their special application briefly considered.

Psychoanalytic therapy aims at repairing ego functions the weakness of which manifests itself in neuroses and behavior disorders.

It has been stated before that a neurosis is not an absolute characteristic of an individual but the result of interaction with the environment. A person might become neurotic in one environment and remain healthy in another. Adjustment can at least theoretically be achieved either by changing the person to fit his environment or by changing the environment to fit the person.

An important factor discussed previously is the ability to adjust to different environmental conditions. Less adaptability does not necessarily mean that a person will develop a neurosis, because his inflexibility may remain unchallenged by life. He will, however, be more likely to develop a neurosis than one who can adjust himself flexibly to changing conditions. Persons who are inflexible might therefore be described as potential neurotics. Early traumatic experiences resulting in fixation and retarded emotional development cause most severe chronic neuroses, but some neuroses are occasioned by trying situations in later life. These are the more acute cases and are most amenable to therapy.

Psychoanalysis was at first applied almost exclusively to severe chronic neuroses the victims of which consulted a psychoanalyst as a last resort. With a more general acceptance of psychoanalysis, both the mild and the acute cases were treated by this method. The war necessitated the psychoanalysis of many patients who in ordinary life would probably not have developed pronounced symptoms. This greater variety of patients encouraged flexibility in the therapeutic application of psychoanalytic principles. In this chapter we shall describe the application of basic psychoanalytic principles to all kinds of neurosis. It is a matter of definition whether or not only the original method applied to chronic cases should be called psychoanalysis. We shall take the position that psychoanalytic principles lend themselves to different therapeutic procedures which vary according to the nature of the case and may be variably applied during the treatment of the same patient.

Certain therapeutic factors are constant in all forms of psychotherapy.

1. UNIVERSAL FACTORS IN PSYCHOTHERAPY

EMOTIONAL SUPPORT

Neurosis implies an inadequate substitution of symptoms for realistic gratifications, and frustration is one of its inevitable results. Because symptoms represent regression to earlier forms of gratification, the early conflicts connected with them are aroused. This results in anxiety and guilt, which other symptoms attempt to relieve by self-punishment. Frustration results from the inadequacy of substitutive gratifications, and suffering is the response to guilt, which arouses a need for punishment. Because of frustration and suffering the patient feels the need for help. In therapy he hopes for relief and finds opportunity to gratify some of his regressive need for dependence. This may reduce the need for gratification through symptoms. This explains why all forms of treatment in which the physician offers help and gives emotional support may have a therapeutic effect.

INTELLECTUAL SUPPORT

Because of anxiety and a preoccupation with his symptoms, the patient is unable to handle adequately the practical problems of life. Here the therapist gives emotional support and reduces anxiety so that the patient may use his own intellectual capacities to handle practical problems. By giving the patient an opportunity to discuss his problems objectively the therapist further contributes to their intellectual clarification.

Emotional and intellectual support is to some degree present in all forms of treatment. It results from the therapeutic situation itself, independently of the special techniques employed, provided the therapist instills confidence in his patient and listens with benevolent understanding to his patient's complaints.

In acute cases in which the neurotic disturbance is merely a reaction to a current situation, this support is sometimes sufficient to strengthen the failing functions of the ego.

EMOTIONAL DISCHARGE

In addition to emotional and intellectual support, every form of psychotherapy gives the patient an opportunity to express his emotions. This in itself relieves emotional tension and prepares the way for insight. The patient becomes capable of talking about his problem more objectively and of looking upon it from a distance.

The diagnostic appraisal of the case and therapeutic trials will decide whether more penetrating work is needed. This requires psychoanalytic competence, although the treatment indicated may not be analytic. Emotional support, the intellectual clarification of the patient's actual problem, and emotional abreaction in themselves do not necessarily require the application of the specific principles of psychoanalysis.

OTHER SUPPORTIVE MEASURES

There are other supportive measures, which are not discussed here in detail because they are not common to all forms of psychotherapy, both the psychoanalytic and the non-psychoanalytic. These measures consist in aiding the existing ego-defenses when they begin to fail. Inferiority feelings, for example, are dealt with by reassurance, guilt feelings by absolving the patient and supporting his attempts at self-justification. These measures can be called *repressive measures* (Knight); they are used in severe cases in which the therapist does not consider the patient's ego capable of withstanding any uncovering approach requiring insight.

2. PSYCHOANALYTIC TREATMENT

Psychoanalysis aims to effect permanent changes in the personality by increasing the ego's integrative power. If this is only temporarily impaired by emotional stress, it is usually sufficient to reduce the emotional tension by temporary support and by giving an opportunity for abreaction. Psychoanalysis, however, tries to change the ego by exposing it to conflictful and repressed material within the personality. It requires both intellectual insight into unresolved conflicts and their emotional rehearsal. In different phases of the historical development of psychoanalysis intellectual and emotional factors have been variously emphasized. When Freud first experimented with cathartic hypnosis, the emotional component was stressed. Then followed a period in which the intellectual reconstruction of the origins of the disease was given special prominence. After Freud discovered the significance of the patient's emotional reactions toward the therapist, the transference, emphasis was placed again on the emotions. Ferenczi and Rank, in a remarkable brochure published in 1925, elaborated consistently the significance of the emotional content of the transference. On account of certain erroneous conclusions contained in this brochure, it has long been neglected. The Chicago Psychoanalytic Institute's experiments with therapy have resurveyed the therapeutic process and re-emphasized the significance of emotional experiences during treatment, both in the transference and outside of the therapeutic situation, as the main therapeutic factor. Modern psychoanalytic therapy relies mainly on the handling of the transference.

INTRODUCTION TO THE TREATMENT

Before discussing details we shall have to describe briefly the whole procedure. As in all forms of medicine, the physician must first diagnose the patient's condition before he can plan the treatment. Psychoanalytic diagnosis requires a psychodynamic understanding of the patient's condition. The psychoanalyst, like the surgeon, cannot be sure in the initial diagnosis of what he will ultimately find, and he must modify his views to fit his discoveries in penetrating the unconscious layers of the personality. To gain a preliminary view of a patient's illness several anamnestic interviews are usually necessary. In these the patient is asked to describe his complaint, its origin, and any outstanding facts in his past development and present circumstances that he may feel to be important. It is a great mistake to begin with free associations before a general picture of his illness, personality, and history has been obtained in preliminary interviews. Even in preliminary interviews, however, if spontaneity is encouraged in the patient, better insight will accrue to the therapist. There are always gaps in the story; these must be filled in by direct questioning so that before the actual treatment begins the physician will have a reasonable notion of the patient's history and of the present circumstances of his illness and its beginning. The experienced analyst has usually no difficulty in obtaining from a neurotic patient a general view in a few preliminary interviews. In many cases it is helpful to receive information also from persons who play important roles in the patient's life and are interested in helping him. It is impossible to indicate in which cases initial interviews with others are advisable and in which they must be avoided in order not to interfere with the patient's confidence in the therapist. The nearer a patient's condition is to a psychosis, the more necessary it is to resort to the patient's relatives and associates. Only after the therapist has gained a comprehensive view of the patient's illness and personality can he proceed to the next step, free association.

THE METHOD OF FREE ASSOCIATION

In free association the therapist is counting on the tendency of the unconscious to betray its repressed content. The patient is asked to abandon conscious control of his ideas and give in to free spontaneous association. Once this is done the repressed tendencies begin to come into the open. Freud at first tried to eliminate conscious control by hypnosis. In free association hypnosis is replaced by a partial elimination of control. Gradually, in long and frequent interviews, the patient will reveal more and more of his hitherto repressed tendencies. This self-revealing process may be greatly encouraged by the therapist's objective attitude toward the experiences, desires, ideas, and tendencies which the patient had been unable to admit to himself because of their objectionable character. He learns that the therapist's only interest is to understand why the patient has felt or feels in a particular way, and this encourages self-revelation. The whole procedure is based upon theoretical views which have been discussed in preceding chapters.

The ego of the adult psychoneurotic, which is usually well developed, could easily digest and modify the original tendencies and could also renounce some of them if it only knew about them. Through repression, however, the ego is separated from the instinctual life, and this situation is reflected in the diminished amount of freely dispensable mental energy in the neurotic personality. Repression is a more comfortable way of controlling unadjusted tendencies than conscious rejection, denial, or modification, but it is too radical a method. The price which the neurotic pays for this comfort is his mental health, and it is too high. He spares himself the painful struggle between temptation and its denial, but in doing so he sacrifices most of his freely dispensable mental energy.

The technique of psychoanalytic therapy follows from these premises. The therapy aims at replacing the automatic restrictions of repression by conscious judgment. Wide therapeutic experience has shown that this can be undertaken with psychoneurotics without danger, for their egos are capable of controlling their instinctual life if they establish contact with it. Naturally, the removal of repression burdens the conscious personality with painful insight and new problems which create conscious conflict. It also increases the responsibility of the conscious personality by extending its activity over hitherto unconscious portions of mental life. This, however, is the only way of changing those dynamic conditions in the personality which cause psychoneuroses.

As long as tendencies remain unconscious they cannot undergo modification and sublimation, because sublimation is precisely the result of the interplay between original drives and the environment and of adjustment to external reality. The conscious ego is the portion of the personality which is in touch with the environment. All instinctual demands and wishes excluded from consciousness remain, therefore, infantile and isolated from environmental influences, since they cannot undergo those transformations which we call adjustment to reality. Repression makes the adjustment of instincts impossible. When it has been overcome the ego can modify and sublimate the mental energy expended on psychoneurotic symptoms.

It has been mentioned that the important psychodynamic factor in free association is that conscious control over trains of association is eliminated. The effect of this can be roughly described. In excluding certain tendencies from consciousness there is, in addition to unconscious repression, a conscious and voluntary selective process, called "suppression," which eliminates everything even loosely connected with unconscious material. Suppression also eliminates all kinds of irrelevancies which would distract attention from the topic which is at the focus of interest at any given moment. The elimination of conscious control over trains of thought is a technique easy to acquire and is, in fact, nothing but overcoming suppression. When this is done, the unconscious has to contend only with repression, and unconscious material may therefore enter consciousness. The situation is analogous to that of a spring compressed by two weights. If one weight is removed, the spring will expand.

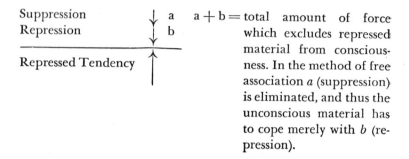

Suppression — a   a + b = total amount of force which excludes repressed material from consciousness. In the method of free association *a* (suppression) is eliminated, and thus the unconscious material has to cope merely with *b* (repression).

Repression — b

Repressed Tendency

THE TRANSFERENCE

It is only natural that the neurotic patient will sooner or later direct his typical neurotic attitudes toward his therapist. In psychoanalysis this repetition of neurotic reactions is favored by the therapist's encouraging the patient to be himself as much as he can during the interviews. Free association is by no means merely an intellectual procedure for the patient, because he is increasingly encouraged to express repressed emotions and turn them toward the analyst. In a sense, the process of growing up is reversed in analytic treatment. Much of the process of growing up is based on repressing attitudes incompatible with maturity. The ideal development of a personality would consist of gradually modifying, transforming, and utilizing in a new and acceptable form the original emotional tendency so that nothing has to be drastically repressed. This, however, never occurs even in the best-adjusted persons. Many infantile emotional reactions are repressed and conserved in unaltered form in the unconscious. In the conscious personality only the defenses by which they are kept in check and out of consciousness are observable. It is important to keep in mind that repressions have taken place, in the last analysis, as a result of parental disapproval. In the course of analytic treatment, because of the prevailing permissive atmosphere, these emotional factors which have been repressed or at least checked by inhibitions are encouraged to free expression. The analyst is the natural target for these regressive emotions. The core of these reactions is a dependent attitude. This is only natural, because the patient comes for help from someone in whom he places his confidence. The patient's conscious ego defends itself in different ways against these dependent wishes. It may overcompensate for them with an aggressiveness by which it tries to eliminate the sense of inferiority caused by extreme dependence. These aggressive hostile reactions again may cause guilt, which in turn may lead to provocative behavior or to a masochistic distortion of the analytic situation. The patient does not feel guilty if he can provoke the analyst to express his impatience or if he succeeds in interpreting the treatment as a method of torture. The hostile impulses may also be turned against the analyst or turned against the patient's self, leading to depressive manifestations. In each case the reaction of the ego to the emotional conflicts aroused by the analytic process is characteristic of the patient, and it takes different forms in the different types of neurosis. The paranoid patient uses projection. The depressive patient turns his hostility against himself. The neurotic character begins to act them out in relation to the analyst or outside the analytic situation. The compulsive neurotic defends himself against his ambivalence by intellectualizing and standardizing the treatment, thus making it a ritual. In anxiety neurosis the therapy may temporarily even increase anxiety.

This repetition of neurotic patterns in relation to the therapist is called the transference neurosis. Its resolution is considered the essence of psychoanalytic therapy, which consists roughly of two parts: (1) the development of the transference neurosis, and (2) its resolution. Assuming a tolerant attitude and avoiding any evaluation of the patient's material suffices after a time to encourage the development of a transference neurosis. It requires no particular activity on the part of the analyst; the prevailing neurotic tendencies within the patient take their free course and express themselves uninhibitedly.

The real therapeutic problem is the resolution of the transference neurosis. In my opinion we are still improving techniques of handling the transference neurosis, and principles suggested here are not final.

In Freud's early view the transference neurosis is a less intensive repetition of the original neurotic pattern and contains its infantile reactions but is experienced in relationship to the therapist. Its intensity is reduced because the transference emotions are reactions to previous situations and not to the actual patient-physician relation. The only actual relationship between the patient and doctor is the fact that the patient comes to the physician for help. When in the patient's mind the therapist assumes the role of the father, mother, or older or younger sibling, he is actually none of these, and the transference relationship reflects the distortions in the patient's fantasies of the real situation. The nonpsychotic patient whose ego retains its capacity to test is aware of the imaginary character of the transference, and this serves to reduce its intensity. Infantile conflicts are viewed openly in the personal relations with the analyst and are faced by the adult ego. Originally, when they were first repressed, the child's weak ego could not cope with them. These quantitative factors, the stronger adult ego facing a weaker edition of the original conflicts, constitute the dynamic basis for the treatment.

These views have been proved by many years of experience. But there are other important considerations which enable the therapist to meet the difficult problem of dissolving the transference neurosis. All these therapeutic factors are quantitative and have been used intuitively by analysts, but they have only recently been suggested as integral parts of the psychoanalytic treatment.

QUANTITATIVE FACTORS IN THERAPY

It has often been stated that the transference should be on an optimal level. If the emotional involvement of the patient is insufficient, the treatment may be greatly retarded and the analysis may become an intellectual exercise. If, however, the transference neurosis becomes too intense, the patient's ego may face a situation similar to the one it could not meet originally. He will then be unable to exchange his neurotic pattern for one more healthy and mature. The ego's integrative functions are impeded by excessive emotion. Too violent anxiety, rage, or guilt may become so formidable that the ego's co-ordinating functions cannot master them. The problem is how to keep the transference on an optimal level.

a. Frequency of Interviews

Experience shows that the transference neurosis develops spontaneously as the result of continued contact with the therapist. The outlook for a prolonged treatment favors the patient's procrastination and disinclination to face the problems from which he escaped into neurosis. The transference neurosis soon loses many of the unpleasant features of the original neurosis because it is seen to be a necessary part of the treatment and the conflicts provoked by the regressive tendencies are reduced by the analyst's attitude. This allows the patient to be neurotic during treatment without too much conflict. It must be remembered that the transference neurosis develops naturally and that effort is required on the part of the therapist to counteract it. Reducing the frequency of interviews is one of the simplest means of preventing the transference from becoming too powerful an outlet for the patient's neurosis; if the dependent tendencies are frustrated, they are thrown into relief and the patient is compelled to resist them consciously.

It is unwise to generalize; experience and skill are required to estimate when and how to reduce the frequency of the sessions. In many cases it is advisable to see the patient once, twice, or three times a week instead of daily to prevent too much dependence.

b. Interruptions

In the early twenties Eitingon's experiments with interrupted analyses were made in the outpatient clinic of the Berlin Psychoanalytic Institute. Since then this device has been tested systematically in the Chicago Institute for Psychoanalysis.

Interruptions of shorter or longer duration, if correctly timed, increase the patient's confidence in applying what he has learned during his treatment. The neurotic is inclined to sidestep renewed attempts to cope with life, and he retreats into fantasy and forms symptoms. During the intervals in which his analysis is interrupted, the patient translates his insight into practice without the help of his therapist. This counteracts the tendency of the patient to postpone the solution of his problem. It is one of the strongest checks against perpetuating the transference neurosis. Interruptions must usually be imposed tentatively, since there is no clear indication when the patient is ready to accept them without relapsing.

c. Extra-analytic Experience

It must be remembered that an analysis is not a substitute for the patient's ordinary life but a complement to it. His other relationships continue as before. Many of his neurotic needs will be met in the transference, and this may permit him to behave more rationally outside.

One of the most effective ways of counteracting the patient's tendency to perpetuate a comfortable transference neurosis is to encourage experiences parallel with those which occur within the transference. The therapist must constantly direct the patient's attention to his outside relationships and not allow him to withdraw completely into the therapeutic situation. The patient comes to the therapist with actual problems, and to allow him to evade them would encourage him to retreat from life into the ivory tower of transference. It is an error to suppose that a patient may postpone the solution of his real problems for months or years, withdraw into the world of the transference, and suddenly return, successfully adjusted, to the world of reality. If the patient works through his resistances he becomes able to express his neurotic inclinations more and more frankly in the transference. This does not mean, however, that he has learned to modify them. This is the real therapeutic problem. The analytic process cannot be divided rigidly into two parts, the first of which encourages the transference and the second of which forces a return to actuality with modified attitudes. The two must take place more or less simultaneously. It is therefore very important to encourage similar experiences within and outside the analysis at the same time. When the patient changes his neurotic pattern toward the analysis—if, for example he dares, contrary to his previous attitude, to express his opinions freely and renounce his dependence—the same behavior should be encouraged outside toward an employer, a father, or an older brother. Steady pressure must be exerted on the patient to apply every analytic gain to his life outside the analysis. This takes place to some degree automatically, but the neurotic's tendency is to delay the attack upon his actual problems. This is what made him neurotic. To increase the ego's self-confidence and thus counteract regression is one of the main therapeutic problems, and it can be solved only in actual practice, not by words alone.

CORRECTIVE EMOTIONAL EXPERIENCE

It must be clear by now that the essence of psychoanalytic therapy consists in exposing the conscious ego to the repressed emotions which underlie the neurosis and in teaching it how to reconcile them with internal and external conditions.

It would be a mistake, however, to consider this learning primarily an intellectual process. It is usually easy for the patient to figure out what would be the rational and healthy emotional reaction to any given situation. He cannot apply this knowledge because of his anxiety, lack of confidence, guilt or intense hatred, or possessive love. Therapy may be compared to a kind of emotional gymnastics; the ego is repeatedly exposed to its crucial emotional conflicts, reduced in intensity, until the patient finally begins to act differently.

An important consideration in this connection has only recently been emphasized. Neurotic patterns do not develop in a vacuum. They are adaptive reactions to parental attitudes. The simplest example is the repression of self-assertive and aggressive attitudes, due to parental intimidation, which encourages dependence and causes all kinds of inhibitions in human relationships. When the early conflictful relationship is repeated in the transference, the therapist's attitude must reverse that of the intimidating parent. He can be objective and understanding because he is not emotionally involved, and this permits the patient to express himself more freely. The parental intimidation is corrected by the more tolerant and sympathetic attitude of the therapist, who replaces the authoritarian parents in the patient's mind. As the patient realizes that his modest self-assertion will not be punished, he will experiment more boldly. At the same time he can express himself more freely toward persons in authority in his present life. This increases the ego's capacity to deal with aggressive attitudes which anxiety had previously repressed. It is actually a much more complicated process, but this simple example may explain the principle of corrective emotional experience. The same principle is applied, *mutatis mutandis*, to cases of parental overindulgence.

To summarize, the principle of corrective emotional experience is a consciously planned regulation of the therapist's own emotional responses to the patient's material (countertransference) in such a way as to counteract the harmful effects of the parental attitudes.

THE THERAPEUTIC IMPORTANCE OF RECOVERED MEMORIES

Before Freud recognized the significance of the transference but after he had abandoned hypnosis, his main interest lay in reconstructing the early emotional development by resolving what he called the "infantile amnesia." In cathartic hypnosis, patients can remember forgotten events connected with the repressed emotions underlying their symptoms. When Freud substituted free association for hypnosis he tried to make the patient recall such memories when awake. It was natural that his interest was focused at this time upon the genetic understanding of neurosis and personality development in general. He had first to understand the natural history of neuroses. He supposed that the course of his investigations set also the course of therapy. Both required recovery of forgotten memories, and this became for a time the main therapeutic device. He came only gradually to realize the therapeutic significance of transference and the importance of the patient's reliving, not merely recalling, his early conflicts. His first impression, however, was so strong that the belief in the primary therapeutic significance of genetic reconstruction was perpetuated.

We now know that the recovery of memories is a sign of improvement rather than its cause. As the ego's capacity to deal with repressed emotions increases through experience in the transference, the patient is able to remember events repressed because of their similar emotional connotations. The ability to remember shows the ego's increased capacity to face certain types of psychological content. This change in the ego is achieved through the emotional experiences of the treatment—although it cannot be denied that remembering and understanding the origin of neurotic patterns has also a therapeutic significance and helps the reintegration of repressed psychological content into the total personality.

INTELLECTUAL INSIGHT

It is difficult to make general statements about the therapeutic effectiveness of a patient's insight into the nature and origins of his disease. It was customary to distinguish three therapeutic factors—abreaction, insight, and "working through." *Abreaction* means the free expression of repressed emotions. *Insight* was considered to be effective only when it coincided with emotional abreaction. As Freud expressed it, "An enemy cannot be licked who is not seen." The patient must feel what he understands. Otherwise he could be cured by a textbook. *Working through* describes the repetition of all the details of the emotional pattern, including abreaction and insight, during analysis, when the ego's defense measures are gradually reduced. It consists of experiencing and understanding each aspect of the neurosis as it is revealed under treatment and as the patient's resistance to self-expression diminishes.

Often quite definite changes in the emotional pattern can

be observed in patients without intellectual formulation by the analyst or patient. The corrective emotional experience in the transference alone may produce lasting therapeutic results. A purely intellectual understanding of the neurosis has seldom much therapeutic effect. Too sweeping generalizations should, however, be avoided. As a rule intellectual insight based on and combined with emotional experiences stabilizes emotional gains and complements corrective emotional experience. Moreover, intellectual insight through interpretation facilitates and prepares the way for emotional experience. Understanding gives the patient the feeling of mastery and encourages emotional expression. The ego is prepared to face repressed emotions, knows their nature in advance, and is not taken by surprise when they actually appear in consciousness. Intellectualization should, however, not be carried too far. Interpretation of content can actually retard the analysis, especially of obsessive and compulsive neurotics. The substitution of understanding for feeling is a characteristic defense of the compulsive personality. In these cases every effort must be made to have the patient experience his basic ambivalence emotionally and to promote corrective emotional experience by definite well-planned attitudes of the therapist.

DREAM INTERPRETATION IN PSYCHOANALYTIC THERAPY

Psychoanalysis by its very nature mobilizes repressed forces. The whole therapy is based on the expression of repressed desires, ideas, and trends. Only in this way can their reintegration be achieved.

Dreams express externally or internally frustrated desires and guilt with which the patient reacts to his alien tendencies. It is only natural that a treatment which mobilizes repressed material will stimulate dreams. Many patients who maintain that they almost never dream or cannot remember their dreams begin under analytic treatment to report dreams in every interview. The study of these dreams gives direct access to unconscious content.

The significance of the first dream reported by a patient has often been stressed. The patient comes to the therapist for help and learns that he can obtain this only by revealing the most intimate details of his life. He is caught between this necessity and his resistance to exposing material which he has not been able to admit even to himself. The first dream is often a product of this conflict. The following example reported after a preliminary interview may serve as an illustration.

The patient was a young student who had been sent by his father to a university away from home. He had been unable to work and idled about for a long time. He stayed in bed until noon reading cheap detective stories and in the afternoon frequented poolrooms and played billiards but had no significant social contacts or relations with girls. He lived an entirely purposeless life. He would have been called extremely lazy, but his laziness was the expression of a latent compulsion neurosis. In preliminary discussion he justified his idleness by a peculiar argument. He stated that his father had never loved or cared for him and had never given him anything of value. Since his laziness was the result of bad education, his father must now suffer the consequences and support him. He felt no obligation to become independent. This picture obviously did not present the whole truth, or he would never have called on me. His argument was a rationalization of his compulsive laziness in which he felt depressed and despairing. He began his first analytic session by reporting the following dream:

"I wanted to sell my diamond ring but the jeweler, after testing the stone, declared it was false." He immediately remarked that the dream was silly because he knew that his ring was genuine. In the course of further associations it transpired that the ring was a present from his father.

The content of this dream could not be understood as the fulfillment of a wish without knowledge of the patient's attitude toward his father. His favorite formula was, "I never received anything of value from my father, so I do not need to exert myself. My father wants me to study, but I owe him nothing." His belief in this assertion was necessary to excuse his laziness and passive attitude toward life. The diamond ring which he had received from his father was of real value. He proved in the dream, however, that even this present from his father was false. He began his analysis by defending his conduct. The significance of this dream lies in the fact that he had it after he had made up his mind to start analysis. It was a sign of resistance, since in the dream he wanted to prove the truth of his theory of life which the analysis might destroy.

It was almost a year later that I could make use of this dream which expressed the patient's basic neurotic pattern. He was forced by external circumstances to break off his analysis a week after he had begun because he had to move to another city. I advised him to continue with a colleague who lived there. Six months later he returned to me, but I had no time and proposed another colleague. A few months later he appeared again in my office and declared that he was unable to continue with the analyst I had recommended to him because he felt that this analyst disliked, indeed hated him, although he could complain of no bad treatment. On the contrary, the analyst was always kind and polite to him and denied any negative feelings toward the patient. He felt, however, that his kindness was merely a mask which covered the analyst's genuine feelings. He asked me to resume his treatment, and I rang up my colleague and asked his opinion. To my surprise he corroborated the patient's statement that he really felt a strong aversion to him. He had tried to conceal his feeling but without success, and begged me to continue the analysis. I agreed, and soon after I began the treatment I understood my colleague's feelings. The patient was really the most disagreeable person imaginable. He usually came unwashed, unshaven, and unbrushed to the analysis, bit his nails, spoke in a scarcely intelligible mumble, criticized everything, and paid a very low fee. If I kept him waiting a minute he immediately accused me of doing so because he paid less than others. He was unpleasant in every possible way, and it was difficult to like him. One day I happened to answer in a somewhat impatient tone. He jumped up from the couch and exclaimed, "You are just like your colleague. Do you deny that you dislike me and do you call it analysis being impatient with your analysand?" I answered, "Well, you are right, but I must ask you how you can expect anyone to like you when you behave as you do. Do you think that an analyst has no genuine emotions and reactions?" I then explained to him that his whole behavior was calculated to provoke me, to make me dislike him and to establish the same relation with me which he had had in his youth with his father. He wanted to prove that the analyst did not like him, just as he had thought his father had not, and that he had not received anything of value from the analyst. Finally I reminded him of the first dream about the diamond ring in which he had wanted to prove that the ring, his father's present, was false. This emotional experience and the interpretation was the turning point in a difficult treatment, which could then be continued to a successful end.

The greater part of the treatment often consists in a kind of dialogue between the analyst and the patient's unconscious. If the analyst's interpretation of a dream is still unacceptable to the patient's ego, he may respond with another dream which rejects the insight provided. The nature of the denial may give the therapist valuable clues to the character of the patient's resistance.

An example may illustrate this more concretely. The patient was a fifty-year-old physician who was suffering from a severe compulsion neurosis and phobia. He was an excellent physician, very able, and only his neurosis was responsible for the mediocrity of his medical career. He had an extensive practice in a poor district of the city. In an early interview we discussed his relationship to his older brother. He spoke about him in a tone of great respect and admiration, emphasizing the fact that his brother had always been very good to him. He was a businessman who had made much money and had helped my patient generously and tactfully. He had, for example, invited my patient to invest money in his business and paid him a very high rate of interest. In point of fact the business did not need any more capital, but in this way he could help his brother while giving the appearance of receiving instead of doing a favor. My patient had conscientious scruples in accepting this masked financial aid and had often considered whether he should not put an end to it. In other respects also he had guilt toward his brother, which he displayed in many ways during his analysis.

I tried to make him conscious of the repressed motives which lay behind his bad conscience about his brother. I pointed out that he envied his successful brother and that even in childhood he had regarded him as a competitor. He denied this and would not admit any hostile feeling. He emphasized again and again his positive feelings of gratitude toward his brother. Nevertheless my interpretation aroused guilt, and in the next hour he responded to it with the following dream:

"I meet my colleague N. on the street, and he asks me to substitute for him and see a very prominent patient of his, who is a senator." I asked him to associate to substituting for a colleague in his practice and he answered: "Oh, that is a thankless job; it is a favor which you have to do if a friend asks you, but for my part I don't like it at all." Then I asked him to talk about his colleague and learned from his associations that N. was a very prominent physician, an old friend and schoolmate of my patient, and had had much greater success than he. He lived in a fashionable district, and as time went on they had seen less and less of each other.

I then explained to him that the dream was an expression of a repressed envy felt toward his colleague. In the dream this colleague asks him to see one of his patients, but in reality he would like to have his colleague's practice. He disguises this wish in the dream by making his colleague ask him a favor and so represents his real wish to take away his colleague's practice by a favor. At first my patient would not accept this interpretation and defended himself by the same arguments which he had used in the dream, namely, that substituting for his colleague was a very disagreeable task. But on further discussion he gradually admitted that he felt it to be an injustice that his colleague with his inferior knowledge had a fine practice and that he often compared himself with him and thought that he deserved the greater success. After he had become conscious of his repressed envy toward his friend N., I was able to return to a topic discussed in a previous analytic session, the relation of my patient to his older brother. I showed him that he had displaced the whole conflict from his older brother to his colleague because his feelings toward the latter were similar but less objectionable. The advantage of this displacement was evident. The emotional conflict with his colleague was identical in quality but much less intense. It was less objectionable to envy a colleague than to envy his own brother, who had always helped him and been so good to him. His colleague N. behaved in the dream in the same way as his brother had in reality. He referred to him a very desirable patient but arranged it so as to appear that he was asking a favor. By the interpretation of this dream I gained much ground in exposing his envy of both his colleague and his brother. I could thus convince him at least intellectually that the guilt toward his brother was based on repressed hostility and envy. In the next hours he produced confirmatory material from childhood concerning his competition with his older brother.

Dreams provide the best possible estimate of the psycho-dynamic situation at every phase of the treatment. They even reveal the relative strength of the conflict in the ego's increasing capacity to face hitherto repressed material and indicate the degree of the progress effected by the treatment.

Dream sequences in analysis disclose the progressive integrative accomplishments of the ego that French has called the dream's *problem-solving function.* He illustrates this by citing two dreams from an analysis by a woman.

The first was the first dream in the patient's analysis. It was reported in the tenth analytic hour. In the first hours of his analysis the patient had found it difficult to talk freely about personal matters and was very uncomfortable because of severe asthmatic wheezing. In the sixth hour he experienced much relief when he was finally able to voice freely his resentment against his wife, who, he complained, was fat, sloppy, and quarrelsome and neglected her two children and himself.

In the ninth hour, the analyst expressed an interest in dreams, and in the tenth hour the patient reported the following dream, prefacing it with the remark, "This is what you want."

"I dreamed of my school days. One week end I was going home, for we always walked unless someone picked us up. I walked alone until I got to a bridge. A girl was there leaning on the bridge watching the boats. I stopped and pinched her on the back and we walked on home. Dusk came on. Her mother met her and thanked me and asked me in and gave me a glass of milk."

The other dream, reported six weeks later, deals more plainly with the same problem. "I was walking along a street. A lot of people were digging up the surface of the street. I reached a corner and saw a girl who seemed at first like a child. She was carrying a big milk can full of water. She was standing at a fireplug and asked me to help her carry the can home. She then turned into a grown woman. I carried one side of the can and we carried it home. She thanked me and offered me a kiss. I kissed and embraced her and woke up." Later he added, "While we were embracing her mother called her and we broke away and I went home."

Without citing the associations it is evident that in this dream the patient is in conflict between sexual impulses and fear of the disapproval of a mother. It is clear that in the earlier dream the conflict was also one between sexual wishes and fear of the mother's disapproval. Evidently sexual impulses were aroused by this treatment by a woman therapist and provoked the conflict in each case. Although the basic conflict is the same in the two dreams, it will be noticed that in the second dream the patient acts upon his sexual impulses more boldly. In the second dream it is only after he has kissed the girl that the fear of the mother emerges and induces him to let the girl return to her mother. In the earlier dream he interrupts his erotic overtures immediately after a playful pinch and escorts the girl home to her mother.

In this difference the patient's increased confidence in the analyst's kindly and nonpunitive attitude can be seen.

The patient may continue to defend himself against the insight opened by the analysis and try to veil this insight by different means of self-deception. The analyst counteracts this tendency by a persistent correction of all these self-deceptions. As the patient's insight increases, it becomes increasingly difficult for him to ignore it. "The voice of the intellect is soft, but persistent" (Freud). How this struggle against insight is reflected in dreams has been illustrated above by a dream expressing the ego's resistance to an interpretation which the patient was not yet ready to accept. As the analytic process advances, the neurotic conflict under the pressure of insight becomes more and more circumscribed and isolated from the rest of the personality in a process which can be compared with sequestration.

The following example may illustrate this. A patient, after analytic sessions in which he had been forced to recognize his repressed acquisitiveness, dozed off in a hypnagogic state and had a fantasy that in the neighbor's courtyard there was gold, and that he dug up a great quantity of it and hoarded it in the back of his car. He was only half asleep, and the idea came to his mind: "What can I do with all this gold? Hoarding is prohibited. And I have enough; why do I want to accumulate more of something which I cannot use?" This immediate afterthought shows that he could not even in fantasy gratify his wish to have everything for himself and that he rejected his insatiable acquisitiveness. The wish to acquire and retain in order to grow is inappropriate in an adult. The mature personality rejects these pregenital tendencies, which had played legitimate roles in the growing organism. Here the sequestration of conflict can be observed in operation, for the patient reacted promptly with insight into his frankly acquisitive fantasy.

Another manifestation of this process of sequestration was a dream in which he was about to do a post-mortem on the body of an idiot. He felt some anxiety. The patient recognized immediately that the idiot represented a part of himself, the irrational emotions which he had learned to understand but which were not quite dead and still threatened him.

One part of his person is sharply defined as a person living outside himself and about to die. The dominant portion of his personality is the one who looks upon neurotic mechanisms with curiosity and from a distance.[1]

Sequestration dreams which indicate real improvement must be distinguished from those in which the patient pretends to have improved in order to please his analyst. Real sequestration dreams occur in the end phase of a treatment. The patient's behavior shows marked improvement. This manifests itself in various ways, in human relationships and in a changed attitude toward himself. He is capable of more detached attitudes, sometimes humorous ones. Humor implies detachment and tolerance and is possible only when the ego feels relatively secure. As long as it is weak it must protect itself by repression and projection from anything which might affect its integrity. Both the process of sequestration and humor about oneself indicate security and objectivity. Sequestration dreams are therefore valuable indications of the equilibrium between the ego and tendencies alien to it, and occur when the ego recognizes such tendencies openly and begins to discard them or assimilate them in modified form. They indicate that the ego is maintaining its integrity even when it recognizes repressed alien tendencies. These become part of the conscious personality, which deals with them by control, renunciation, and modification but no longer needs to deny or repress them.

SUMMARY

Psychoanalysis aims at improving the ego's capacity to deal with internal and external conflicts. The ego's failure is occasioned by the previous repression of conflicting impulses when

---

[1] Both dreams were originally discussed in F. Alexander, "The Voice of the Intellect Is Soft . . . ," *Psychoanalytic Review*, 28:12, 1941.

their satisfactory release might have been effected by continued efforts. Under the influence of the failure, the ego retreats from further attempts, and its repair requires the restoration of the ego's lost confidence in meeting new trials. Psychoanalysis achieves this by re-exposing the patient's ego to the conflicts it earlier repressed. It does this not merely by intellectual reconstruction but by making the patient re-experience emotionally the unsolved conflict under more favorable conditions. This re-experiencing takes place both in the transference and in the patient's other relationships. The latter, however, is now also under the control and guidance of the therapist. The core of the treatment lies in the transference situation. The most important therapeutic factor is that the therapist's response to the patient's neurotic reactions is different from that of the persons with whom the conflicts were originally connected. The objective, understanding attitude of the therapist is for the patient a novel response. No relations in actual life are quite as objective and understanding or exclusively concerned with helping another. The corrective experience can be made even more effective if the therapist assumes an attitude opposite to that of the parents, which caused the neurotic development.

There is no doubt that intellectual insight assists and stabilizes reorientation. The therapist's attitude encourages the patient to change his own behavior, which was originally conditioned by his parents. This explains why simply listening understandingly to the patient may lead in some cases to remarkable improvement. Adequate interpretation, however, and a suitable emotional attitude toward the patient not only accelerates the cure but is in most cases indispensable. Without these measures mere listening will sooner or later lead to emotional complications. Most patients will automatically involve themselves in transference conflicts, the solution of which requires interpretation and a deliberate creation of the most suitable emotional atmosphere in the treatment situation. All this aims ultimately at encouraging corrective emotional experiences suitable to undo the traumatic effects of previous pathogenic experiences.

Finally, it should be emphasized that psychoanalytic theory and practice are in process of development. To further this development a continuous revision of theoretical assumptions and generalizations, as well as experiments with therapeutic procedure, is imperative.

BIBLIOGRAPHY

AICHHORN, A.: *Wayward Youth*. New York, Viking Press, Inc., 1935.

ALEXANDER, F.: "Indications for Psychoanalytic Therapy," *Bull. New York Acad. Med.*, 20:319, 1944.

———: "Individual Psychotherapy," *Psychosom. Med.*, 8:110, 1946.

———: "A Metapsychological Description of the Process of Cure," *Internat. J. Psycho-Analysis*, 6:13, 1925.

———: "Metapsychologische Betrachtungen," *Internat. Ztschr. f. Psychoanal.*, 7:270, 1921.

———: "On Ferenczi's Relaxation Principle," *Internat. J. Psycho-Analysis*, 14:183, 1933.

———: "The Problem of Psychoanalytic Technique," *Psychoanalyt. Quart.*, 4:588, 1935.

———: " 'The Voice of the Intellect Is Soft,' " *Psychoanalyt. Rev.*, 28:12, 1941.

ALEXANDER, F., FRENCH, T. M., et al.: *Psychoanalytic Therapy. Principles and Application*. New York, The Ronald Press Co., 1946.

ALEXANDER, F., and HEALY, W.: *Roots of Crime*. New York, Alfred A. Knopf, Inc., 1935.

EDER, M. D.: "Dreams as Resistance," *Internat. J. Psycho-Analysis*, 11:40, 1930.

FENICHEL, O.: *Problems of Psychoanalytic Technique*. Albany, The Psychoanalytic Quarterly, Inc., 1941.

FERENCZI, S.: *Further Contributions to the Theory and Technique of Psycho-Analysis*. London, Hogarth Press, 1926.

FERENCZI, S., and RANK, O.: *The Development of Psychoanalysis*. Nervous and Mental Disease Monograph Series No. 40. New York, Nervous and Mental Disease Publishing Company, 1925.

FRENCH, T. M.: "A Clinical Study of Learning in the Course of a Psychoanalytic Treatment," *Psychoanalyt. Quart.*, 5:148, 1936.

————: "The Integration of Social Behavior," *Psychoanalyt. Quart.*, 14:149, 1945.

FREUD, S.: *A General Introduction to Psychoanalysis*. New York, Boni & Liveright, Inc., 1920.

————: "Analysis Terminable and Interminable," *Internat. J. Psycho-Analysis*, 18:373, 1937.

————: *New Introductory Lectures on Psycho-Analysis*. New York, W. W. Norton & Company, Inc., 1933.

————: Papers on Technique in *Collected Papers*, II. London, Hogarth Press, 1924, p. 285.

GLOVER, E., Ed.: *An Investigation of the Technique of Psychoanalysis*. Baltimore, Williams & Wilkins Company, 1940.

GLOVER, E., FENICHEL, O., STRACHEY, J., BERGLER, E., NUNBERG, H., and BIBRING, E.: "On the Theory of Therapeutic Results of Psychoanalysis" (Symposium), *Internat. J. Psycho-Analysis*, 18: 125, 133, 139, 146, 161, 170, 1937.

GRINKER, R. R., and SPIEGEL, J. P.: *Men under Stress*. Philadelphia, The Blakiston Company, 1945.

HARNIK, J.: "Resistance to the Interpretation of Dreams in Analysis," *Internat. J. Psycho-Analysis*, 11:75, 1930.

KNIGHT, R. P.: "Psychoanalytically Oriented Psychiatry," G A P Therapy Committee Symposium, April 1948. (Not published.)

KUBIE, L.: *Practical Aspects of Psychoanalysis*. New York, W. W. Norton & Company, Inc., 1936.

LEVINE, M.: *Psychotherapy in Medical Practice*. New York, The Macmillan Company, 1942.

LORAND, S.: *Technique of Psychoanalytic Therapy*. New York, International Universities Press, 1946.

OBERNDORF, C. P.: "Consideration of Results with Psychoanalytic Therapy," *Am. J. Psychiat.*, 99:374, 1942.

———: "Factors in Psychoanalytic Therapy," *Am. J. Psychiat.*, 98:750, 1942.

Proceedings of the Brief Psychotherapy Council, 1942. Chicago, Institute for Psychoanalysis.

Proceedings of the Second Brief Psychotherapy Council, 1944 (Section I: War Psychiatry, Section II: Psychosomatic Medicine, Section III: Psychotherapy for Children, Group Psychotherapy). Chicago, Institute for Psychoanalysis.

Proceedings of the Third Psychotherapy Council, 1946. Chicago, Institute for Psychoanalysis.

SAUL, L. J.: "The Nature of Psychogenic Cure," *Am. J. Psychiat.*, 101:91, 1944.

———: "Utilization of Early Current Dreams in Formulating Psychoanalytic Cases," *Psychoanalyt. Quart.*, 9:453, 1940.

STRACHEY, J.: "The Nature of the Therapeutic Action of Psycho-Analysis," *Internat. J. Psycho-Analysis,* 15:127, 1934.

WEISS, E.: "Emotional Memories and Acting Out," *Psychoanalyt. Quart.*, 11:477, 1942.

WHITEHORN, J. C.: "Psychotherapy," in *Modern Medical Therapy in General Practice.* Baltimore, Williams & Wilkins Company, 1940, p. 3.

Index

SALVE REGINA COLLEGE LIBRARY
OCHRE POINT AVENUE
NEWPORT, RHODE ISLAND 02840

In the Norton Library

Norton Books

ON PSYCHIATRY AND PSYCHOLOGY